Key Concepts

Barbara Adam, *Time*
Alan Aldridge, *Consumption*
Alan Aldridge, *The Market*
Jakob Arnoldi, *Risk*
Colin Barnes & Geof Mercer, *Disability*
Darin Barney, *The Network Society*
Mildred Blaxter, *Health* 2nd edition
Harriet Bradley, *Gender*
Harry Brighouse, *Justice*
Mónica Brito Vieira and David Runciman, *Representation*
Steve Bruce, *Fundamentalism* 2nd edition
Margaret Canovan, *The People*
Alejandro Colás, *Empire*
Anthony Elliott, *Concepts of the Self* 2nd edition
Steve Fenton, *Ethnicity* 2nd edition
Katrin Flikschuh, *Freedom*
Michael Freeman, *Human Rights*
Russell Hardin, *Trust*
Geoffrey Ingham, *Capitalism*
Fred Inglis, *Culture*
Robert H. Jackson, *Sovereignty*
Jennifer Jackson Preece, *Minority Rights*
Gill Jones, *Youth*
Paul Kelly, *Liberalism*
Anne Mette Kjær, *Governance*
Ruth Lister, *Poverty*
Jon Mandle, *Global Justice*
Judith Phillips, *Care*
Michael Saward, *Democracy*
John Scott, *Power*
Anthony D. Smith, *Nationalism*
Stuart White, *Equality*

Ethnicity

Second Edition

Steve Fenton

polity

The right of Steve Fenton to be identified as Author of this Work has been
asserted in accordance with the UK Copyright, Designs and Patents Act 1988.

First published in 2010 by Polity Press

Polity Press
65 Bridge Street
Cambridge CB2 1UR, UK

Polity Press
350 Main Street
Malden, MA 02148, USA

ISBN-13: 978-0-7456-4265-9
ISBN-13: 978-0-7456-4266-6(paperback)

A catalogue record for this book is available from the British Library.

Typeset in 10.5 on 12 pt Sabon
by Toppan Best-set Premedia Limited
Printed and bound in Great Britain by MPG Books Group Limited, Bodmin,
Cornwall

The publisher has used its best endeavours to ensure that the URLs for
external websites referred to in this book are correct and active at the time of
going to press. However, the publisher has no responsibility for the websites
and can make no guarantee that a site will remain live or that the content is
or will remain appropriate.

Every effort has been made to trace all copyright holders, but if any have been
inadvertently overlooked the publisher will be pleased to include any
necessary credits in any subsequent reprint or edition.

For further information on Polity, visit our website: www.politybooks.com

Contents

Preface to the First Edition

In this book I have sought to meet the aims of the Key Concepts series. This is to provide an introduction to a key concept in the social sciences; to discuss some of the main literature in this field; and to provide a commentary on important debates within the subject. All this I have sought to do with respect to ethnicity. In addition, I have tried to establish a framework for thinking about ethnicity within the context of 'modernity' or 'late capitalist modernity'. This is an attempt to resituate ethnicity within a much broader sociological canvas.

In the early chapters I argue that an understanding of 'ethnicity' must be set alongside our understanding of 'race' and 'nation'. The meanings of these words are not the same as that of 'ethnic group' but they cover a great deal of the same terrain and it is important to acknowledge this.

In looking at important debates and literature I concentrate in chapters 4 and 5 on the debates surrounding 'primordialism' or the idea of 'primordial identities'; and on the debates about the work of Nathan Glazer and Daniel Patrick Moynihan which set the tone for much of the discussion of ethnicity in the USA. Although many examples are taken from the USA and the UK, I have drawn on materials about Malaysia to show how discourses of ethnicity are articulated in different ways in different social contexts.

In the later chapters, I look at some aspects of 'late capital-ist modernity' and the place of ethnicity within it. This includes global migration, local and global inequalities, the strength of the state, the theme of individualism, and the question of national identity and majority ethnicity. I have tried to cover key areas in ways which will help new readers as well as providing something for more experienced readers.

Preface to the Second Edition

The main purpose of the changes I have made to *Ethnicity* (2003) for this second and revised edition has been to update the material. This is with regard both to new published work and to the social changes of the recent period. The opening chapters are the least changed because they remain as a fundamental review of the key concepts and ideas in the field. In chapter 2, I have added to the discussion of 'discourses of ethnicity' by adding the cases of Japan, Brazil and Singapore, and a world study of ethnic terminology.

Larger changes come in the later chapters. Chapter 5 had previously been an assessment of some key moments in the ethnicity literature, and the 1960s and 1970s work of Glazer and Moynihan formed a large part: this discussion is now much reduced. In the second edition, more space is given to a vital strand in ethnicity conceptualization – the idea of 'threat' or 'competition'. This is well suited to the general argument of my book – that we must look carefully at the material contexts of action, where action is ethnically 'aligned'. I explore the work of Edna Bonacich, who argues that we can understand ethnic antagonism within a context of class conflict and competition. The examples in these case studies are mainly from the USA so that these additions have the secondary effect of examining studies of the historic relationship of 'black' and 'white' in American society.

In chapter 6, I have concentrated on updating material about migration, especially reflecting on increased migration to the USA from Central and South America. The debates about segmented assimilation are connected to the question of Hispanic or Latino migration. New migration to the USA is also apparent in the changes I have made to chapter 7, where the focus is on political and economic power and inequalities. It is in chapter 8 that I have, perhaps, most shifted the argument. In the 2003 edition the emphasis was on ethnicity, racism and the 'discontents of modernity'. Although elements of this argument remain, I am less convinced of it than I was then. If we are to show how and why action comes to be informed by ethnic identities and interest – especially where it is marked by a high degree of antagonism – then we must be more specific about which aspects of the modern world make for a more ethnicized or racialized world. Put another way, we need to show which dimensions of modernity impel actors to act along the lines of ethnic divisions.

The economic and political uncertainties are, in 2009, greater than ever. If I were pushed, I could essay a forward view of the implications of these present uncertainties for ethnic divisions and antagonisms. But that is not my principal purpose here – and may give too many hostages to fortune. I hope the reader of this book will have a broader understanding of the field and the tools with which they can make such judgements themselves.

First Edition Acknowledgements

I am very grateful to Rachel Kerr and Louise Knight of Polity Press who have been very helpful at every stage of the preparation of this book. Their support is very much appreciated.

My colleagues at the University of Bristol, Department of Sociology, have given me a great deal of help. Many thanks to Gregor McLennan for his encouragement. Very special thanks go to Tom Osborne and Harriet Bradley who both read the typescript and gave me excellent critical commentary.

From outside Bristol I have received both important comments and encouragement from John Rex; for this I am most grateful. In recent years I have had the pleasure of meeting up again with my dissertation supervisor, Edward Tiryakian, and this has been another stimulus to my thinking. My email conversations with Michael Banton have also helped me to clarify things and argue them out. I have had a lot of help and encouragement from Stephen May, now at the University of Waikato.

During a period of study leave in Malaysia, I had the most engaging and informative conversations at Universiti Sains Malaysia in Penang and the University of Malaysia at Sarawak; special thanks to Kntayya Mariappan at USM and to Michael Leigh and Zawawi Ibrahim at UNIMAS.

To all these people I am most grateful.

And finally, as ever, my love to Jenny, Alex and Lynda.

Steve Fenton, 2003

Second Edition Acknowledgements

As in 2003 I want to recognize how much I have learnt from Ed Tiryakian, Michael Banton and John Rex.

I have benefited a lot from – and much enjoyed – conversations and emails with other friends and colleagues, including Rohit Barot, Jon Fox, Robin Mann, Bob Carter, Ann Morning and Patricia Fernandez-Kelly. Many thanks too to Karen Paton and Jonathan Skerrett.

Steve Fenton, 2009

Introduction

For a term which only came to be widely used in the 1970s, 'ethnicity' now plays an important part in the sociological imagination, and in policy and political discourses. It is worth attempting to be clear about it. In the present volume I have tackled this question along two different lines. The first task is to establish how we might sensibly use the terms 'ethnic group' and 'ethnicity'. The second is to explore the social conditions under which ethnic identities become significant in social action. The first requires being clear about what it means to speak of a person's 'ethnic identity' or 'belonging to an ethnic community'. We should not assume that all people do either of these things. In many cases, people would look at you quite blankly if you asked them to speak about their 'ethnicity'. The second task requires exploring a wide range of circumstances which influence whether people are at all likely to make ethnicity a relevant category of social action. In pursuing the first task, I have looked at the explicit and implicit meanings of the terms 'ethnic', 'ethnicity' and 'ethnic group', and the related terms 'race' and 'nation'. In the second task, I have outlined, sometimes with full knowledge and sometimes speculatively, the circumstances under which ethnic identities become an important dimension of action. The first part of the book addresses the questions most valuable to new students of the field; the second part will, I hope, appeal to new and experienced students alike.

With regard to the definition of ethnicity, a key debate is whether, for the purposes of sociological theory, the terms 'ethnic group' and 'ethnicity' refer to sociological realities which are substantial, embedded in group life and individual experience; or whether these terms point to some rather more diffuse and ill-defined identities which have fleeting moments of importance, and should be understood as 'socially constructed' rather than profound and 'real'. In theorizing the conditions under which ethnicity becomes sociologically important – even decisive – I conclude that a theory of ethnicity has to be a theory of the contexts under which it is situationally relevant. This conclusion is diffused through the book, but it can be rehearsed at the beginning as well as recapitulated at the end. I conclude that:

> As a general rule it should be understood that there cannot be a theory of ethnicity, nor can 'ethnicity' be regarded as a theory. Rather there can be a theory of the modern social world, as the material and cultural context for the expression of ethnic identities. This is to reject all separation of 'ethnicity' or 'racism' or 'national identity' from the social and theoretical mainstream. It is to re-position the interest in ethnicity within the central domain of the sociological imagination – the structuring of the modern world, class formations and class cultures, and the tensions between private lives, cultures, and the cohesion of communal and public life.

Much of the rest of this book will be an exercise in filling out that argument.

The ontological status of the term 'ethnicity'

The very natural supposition of those who read about ethnicity, or class or nation for example, is that the word refers directly to something 'out there'. The student's wish is to find the definition which is the most precise in capturing this 'thing out there'. In practice, it is rarely as simple as this. One text on ethnicity suggests that the best way of thinking about it is as an intellectual construct of the observers (Banks 1996). And a scholarly article on the 'nation' (Tishkov 2000) advises

that we should stop using the word: 'forget the nation'
Tishkov writes. Of course, to say that something is an 'intellectual construct' is not the same as saying it doesn't exist.
Rather it is reminding us, as Banks rightly does, that whilst
something is happening – people march under banners, form
associations, kill one another, dress up and dance and sing,
follow guidance about whom they should marry – the particular term or terms used to describe these things are the
observers' elaborations. These elaborations can take on a life
of their own. This is not, however, to think ethnic groups or
nations out of existence: it would be dispiriting to think that
you were writing a book about something which doesn't
exist.

I do think there is something 'out there' which corresponds
to what observers call 'ethnicity'. At the same time, I do not
believe that ethnicity is anything more than a broad and loose
denoting of an area of interest; it is not, on its own, a theoretical standpoint, nor is it likely that there can be a unitary
theory of ethnicity. We can make a start by thinking of ethnicity as referring to social identities – typically about 'descent'
and 'cultural difference' – which are deployed under certain
conditions. A further step or two would be to say that ethnicity refers to the *social construction* of descent and culture,
the social mobilization of descent and culture and the meanings and implications of classification systems built around
them. People or peoples do not just possess cultures or share
ancestry; *they elaborate these into the idea of a community
founded upon these attributes*. Indeed, it is entirely possible
for people to elaborate an idea of community despite the
fact that claims to sharing descent and culture are decidedly
questionable. Two books on *national* 'descent and culture
communities' have had great impact with their titles of
the *Invention of Tradition* and *Imagined Communities*
(Hobsbawm and Ranger 1983; Anderson 1983). For all that
there is a difference between 'imagined' and 'imaginary',
these words 'imagined' and 'invention' have loomed large in
the study of ethnic groups, nations and nationalism. Nations
and ethnic groups are frequently viewed as socially constructed, imagined or invented, and certainly not as merely
groups who share descent and culture. So when we start with
this phrase 'descent and culture communities', we should

recognize the danger of over-concretizing the communities. But in another sense, there really are white Americans of European descent; there really are Malaysians of Chinese descent. When it comes to viewing groups as 'real' and viewing them as 'constructed', we want to have our cake and eat it. An example may help.

An example of groups and names

In a report on Sarawak's population – Sarawak is part of Malaysia in the north of the island of Borneo – in 1968, Michael Leigh listed some 25 ethnic groups and 47 sub-groups (Leigh 1975). Leigh nowhere uses the term 'Dayak' to describe the population although many of the references he cites do. *Dayak*, a Malay word meaning 'up-country', certainly continues to have currency but is a very loose descriptor for peoples living both sides of the Malaysia–Indonesia borders. When in 2001 local groups in Kalimantan, Indonesia (on the southern and Indonesian side of the border in Borneo), fought and killed to drive out Madurese immigrants, these local groups were widely referred to, in the international press, as 'Dayaks' or 'Dayak tribesmen'. On the Malaysian side of the border in Sarawak, it is common to hear people described as, for example, Iban or Bidayuh – two 'Dayak' groupings – but the broad term Dayak is often used too, and one of the state's political parties is the Parti Bangsa Dayak Sarawak – the Dayak People's Party of Sarawak. In what sense, we could ask, are 'Dayaks' really an ethnic group?

To put the same question in the western world, we could ask – in what sense are 'Irish Americans' truly an ethnic group?

Fixed categories and diffuse identities

How fixed are these ethnic categories and what do they rely upon? In the Sarawak case they could be said to rely on some of the characteristics of the groups themselves – the language and dialect differences, for instance, are actual and

important; people of a particular grouping are identified with
certain areas 'up-country', and there are, for example, more
Bidayuh to the south of the capital Kuching and more Iban
in the districts north and east of Kuching; and traditionally
there are differences of custom in, for example, the style of
construction of longhouses. Certainly, an individual Iban or
Bidayuh will describe herself or himself as such, although
intermarriage across these groups is common. In some
respects, the real boundary is with Malays and the real sustaining of the boundary is through Islam; thus the distinction
between Malays and other Sarawak native peoples is between
Muslim and non-Muslim – leaving some eight Chinese dialect
groups out of the equation for the moment. But about two-
thirds of one 'native' group – the Melanau – *did* adopt Islam
when other 'Dayak' peoples resisted, and this has made the
Melanau an important group whose elite political players
may in effect identify with Malays, especially when in penin-
sular Malaysia.

But, partly, the answer is not in the characteristics of the
groups but in the behaviour of political elites. If there are
occasions for appealing to all Dayaks then an astute political
leader will do so. No single group – say Bidayuh – is really
a large enough group on which to build a political career. So
politicians may appeal to Dayaks, or to *bumiputeras* (indigenous 'sons of the soil'), a status which native peoples of
Sarawak share with Malays. So if we think of groups as classifications marking one from another, there is any number of
boundary lines involved: between Iban and Bidayuh, between
Malay and non-Malay, between Muslim and non-Muslim
and between *bumiputeras* (groups considered to be 'native'
to the country which would include Malays *and* Dayaks but
not Chinese) and non-*bumiputeras*. Just which boundaries
are important will depend on social context and sometimes
on political or other advantage. Judith Nagata made this
point about Malays and non-Malays in a classic study of
Penang (Nagata 1974). All this impels us to conclude that
'groups' are both actual and constructed. It is a mistake to
argue that there is 'nothing there' – there clearly is. But at the
same time it would be a mistake to think that the 'groups'
are self-evident population and community sub-sets with a
clear line drawn round each one. And it would also be wrong

to think that, for all this ethnic complexity, people's lives are governed by something called 'ethnicity'.

Do people act by reference to their ethnic identity?

As well as addressing what 'ethnicity' is and what 'ethnic groups' are, we are bound to address the crucially important question that follows: how important are ethnic groups thus defined and in what sense is 'ethnicity' a causal factor in societies and social action? 'How causal is ethnicity' could be rephrased as 'do these identities and social attachments which we call ethnic play an independent part, even a leading part, in social action?' If people assume an ethnic identity, does it in any sense become a real guide to action? How important are markers of ethnic difference in social transactions?

The answer to both these questions is conditional. To the first we would say 'under some circumstances, people take cultural and descent identities very seriously, in some societies these types of group boundaries play a key role in the social order; in other circumstances, they are trivial, unimportant and barely surviving'. To the second question we would say 'do not be misled into thinking that, because something called "ethnic groups" are involved, that action, conflict and social relations are primarily determined or "driven" by ethnicity'. A very straightforward illustration would be the intense conflict which was played out throughout the 1990s in the former Yugoslavia, and persists into the new millennium. This was very commonly described as ethnic conflict with the more or less clear assumption that the differences and dislikes between the groups were the causes of the conflict. This is almost implied in simply using the term 'ethnic conflict'. As Michael Banton has pointed out, the danger with the term 'ethnic conflict' is that we assume that the conflict referred to is primarily 'ethnic' in nature and cause (Banton 2000). Often it is not. In the Yugoslavia of 1990 we would at least have to answer the question as to why these same suspicions and dislikes had not caused conflicts in the preceding forty years on anything like the scale of the 'break-up period'.

Ethnic cleansing or racial segregation?

One of the notable things about the conflicts in Yugoslavia is that the press – in English – always referred to *ethnic* conflict and *ethnic* cleansing. But conflicts in the US which bear some similarities (without being full scale civil war) are described as *racial* conflict and *racial* segregation. Is there some special feature which makes American conflict racial and Yugoslavian conflict ethnic? There are, of course, real differences in the circumstances of America and the former Yugoslavia, but there is no obvious reason, in describing these conflicts, why one is racial and the other ethnic. The answer lies in the fact that different countries, regions and contexts have given rise to different discourses to describe 'local' events and history. In the USA, a race discourse is very powerful and the word 'races' continues to be used routinely, despite the discrediting of all social theory based on ideas of racial difference. This difference of discourse (cf Fenton 1999) has elsewhere been described as an 'idiom of race' and an 'idiom of ethnicity' (Banton 2000). To these two idioms we must add the idiom of nation. Race, nation and ethnic group belong together in a family of concepts and bear strong family resemblances. They do not all 'mean the same thing' but they do share a common reference to the idea of a people, or 'people of this kind'. Furthermore, social attitudes, social groups and cultural meanings which have been described as 'racial', 'national' and 'ethnic' are *not* a series of distantly related or unrelated topics. They 'sit together', in fact, in theory and in everyday discourse.

In particular, in **chapter 1**, we look at the English-language etymologies of race, nation and ethnic group. No amount of peeling back the layers of meaning of these terms reveals a decisive set of markers. Rather, there is a core and shared meaning among all three, with each having particular connotations which are not fully shared with the others. In chapter 2, we examine the way in which particular countries develop discourses of ethnicity which are peculiar to the history and circumstances of that country. To show that even an English-language discourse of descent and culture communities can vary within different national traditions, the British and American discourses of race and ethnicity are compared. The case of Malaysia is examined in order to illustrate a non-English-language discourse, along with the interesting cases of Japan, Singapore and Brazil.

In **chapter 3**, we examine some aspects of the usage, within sociology and anthropology, of the terms 'ethnic' and 'ethnicity', with an inspection of related terms such as 'race' and 'tribe'. The last two gradually but irretrievably lost favour. In the case of both race and tribe, the long-run tendency has been to replace them with 'ethnic'. We begin by looking at the gradual demise of the term 'race' as critiques of its nineteenth-century scientific meaning of 'anthropological classification' began to mount.

In **chapter 4**, we look at a number of leading controversies in this field of study, and the principal one – by some distance – is the dispute surrounding the word 'primordial'. This is not just an extension of defining what 'ethnicity' is, which we treat in chapters 1 and 2. It goes right to the heart of how we think about ethnicity within sociological theory and how we think about society. The simplest way of thinking about 'primordiality' is to think of 'first order' as the word implies: sentiments, ties and obligations and an unquestioned sense of identity which are embedded in the individual from an early age and remain as a fixed point of reference. This is contrasted with a view of ethnicity as a matter of circumstance, convenience and calculation – a kind of 'English when it suits me' or 'Serbian when it benefits me'.

On this circumstantialist view, ethnic groups are not simply groups of people who share a culture and have a shared ancestry. Rather, ideas of descent and culture are mobilized, used and drawn upon to give force to a sense of community, of 'group-ness' and of shared destiny. But if groups are, in some sense, socially 'constructed', we are bound to ask who does the construction? If myths of group belonging are being created who is doing it? One simple answer would seem to be: the people themselves who belong to the group.

Curiously, this is often a misleading if not frankly wrong answer. There are at least three other prime suspects.

One is that the idea of a group is not constructed by 'us' but constructed 'for us by others'. In colonial situations, a powerful settler or ruling group established the names for 'natives' and these created groups came to take on, over a long period, a distinctive and actual character. Wherever we look in the postcolonial world, we find groups whose names and formation are a direct consequence of the colonial encounter. Even in relatively 'free' migrations, as in workers and families from Europe to the USA in the nineteenth century, new immigrants were categorized and often despised by those established in the country (Jacobson 1998). Second, the building of a group identity may be not so much the work of all members of a group, as of an elite within it, or of a party and organizational leaders. The third possible answer is that groups are formed as a consequence of *state* actions, power and administrative fiat. Many constitutions of states in the contemporary world contain laws and executive guidelines and regulations which have the function of, if not quite creating groups, giving them a kind of permanence and substance as socio-legal realities. If you pass laws bestowing privileges or rights on indigenous peoples, you must have some way of deciding who is indigenous and who is not. If you forbid marriage or sexual relations between As and Bs, you must be able to define the As and the Bs.

Ethnic categories are frequently put to some political purpose. In **chapter 5**, we explore the literature to see how the idea of 'ethnic groups' has been applied, beginning with the anthropologist Fredrik Barth's view of ethnic groups as constituted by the maintenance of 'boundaries' between socially contiguous groups. The ideas of 'group boundary' and ethnic group interest are imported into competition theory. On this theoretical view, action is seen to be ethnically motivated if (people in) group A respond to perceived threat or competition from Group B. This theoretical view partially overlaps with Bonacich's (1972) class-based model of explaining ethnic antagonism. Brubaker (2004) has captured the 'non-groupist' conception of ethnicity in his book titled precisely that: ethnicity without groups.

In **chapter 6**, we begin by looking at the importance of the historical migration of labouring populations in the 'making of ethnicity'. Former slavery societies depended on workers who were captured, and migrated because they were forced to; this violent beginning has marked all subsequent social relations. In societies which were colonized, the colonial power often imported workers in semi-free conditions, as the British did, for example, in Malaysia, Fiji, Trinidad and the countries of East Africa.

Throughout the nineteenth and twentieth centuries, the USA was a great destination for migrating workers and people fleeing persecution. By the end of the twentieth century, many countries and regions had become destinations in a great globalization of population movements. So here we look at the effect of migration and social mobility on the sustaining of ethnic identities. We discuss how there have been some significant changes in the pattern of migration to the USA. These changes have begun to open up the possibility of changes in the way ethnic and racial difference are understood in the USA, especially in regard to the growing Hispanic and Asian American populations.

In **chapter 7**, we look more directly at the global context of economic inequalities both within and across countries. The hardening of the lines of economic inclusion and exclusion, of security and insecurity, produces divisions which frequently *broadly approximate* to ethnically identifiable populations. In the USA, there are important overlapping boundaries of, on the one hand, ethnic or racial groups and, on the other, social classes. This means that class situations and class interests 'condition' ethnically informed action. Many recent Hispanic immigrants fill very specific low-wage labour market positions; this we partly explore by looking at migration, class and ethnicity in Los Angeles.

Similarly, state regimes differ greatly in the degree to which they can guarantee any measure of physical, legal and economic security to their citizens. In this part of chapter 7, our attention shifts towards the political bases of ethnic action. Much attention has focused on 'precarious' or unstable states, political systems where the state cannot or does not provide protection for groups of its citizens. Ethnicity in a precarious state takes on meanings scarcely found in more secure states.

But the state, as Mann (2005) has argued, may itself prompt or carry out ethnically motivated action, including genocidal attacks on targeted populations.

In **chapter 8**, we take seriously the term 'ethnic majority'. In most discussions the term 'ethnic minority' is familiar. Logically as well as sociologically, the term 'ethnic minority' suggests an ethnic *majority*. In societies like Britain, which have only recently developed an awareness of themselves as 'multi-ethnic', the ethnic majority is also the 'silent majority', scarcely conscious of itself as 'ethnic' at all. It is not inevitable that this situation should produce tensions, and racisms, but very regularly it does. In a diffuse sense of hostility towards change and modernity, minority ethnicities are targeted as unwanted along with other symptoms of modernity. In several European societies new populist parties have emerged, with strong anti-immigration ideologies. Some class segments of the ethnic majority are particularly likely to support these typically xenophobic parties. In the final chapter, we set out some of the most besetting contradictions of 'late capitalist modernity'. These relate to the economic sphere, especially in the social production of inequality and unsatisfied expectations. They relate to the sphere of the individual and the social or 'communal' in the tension between a wish for security and the onward rush of individualization. And these contradictions relate to the moral sphere in the tension between a 'universalist' regard for the dignity of the individual and the periodic resurgence of 'control' moralities. This is an outline of a sociology of capitalist modernity which evokes some of the principal themes around which ethnic identities and ethnic antagonisms are played out.

1
Ethnos: Descent and Culture Communities

Ethnic group, race and nation are three concepts sharing a single centre – or 'core' – with some notable and important differences at the periphery. Common to all is an idea of descent or ancestry and very closely implicated in all three we find the idea of shared culture. Ideas about culture will include myths about the past, beliefs about 'the kind of people we are' and the idea that 'culture', language, dress and custom, define a group. All three terms relate to 'descent and culture communities'. Ethnic group, race and nation are all viewed, by themselves or by observers, as peoples who have or lay claim to shared antecedents. This idea of shared ancestry may not be as precise as the genealogies of extended families (though how can we tell how much imprecision is concealed in family trees?) but there is nonetheless a repeating theme of 'people coming from the same stock'. In English, this word 'stock' is mostly used with reference to animals, so in its use with reference to people it has a strong biological sense, a strong sense of genealogy and type. This sense of shared ancestry can certainly be found in the dictionary definitions of all three of these terms:

> Race: a group of persons (animals or plants) connected by *common descent* or origin; a tribe, **nation** or people regarded as of common stock. [my emphasis]

Nation: an extensive aggregate of persons so closely associated with each other by *common descent*, language or history
as to form a distinct **race** of people usually organised as a
separate political state and occupying a definite territory. [my
emphasis]

Ethnic: (an adjective) pertaining to nations not Christian;
pertaining to **a race or nation**; having common racial, cultural,
religious or linguistic characteristics especially designating a
racial or other group within a larger system. [my emphasis]

(*Compact Oxford English Dictionary*, 1993)

Shared references

'Ethnic', the only adjective, refers to the previous two by
listing race and nation and 'common racial, cultural, religious
or linguistic characteristics'. The definition of 'nation' refers
to common descent and a distinct race of people. And that
of 'race' refers to common descent and tribe, nation or people.
Clearly, all three occupy very much the same territory of
meaning; not precisely the same but so close as to make it
impossible to consider them separately.

Much of the sociological literature on these terms has been
concerned to distinguish them by means of separation, that
is by distinguishing them in such a way that one makes a
clean break from the other. It is far better to start by saying
that all occupy the same terrain. Having said this, the next
step is to show the respects in which, as we move from the
core outwards, they diverge. What they all convey is a sense
of a people. This is precisely the meaning of the term in which
'ethnic' has its origins: the classical Greek word *ethnos*.
The word has preserved this meaning in modern Greek, covering the English sense of both nation and ethnic group
(Triandafyllidou et al. 1997).

Liddell and Scott's *Greek–English Lexicon* (1897), the
authoritative source on classical Greek usages, cites a number
of meanings which are shifts in emphasis in different contexts
and at different periods of ancient Greek history. They are:

Ethnos: Number of people living together, body of men; particular tribes; of animals, flocks; (after Homer) nation, people;

(later) foreign, barbarous nations; non-Athenians, (biblical Greek) non-Jews, Gentiles, class of men, caste, tribe.

The adjectival form, *ethnikos*, has two principal meanings: national and foreign.

So, the Greek *ethnos* has the meanings which are attached to modern English usage of nation, peoples, especially foreign peoples, or tribes and castes plus the adjectival national and foreign. For tribe we might now read 'ethnic group'. We could have added 'race' in its pre-nineteenth-century forms when it had similar connotations of nations, peoples and even classes. It was the rise of biological and anthropological science in the nineteenth century which gave to 'race' its special meaning of grand divisions of humankind.

The word 'ethnic' found its way into English (after a number of early spellings such as 'aethnycke') and appears to have long had the sense of 'foreign' and the sense distinguished from Jewish (i.e. Gentile) and distinguished from Jewish *and* Gentile (i.e. heathen). In fact the *Compact Oxford English Dictionary* (1993) states that 'ethnic' derives from the Greek *ethnikos*, 'heathen', citing this heathen sense despite the fact that the Greek adjective also clearly had the more neutral sense 'national'. Once 'ethnic' or equivalent establishes itself in English, with the first citation from a written work of 1473, it regularly has the meaning of 'heathen and foreign'. The *Oxford Dictionary* then cites a second set of meanings, mostly dating from the nineteenth century, when it becomes generalized, losing the special 'heathen' sense. Thus we have this definition: 'ethnic': *pertaining to race, common racial or cultural character*. By 1935, they are citing Huxley and Haddon (of which more later) and their famous argument for the abandonment of the term 'race' and its replacement by 'ethnic'. The *Oxford Dictionary* also cites the term in its combination with (ethnic) minority group and as a *noun* meaning one who is not a Christian or Jew. In both the USA and Britain, the noun form 'ethnics' is used to mean something other than majority.

Before leaving the Greek dictionary we should note three other ancient Greek terms which have a meaning approximating to people or 'class' of people. One is *phylon*, for which Liddell and Scott give the meaning 'race, tribe or class' followed by a second meaning, 'nation'. *Phylon* too has a meaning as a class within the animal kingdom. *Genos* is defined as 'race, stock or kin'. This latter term has a closer link to the notion of family, offspring and descent. But it too can mean tribe 'as a sub-division' of *ethnos* and can mean classes in the animal kingdom. All these words – *ethnos*, *phylon* and *genos* – encompass shared meanings of people, tribe, nation and class, with shades of difference from one to another. The word for people in Greek, which moves away from all these three but nonetheless could be translated as 'people', is *demos*. It is, in Liddell and Scott, given a first meaning of district, country, land, but subsequently 'the people, the inhabitants' of a district or land. It has two further meanings. One is its meaning as 'common people' as against aristocracy, the people of 'the country' as opposed to the elite people of the city. The other is 'in a political sense' the 'sovereign people, the free citizens', this being the sense which modern English users know in the word 'democracy'.

Stock, type, people, breed

Four things are of special interest in this examination of one language (Greek), a language which happens also to be the source of a good deal of modern terminology. *First*, all these terms mean something like 'people' and all except *genos* were used in ways which today might be translated as 'nation'. The meaning of *genos* as specific descent group and sub-group, and as 'less than a nation' is fairly clear. However, *genos* and the Latin equivalent *genus* have provided the English 'genus', which has been used in biological sciences to mean 'stock, race, kind'. *Second*, all of them, bar *demos*, could have the meaning of a 'class' of animals or people; in the animal and plant kingdom, modern biology has adopted *phylon* and *genos*, neither of which, in common usage, has given us words meaning anything like people or nation. *Genos*, though, appears in 'genocide', 'the deliberate extermination of an ethnic or national group'. *Third*, an idea of cultural difference is conveyed by the way in which these words for people, and particularly *ethnos*, were used to mean *other*

peoples, who spoke other languages, lived in different countries and, in a later context, were not Jews, or were neither
Jews nor Christians. *Fourth*, the words make distinctions
which had significance within the societies and periods from
which they emanate. The Greeks in general and the Athenians
in particular expressed this strong sense of difference between
themselves and other peoples. Later, distinctions of Jew,
Gentile or Christian and others became important. And in
the word *demos* for people, the distinction between citizens
(free) and unfree persons was the important one.

Nation

The word 'nation' came into English via French from the
Latin root *natio*, which has provided the word for 'nation'
in virtually all Romance languages. It too has an original
meaning of a 'breed' or 'stock' of people who share a common
descent or were regarded as so doing. The fact that it has
something to do with descent is betrayed by the word *natio*'s
own root in the verb *nasci*, 'to be born'. The *Oxford Dictionary* gives references to usages of 'nation' as early as 1300.
The idea of common descent and the idea of people of a territory were both present. Its earliest uses were not solely – as
some have implied – in the context of student groups (*natio-
nes*) in medieval universities, identified by country of origin
(cf. Greenfeld 1992). The Latin *natio* is clearly quite close in
meaning to the Greek *ethnos*. It even shares the biblical sense
of *ethnos*; the *Oxford Dictionary* cites English usage of
'nations' meaning 'heathen nations' in biblical use as early as
1340.

The first part of the *Oxford English Dictionary* section on
'nation' essays a general definition that we cited earlier:

> An extensive aggregate of persons, so closely associated with
> each other by common descent, language or history as to form
> a distinct race or people, usually organised as a separate politi-
> cal state and occupying a definite territory.

The source goes on to say that early uses showed more of
'the racial idea' and later uses, the political. Early (1300–86)

references described Englishmen ('Ingles man') as a nation. And the *Dictionary* cites Fortescue in 1460 referring to the King being compelled to make his armies of 'straungers' such as 'Scottes, Spanyardes . . . and of other nacions'. In a history of Carolina in colonial America (1709), the writer says that 'two nations of Indians here in Carolina were at war'. But 'nation' has also had the meaning of a class of persons or even animals. A 1390 cited work refers to lovers, or gentle people, as a nation ('Among the gentil nacion love is an occupacion'), and similarly schoolboys are described as a nation in late seventeenth-century usage. An early eighteenth-century usage refers to animals as 'the nations of the field and wood'.

Race

Finally in this trio we come to the word 'race', again a word which appears in most Romance languages and is cited as deriving from the French *race* and the earlier French *rasse*, matched by the Italian *razza* and Portuguese *raça* (*Compact Oxford English Dictionary*, 1993). Its earliest uses in the sixteenth century have a sense of 'breeding', persons of the same family or bred from the same ancestors and, like many of the other words we have traced, it could be applied to animals as well as humans. In 1600, it was used to mean 'a nation or tribe of people regarded as of common stock' and there are indications that it was used to mean simply a people of a land or even just a class of people as in 'a race of heroes'. It was not until the late eighteenth century and early nineteenth century that it began to acquire the meaning of 'one of the great sub-divisions of mankind'. By the late nineteenth and early twentieth centuries, it had become the key term in a whole science of classifying the divisions of humankind by physically defined races which were also widely believed to be the basis of differences in ability and temperament in a global racial hierarchy (Balibar and Wallerstein 1991; Banton 1987; Malik 1996). After challenges to this race science in the early part of the twentieth century, by the 1950s the term 'race' was in retreat. The

1986 *Oxford Reference Dictionary* states that the notion of 'race as a rigid classificatory system or system of genetics has largely been abandoned'.

Looked at etymologically and historically, the usages of these three terms, 'ethnic', 'nation' and 'race', support the suggestion that all three have a great deal of common ground. Contained in their past and present usages are ideas of common descent, a common belief in shared descent, ideas of class or type and about the people of a place, country, kingdom or other form of state. Closely associated or implicated in these terms – and especially in *ethnos* and 'ethnic' – are notions of cultural character, language and difference and foreignness. Despite the fact that they are such closely related ideas, race, nation and ethnic group are frequently considered to be quite different topics: race and racism, nation and nationalism and ethnic groups and ethnicity. Remarkably, one recent publication dealing with 'racism' states that it does not 'deal with "ethnicity", a topic covered by a different volume' (Bulmer and Solomos 2000).

The demise of race

We have referred to the decline of the term 'race' and this is certainly true by contrast with what may be regarded as the high point of racial terminology and race thinking – somewhere in the last quarter of the nineteenth century and the first quarter of the twentieth. The Nazi regime in Germany, through to the end of the Second World War in 1945, adopted race science as the guide to its genocidal politics, although academic and scientific attacks on race thinking had already begun. Race thinking had four main characteristics. *First*, that it was possible to classify the whole of humankind into a relatively small number of races defined primarily by physical and visible difference. The *second* was that races so defined shared not just appearance type but also temperament, ability and moral qualities. The *third* was that there was something that could be called 'racial inheritance', whereby the physical and moral qualities of the race were preserved through racial descent. And the *fourth* was that the

races of the world were hierarchically ordered with something referred to as the White race, the Caucasian race or
sub-division of these (Nordic, Anglo-Saxon) being superior
to all others.

All four of these 'propositions' are now either rejected or
not regarded as having any social scientific value. Although
physical characteristics (such as skin colour and eye and hair
formation) are clustered in particular populations, the attempt
to arrive at final classifications of races has largely been abandoned. This is both because we know that there is significant
variation within populations referred to as 'races' and because
of the sheer difficulty of determining boundaries between
races, not least because of the movement and mingling of
populations. It is, however, the second and third propositions
that are most roundly rejected – the idea that racial difference
'predicts' social and moral qualities. There never was anything but speculative support for such arguments and anthropology and sociology now adopt the contrary argument – that
social and cultural qualities are socially and culturally transmitted. All these first three taken together were components
of the fourth proposition, the equally discredited white
supremacist line of argument. (Students who wish to follow
some of the points raised here should consult Banton 1977;
Barzun 1965; Jacobson 1998; Malik 1996.) It is also important to understand that this basic set of propositions about
races, and the very idea that racial difference was so important, made other subsidiary propositions possible. Most
significantly, the belief among 'white' western populations
in the superiority of the Caucasian race was important in
supporting two positions: that white peoples had some historic destiny to rule over or even supersede and eliminate
lower races, and that race mixing was dangerous.

Culture and ethnicity are not the same

We have referred to 'descent and culture' as common points
of reference, but they are not of equal weight. Descent, the
belief in common descent and the importance attached to
common descent are unmistakably components of race,

nation and ethnicity. Culture is more problematic. Nations and ethnic groups are not, for example, 'culture groups' in the sense that the boundaries of some cultures are co-terminous with the boundaries of the nation or ethnic group. Cultures are both wider and narrower than, for example, nations. This can be seen if we think of culture and religion. We can distinguish analytically between cultures and religions, the first referring to custom and practice often with reference to a particular group, and the second referring to communities of faith. In practice, culture and religion are very much bound up with each other, and are implicated in the definition of boundaries around groups. Thus religious cultures such as Islam and Christianity are part of the cultural definition of some nation-states; but they have also a global presence in the shape of Christians or Muslims *beyond* any particular nation-state. But cultures may also be *narrower* than nations in the sense that all societies, or rather nation-states, are not comprehended by a single culture. They are divided and differentiated by class and regional cultures and differences of language and religion. And it is also possible to speak of culture without attaching it to groups defined by descent; as in civilizational culture, youth culture and class culture. Danielle Conversi nicely puts the conflation of 'ethnicity and culture':

> In the literature on nationalism, the terms ethnic and culture are often confused. . . . By ethnicity we refer to a belief in putative descent. Ethnicity is thus similar to race. Culture is instead an open project . . . [but] since culture is necessarily based on tradition and continuity, it is often confused with ethnicity. (Conversi 2000, pp. 134–5)

The proper emphasis on descent is certainly confirmed by the etymological discussion above – the theme of *descent and common origin is much more central than culture*. However, whilst Conversi is technically correct, some compromise is needed. The association of 'ethnic' and 'culture' has become very familiar and the claim to share a culture is so commonly a key component of the claim to 'sharedness' alongside common descent. People, or nations, or ethnic groups are saying, in effect, 'We are the people, we come from the same stock, we live(d) in the same place, and our customs and beliefs are these.' It is worth noting that this way of thinking about 'groups' and 'cultures' implies a rather crude and dated idea of 'culture'. It is used to mean culture as some*thing* (a list of attributes) which a group 'possesses'. This is as static and simplistic an idea of culture as it is of 'group'; nonetheless, it is commonly found in the sociology of ethnicity. Later we will discuss how social actors deploy cultural 'markers' in the drawing of group boundaries in social relations.

In this volume we shall continue to deal principally with ethnicity but only whilst understanding that the topic cannot be separated from the other two, race and nation. So with a primary focus on ethnicity, we shall continue to be drawn towards 'race, racism, nations, and nationalism'. We shall also be dealing with these three representations of 'descent and culture' in the *modern* world; in several respects they are very much modern topics. Ethnic group identities or ethnicity have taken on new and important meanings in modern nation-states; 'race' was the popular, political and scientific word for most of the nineteenth century and much of the twentieth, and racism (as the attribution of inherent and unequal qualities to peoples) remains important, however much a classificatory and biological idea of 'race' has lost its force. Nations and nationalism are a product of modernity and the nineteenth- and twentieth-century dominance of the 'nation-state' as a political form is the key to this. Anthony Smith (1986) in, for example, his *The Ethnic Origin of Nations*, has long argued for the pre-modern origins of ethnic groups or nations but he also is very clear about the link between 'nation' and 'ethnicity'; the latter is important because of the importance of the former:

> Nationalism extends the scope of ethnic community from purely cultural and social to economic and political spheres; from predominantly private to public sectors. To make any real headway in the *modern* world, ethnic movements must stake their claims in political and economic terms as well as cultural ones, and evolve economic and political pro- grammes. . . . Even dominant ethnic groups must turn a latent, private sense of ethnicity into a public manifest one, if only

to ensure the national loyalty of their members against the claims of other groups. . . . Nationalism has endowed ethnicity with a wholly new self-consciousness and legitimacy as well as a fighting spirit and political direction. (Smith 1981, pp. 19–20)

This is not to say that 'descent and culture communities' are new or specifically modern, as Smith (1986) has brilliantly shown. But the representation of descent and culture communities in this modern and political language of nation, race and ethnicity is new. In the summary below we clarify the exact nature of the shared terrain of the three concepts.

Defining the core and the divergences

Race refers to descent and culture communities with two specific additions:

1   the idea that 'local' groups are instances of abstractly conceived divisions of humankind; and
2   the idea that race makes explicit reference to physical or 'visible' difference as the primary marker of difference and inequality.

Nation refers to descent and culture communities with one specific addition:

The assumption that nations are or should be associated with a state or state-like political form.

Ethnic group refers to descent and culture communities with three specific additions:

1   that the group is a kind of sub-set within a nation-state;
2   that the point of reference of difference is typically cultural difference, and cultural markers of social boundaries, rather than physical appearance; and
3   often that the group referred to is 'other' (foreign, exotic, minority) to some majority who are presumed not to be 'ethnic'.

Summary

In this chapter we have traced the meanings of race, ethnic (group) and nation, mainly through their etymological history – the record of usages and meanings recorded in dictionaries. We have concluded that the idea of an ancestry group, of a people linked by common descent, however loosely that is thought of, is the core idea of all three terms. These terms also have connotations which are peculiar to the individual word – a core of shared meaning and some word associations which are not shared. Only the word 'race', for example, has a strong association of biological difference linked to a universal classificatory system. The meanings of the words have also changed and some new meanings are relatively recently acquired. In the next chapter, we turn to a related theme – the fact that the actual import of the words is found to be different in different societies. By import, we mean the force of meaning which the term carries, the emphasis and importance contained within the term. In different cultures and contexts, the import of the words varies accordingly. This we examine by looking at discourses of race and ethnicity in the USA, the UK, Malaysia and other examples around the world.

2
Multiple Discourses of Ethnicity: Differences by Country and Region

We have discussed how people use the terms 'ethnicity' and 'ethnic groups' in general and formal usage. In this chapter, we emphasize how people use ethnic terminology in different countries and contexts; there is thus a discourse of ethnicity in the USA, in Britain, in East Asia, in Latin America and other settings. We begin by looking at the 'language of ethnicity' in the USA and Britain, and then in countries in Asia. In Asia we look closely at the case of Malaysia, where a discourse of race and ethnic groups has been influenced by its colonial British history. We examine other examples, notably Singapore and Japan, where the formation of *national* identity sets the limits for the perception of 'others'. In Latin America, we look at Brazil; and lastly research into the terminology of ethnicity on a world comparative basis.

The USA is an important case study for two reasons. It is an influential country with a highly developed sociology. It is also a primary case of the black/white model of ethnicity, predicated on an idea of fixed racial difference. Britain shares some features with the USA but has shown some greater flexibility, in, for example, the 'acceptance' of categories of mixed-race origins. Malaysia has a colonial history but is now a postcolonial and 'plural' society where ethnic and racial categories oscillate in their social and political significance. Singapore has a multi-ethnic population with a large Chinese majority and is distinctive for becoming a nation-state for the first time in the postcolonial period. By contrast, Japan has a longer established national identity, the strength of which makes it difficult to accept or embrace a multi-ethnic identity. Brazil has long held a critical place in the sociology of race and ethnicity. It shares with the USA a history of enslavement of Africans, whilst in its post-slavery history Brazil has manifested a quite different view of 'races' from that found in the USA. Some areas, notably the African continent, are not discussed in detail here (see Ejiogu 2001), but the chapter ends with a commentary on Morning's (2008) global study of systems of ethnic and racial classification in multiple countries.

There are three milieux within which the terminology of ethnic (and race and nation) is used. These are the *scholarly*, the *political*, civic and public, and the *popular* or 'everyday' discourse. When we discuss the works of social scientists we are exploring the scholarly discourse. But a terminology of ethnic groups is used in public administration, especially in the Census. Government Census bodies will often take advice from academics (see Hirschmann et al. 2000; Lott 1998); they are also influenced by the everyday use of racial terms in the country. The US Census has been very much influenced by the effects of slavery, the position of post-slavery African Americans and the 'black/white' divide. The popular discourse may remain hidden, unless ethnographic or survey data are available. Although we can expect that scholarly and public usages influence popular discourse, the reverse is also the case. Studies of popular discourse have been infrequent but are growing (see Baumann 1996; Billig 1995; Cashmore 1987; Condor 2000; Fenton 2007; Hirschmann et al. 2000; Rodriguez and Cordero-Guzman 1992; Waters 1990, 1999; Wetherell and Potter 1992).

The USA

The American view of races, popular, political and academic, is grounded in slavery. Jordan has traced the way in which the treatment of African ('Negro') servants was, in the latter half of the seventeenth century, distinguished from the treatment of white indentured servants (Jordan 1968). Africans became not servants but slaves *durante viva* (for life) and their offspring were also slaves. Under the independence constitution, slaves were accorded lesser status than 'free men', and for purposes of taxation and population accounting were reckoned as 60 per cent of a person. They were neither regarded as citizens nor capable of becoming citizens, and the equation of 'Negro' African ancestry with social status became almost an exact match. In the last three decades of slavery particularly, the institution was fiercely debated and one key defence of slavery was that 'Negros' were a race apart, were lower in a hierarchy of races and in civilization, and that slavery guaranteed the proper relationship of 'white' and 'Negro' (Fredrickson 1972, 1988).

As Jacobson, one of most prominent social historians of 'whiteness', has observed, the idea of and the practice of whiteness can be traced to the earliest days of the USA, as well as to the prior colonial condition of slavery:

> In 1790 Congress enacted that 'all free white persons who, have, or shall migrate into the United States and shall give satisfactory proof, before a magistrate, by oath, that they intend to reside therein, and shall take an oath of allegiance, and shall have resided in the United States for one whole year, shall be entitled to the rights of citizenship'. So natural was the relation of whiteness to citizenship that, in the debate which followed, the racial dimension of the act remained unquestioned. . . . nowhere did the nation's first legislators . . . pause to question the limitation of naturalized citizenship to 'white persons'. (Jacobson 1998, p. 22)

In colonial America, captured and enslaved Africans provided the answer to an urgent need for a plantation labour force. In the matter of land and labour, both crucial to the success of the colonies, African slaves were property and they were a labour force to be controlled. And Native American Indian peoples were occupants of the land and thus a threat to commercial land ownership and expansion. In the early years of independent USA, the formation of militia of 'free and able-bodied whites' was in view of the potential threat from 'Negro' slaves and native peoples. As Jacobson says, the very notion of 'providing for the common defence' was inherently racial where it applied to slaveholding, on the one hand, and frontier settlement, on the other (Jacobson 1998, p. 25). Thus, from the outset, ideas of freedom and human dignity applied to whites. The ideals of the Enlightenment simultaneously identified the 'enlightened' races and the lower peoples. US citizenship and civic participation were founded on a concept of white and black, of white and red and of enlightened and savage (see Fenton 1999; Jacobson 1998).

The abolition of slavery and the attempt to found a non-racial citizenship failed when white solidarity, class interests (Camejo 1976) and political manoeuvres (Vann Woodward 1964) combined to create a segregated society in which racial status, and the dominant position of whites, became a permanent feature of the social structure of the USA. White Americans and especially white Southerners, who had been protected from direct labour competition with black Americans by slavery, combined politically to ensure continued protection from competition once black men and women were formally free. The idea and concept of race became the language and discourse within which relations between 'white and black' were understood. The two principal groups were thought of precisely in this way: as white and black, as two races, as fundamentally different and as being in a relationship of superiority and inferiority.

Immigration to the USA

In the European colonial period and early United States, that is the seventeenth, eighteenth and early nineteenth centuries, population was largely drawn from Britain, Ireland and the continent of Africa. Then the sources of new population became more diverse. Between 1820 and 1920, some 35 million people came to the USA from almost every corner of Europe. As Oscar Handlin has written, the failure of agricultural economies drew millions of European peasants to America:

> From the heart of the continent (what is now Germany) came six million . . . from the North went two million Scandinavians, . . . from the South went almost five million Italians,

> . . . from the East went some eight million others – Poles and
> Jews, Hungarians, Bohemians, Slovaks, Ukrainians, Ruthe-
> nians, . . . and before the century was out three million more
> were on the way from the Balkans and Asia Minor. (Handlin
> 1973, p. 36)

Many of these immigrants were, in their turn, viewed as
undesirable, in the light of their lowly economic position and
their concentration in the poorest quarters of the growing
industrial cities of the United States. They were the labour
force of expanding industrial capitalism. They were also
viewed as different races, as Matthew Frye Jacobson (1998)
has so comprehensively demonstrated. Early settlers had
included Irish and Scottish, and were therefore, in the racial
lexicon, 'Celts'. But the early citizens of the USA, in the main,
came to view themselves as Anglo-Saxons, and were predominantly Protestant. Above all, Jacobson argues that throughout the nineteenth century, newcomers – not Anglo-Saxon
Protestants – were viewed as representatives of racial divisions *within* Europe – Celts, Teutons, Nordics, Jews and
Slavs. They were viewed both as inferior to Anglo-Saxons
and as a threat to Anglo-Saxon civilization. Gradually,
however, the idea of racial divisions among Europeans gave
way to a pan-European racial identity of whiteness and the
racial concept of Caucasian. Before this seemingly neat racial
conception was confirmed, there were some ambivalent and
ambiguous distinctions to be made in the delineation of
whiteness in the USA.

Italian immigrants to the late nineteenth-century US South,
already in the grip of Jim Crow practices (the name given to
black–white segregation), may not have been quite regarded
as 'black' but they were certainly not unequivocally 'white'.

> In certain regions of the Jim Crow South Italians occupied a
> racial middle ground within the otherwise unforgiving, binary
> caste system of white-over-black. Politically Italians were
> indeed white enough for naturalization and for the ballot,
> but socially they represented a problem population at best.
> (Jacobson 1998, p. 57)

The new Italian immigrants in New Orleans were regarded
as having compromised their racial status by their close rela-

tionships with blacks, which broke Southern codes of racial separateness. They were seen as dark-skinned and 'like Negroes'. According to Jacobson:

> It was not just that Italians did not look white to certain social arbiters, but that they did not act white. In New Orleans Italian immigrants were stigmatized in the post-Civil war period because they accepted economic niches (farm labour and small tenancy for instance) marked as 'black' by local custom, and because they lived and worked comfortably with blacks. (Jacobson 1998, p. 57)

Italians were therefore one of several groups over the long period of immigration to the USA who were viewed as somehow 'in-between' in the racial classification (for fuller accounts see Jacobson 1998; also Barret and Roediger 1997). In the twentieth century, for example, there was the question of classification of Indian peoples from the Indian continent; most of those from the northern areas of India were light-skinned. Anthropologists had also regarded them as being 'Caucasians'. As David Hollinger observes:

> The American sense of whiteness was not simply an application of the Caucasian of classical race theory. Immigrants from India were undoubtedly Caucasian according to physical anthropologists in the early twentieth century, but the United States Supreme Court ruled in 1923 that south Asian immigrants and their descendants were sufficiently 'non-white' to be ineligible for naturalization as whites. (Hollinger 1995, p. 30)

When in 1975 the Federal Interagency Committee on Education was given the task of adopting standard racial classifications, the purpose had shifted to inclusion rather than exclusion. Measurement and counting by race was designed to allow for the assistance of groups who had been and were discriminated against. Asians (on Indians, see Lott 1998, p. 40), including Chinese, Japanese and Koreans, constituted a complication of US classifications. After the liberalization of immigration laws in 1965, these populations all grew through immigration. Only one other broad grouping has had a comparable effect in destabilizing the US conceptions of race and ethnicity, and that is the population officially referred to as Hispanics, a category that is not officially either ethnic or 'racial'.

Changes of the late twentieth century

By the late twentieth and turn of the twenty-first century, these population shifts have become quite dramatic. The most important changes are the increase in the proportion of the population defined as Hispanic (Rodriguez 2000), the increased size of the Asian population, the emergence of a social movement of white ethnicities, a heightened awareness of multi-ethnic or multi-racial categories and the importance of ethnic categories for the distribution of state funds and resources (Lott 1998). These changes have not only led to modification of racial categories but have also begun to prompt a question of the category 'race' itself.

Among key features of 'race' in America is the idea that races have been regarded as naturally occurring and *fundamental* divisions of humankind – and thus of American society. They are seen to be permanent, 'fixed' and real divisions of the population. As a consequence, we begin to speak of 'race relations' – or relations between races as a special type of social relationship. Race relations are also viewed as problematic, which implies a natural antipathy between races. The American discourse of ethnicity began to shift the emphasis.

Ethnicity and changing ideas of race

Publications in the 1970s began to add a new discourse, that of 'ethnicity', to the debates about communities and difference. Indeed, this was a discourse within which 'difference' was the primary idea rather than a hierarchy of (two) races in relationships of conflict and mistrust. The book which popularized the term 'ethnicity' was the edited collection *Ethnicity: Theory and Experience* (Glazer and Moynihan 1975). The perspective was comparative and worldwide, including examples from Asia, the (then) Soviet Union, India, China and South America. American blacks were discussed as a case of 'neo-ethnicity', part of a perceived revitalization of ethnic identities in the USA by whites and non-whites alike. In other contexts, the terminology of 'races' was much more common in relation to 'black' and 'white'. The notion of 'ethnic groups' was frequently applied to differentiate between whites by countries of origin in (white) Europe.

Many people have noted the ambiguities resulting from 'racial' classifications of Hispanics (see Hollinger 1995). Rodriguez and Cordero-Guzman (1992) were among the first to document the shifts in meaning and emphasis in racial classification. They acknowledge that the concept of 'races' as conceived through the nineteenth and at least the first half of the twentieth century is discredited. Where 'race' has survived as a *scholarly* term it reflects the fact that the idea of 'racial difference' persists in *popular* usage. Races are, thus, culturally constructed in local discourses. One such is the US paradigm of 'race as biologically or genetically based' and unchanging, and dominated by the divide between a category 'white' and the 'one-drop' rule for blackness (see F. J. Davis 2001). The white race 'was defined by the absence of any non-white blood and the black race was defined by the presence of any black blood' (Rodriguez and Cordero-Guzman 1992) – an asymmetrical definition reflecting US inequalities of power. The important conclusion is the much wider one that they correctly draw:

> Popular definitions of 'race' vary from culture to culture [suggesting] the importance of historical events, development or context in determining 'race'. That there are different systems of racial classification in different countries (and sometimes within countries) is quite counter to the usual perception that most White Americans hold of race in the US. (Rodriguez and Cordero-Guzman 1992, p. 524)

Their evidence is drawn from a study of the racial or cultural identifications of Puerto Ricans in an interview survey. Their study was able to discount any idea that Hispanic respondents did not understand the question or that they simply searched for an intermediate (between white and black) category to describe themselves. They continued to show that they *understood* race as a cultural category which they connected to their Puerto Rican or Hispanic identity. In the authors' words, 'they emphasise the greater validity of ethnic or cultural identity. Culture is race' (Rodriguez and Cordero-Guzman 1992, p. 524). This definition of race as a 'cultural category' is rare in the USA. The authors are suggesting that it stems from the South American framework for understanding difference.

This is quite at odds with the US Census's own advice on Census completion:

> How should Hispanics or Latinos Answer the Race Question?
>
> People of Hispanic origin may be of any race and should answer the question on race by marking one or more race categories shown on the questionnaire, including White, Black or African American, American Indian or Alaska Native, Asian, Native Hawaiian or Other Pacific Islander, and Some Other Race. Hispanics are asked to indicate their origin in the question on Hispanic origin, not in the question on race, because in the federal statistical system ethnic origin is considered to be a separate concept from race. (US Census Bureau 2000)

In the Rodriguez and Cordero-Guzman study and in the 2000 Census, over half of the respondents chose a category 'other', that is other than the substantive race categories offered. In the US Census population data for 2000, among the non-Hispanic population only 467,770 chose 'some other race', or 0.2 per cent of the total population. But the 'some other race' category attracts a large number of Hispanics/Latinos: 42 per cent of all Hispanics (almost 15 million) described themselves as 'some other race'. Through the increased numbers of Hispanics in America, a contrasting and incompatible conception of race has run up against an established American classificatory system.

Although we do not know what will happen in the future, it shows that the fast-growing Hispanic/Latino minority does not find it easy to work with the US race classification system. The place of Hispanics is complicated by the fact that 47.9 per cent of them describe themselves as 'white'. One result has been that Census authors and others have begun to use the phrase 'non-Hispanic whites', subtracting Hispanics from the total white population. This is because Hispanics are viewed as a disadvantaged group, or a group of whom some may not be socially recognized as 'white'. It is even possible to see the term 'real whites' (López and Stanton-Salazar 2001) referring to non-Hispanic whites, the latest twist in the long US story of defining whiteness (see also Rodriguez 2000).

David Hollinger's *Postethnic America* (1995), subtitled 'Beyond Multiculturalism' adds a contrasting viewpoint. Rather than suggest that the US race classification is breaking up, he is concerned that there are intellectual and political flows in exactly the opposite direction. The *intellectual* flow is in the direction of recognizing that the term 'race' is obsolete; but the *practical* (administrative) and political flow is tending to consolidate the 'recognition' of races in American life. In administrative practice, five racial categories – white, black or African American, Asian, American Indian and Alaska native, Native Hawaiian and other Pacific islander, plus a 'some other race' category – are increasingly deployed not only in the Census but also as instruments of public policy. Hollinger describes the routine nature of these categories, plus the quasi-racial category 'Hispanic':

> On application forms and questionnaires, individuals are routinely invited to declare themselves to be one of the following: Euro-American (or sometimes white), Asian American, African American, Hispanic (or sometimes Latino) and Indigenous peoples (Native American). (Hollinger 1995, p. 23)

This he calls the 'ethno-racial' pentagon, or the five great 'ethno-racial blocs' which resemble the global categories of nineteenth- and early twentieth-century scientific racism – Caucasian, Mongoloid, Negroid, Amerindian – with Hispanic as the outlier. The 'great races' are embedded in the American imagination and are reproduced by the US Census. Hollinger believes this classification persists in popular thought, despite the recognition of the concept of races as a scientific and historical error:

> Although the insight that ethno-racial distinctions are 'socially constructed' is rapidly gaining ground, it is still obliged to struggle against popular, deeply entrenched assumptions that ethno-racial groups are primordial in foundation. (Hollinger 1995, p. 26)

The strong idea of 'great races of the world', following nineteenth-century thinking, has made an imprint on the US Census for some considerable time. Historically, the emphasis has always been on the black–white or 'Negro–Caucasian' division, as Lee has shown in her review of Census categories from 1890 to 1990 (Lee 1993). Skin colour and a belief in pure races has been a constant theme, although in some Census years 'race mixtures' were notably recorded. The main finding of Lee's review of Census usage over this 100-year period was that the actual categories changed and the Census vacillated between offering few categories – presumably for simplicity – and many categories – presumably for fine-tuned sophistication. This can be summarized from Lee's findings thus:

1890: eight groups listed of which four were variants of black.
1900: five groups when the 'varieties of black', e.g. octoroon and quadroon, were dropped.
1910 and 1920 had six classes and in 1930 ten groups were listed.
1950: the groups shrank to seven and 1960 went back up to eleven.
1970 went back down again to nine.
1980 and 1990 listed fifteen groups although the 1980 Census dropped the term 'race' from the Census questionnaire (cf. Snipp 2003).

The 1890 Census listing of mixed bloods reflected 'the concerns of southern politicians over racial purity' but the terms mulatto, quadroon and octoroon, as indicated above, were to drop out of use (Bennett 2000).

The fluctuations betrayed the fact that the Census, and the scholars whom it consulted, not only did not know what the 'final' list of 'races' should be, but also were not sure what a race was. Equally, none of these difficulties was enough to discourage the Census from creating the (changing) categories, or enough to stop calling them 'races'.

If the logical basis for racial classification has come to be seriously questioned and the practice of classification is and has been highly varied, we could ask what the basis of racial classification is and why it persists in more or less the form that it takes in the Census. One answer is that, since the 1960s civil rights legislation, Census data demonstrate a pattern of disadvantage. They are (in some degree) the basis of the allocation of resources in programmes designed to maximize equality of opportunity and to compensate for historical discriminations (see Bennett 2000). In theory, for the first time in American history, racial categories have become a basis for inclusion rather than exclusion.

The tone was set by the US Commission on Civil Rights (1973; see Lott 1998, p. 34), who argued that 'racial and ethnic data are essential tools with which to combat discrimination and plan and monitor affirmative action to remedy past racial wrongs'. In 1978, the Office of Management and Budget issued Statistical Directive 15 that established the 'ethno-racial pentagon' (see Hollinger 1995) classification and became a standard for the collection of data by many public agencies. Federal agencies were more and more required by legislation to collect and use enumerations of the population along the lines of Directive 15 and 'increasingly state and local governmental agencies, marketing firms, private industry, and the non-profit sectors also used this same classification' (Lott 1998, p. 47).

Thus the groups who might benefit from what effectively is recognition as a minority resisted any proposal to end racial enumeration or changes which might harm their interests. The imperative to collect data on 'races' in the American population persists despite the Office of Management and Budget's own finding that:

> There are no clear, unambiguous, objective generally agreed-upon definitions of the terms 'race' and 'ethnicity'. . . . The categories do not represent objective 'truth' but rather are ambiguous social constructs. (Office of Management and Budget 1995, cited in Lott 1998, p. 65)

The construction of races in the USA began as an exercise in the creation of a white society, and a society in which whites were to be, and remain, socially and politically dominant. This society was predicated from as early as the seventeenth century on racialized categories. The single most notable feature of the category of a dominant group (e.g. 'white') is that it is undifferentiated. In the USA, the category 'white' is the numerical majority and is a single category covering, until relatively recently, up to 90 per cent of the population. In category terms this huge population, diverse in language, country of origin, class position from the super-rich to the abjectly poor, is united by a single feature, its whiteness, that is its membership of something called the white or Caucasian race. The same is true of the UK, where the counting of ethnicity in the Census initially created a single ethnic group, 'whites', which included 94 per cent of the population. This suggests that whiteness is viewed as unproblematic, either from the point of view of civic status or from the point of view of discrimination and social inclusion. When whites in the USA *are* differentiated by 'culture and descent' they are classified as ethnic groups according to ancestry. Thus whites have got ethnicity, non-whites have got 'race'. To be a 'race' in the contemporary United States (other than the undifferentiated white race) you need to be a 'minority' in the sense of suffering disadvantage and discrimination. Thus, given the dominance of a 'race' discourse in the USA, *ethnic* groups and ethnic differences often have a 'white' connotation. By contrast, in Britain, where public discourse uses the language of ethnicity, the term 'ethnic group' retains its meaning of minority status and foreign origins; ethnic groups in the UK are 'not white'. Some of the themes discussed in this chapter will be revisited in chapter 5.

Where have all the races gone?
The case of the UK

In the UK, the Census did not record 'race' or 'ethnic origin' at all until 1990. The question of a 'non-white' presence in the UK became a public issue in the 1960s. It was then that an anti-immigrant politics emerged, after immigration into Britain of people from Britain's former colonies in the Caribbean and India. Official documents consistently used the word 'coloured' in attempts to assess the size and characteristics of the non-white population. In the Censuses of 1960, 1970 and 1980, the non-white population was recorded through country of origin, country of origin of parents and country of origin of the 'Head of Household' (see Fenton 1996). By the 1980s, the so-called New Commonwealth population had a much higher proportion born in the UK and so the use of country of birth as a proxy for ethnic group became unworkable. When in 1990 the UK Census did record ethnic group, the word 'ethnic' did not appear on the form; rather categories were provided as responses to a question as to which group best described the individual. But in all reporting of the 1990 data this question was reported as 'ethnic group'. The idea that *everybody* belonged to an ethnic group had entered the public consciousness on an official basis for the first time (Banton 2000). Although the terms 'race relations' and 'racism' remain important parts of the public language of discussion, the word 'race' and certainly the word 'races' in the plural are less part of the public discourse in the UK when compared with the USA. Indeed, the US Census recognizes both 'race' and 'ethnicity' as distinct concepts and both are recorded. The UK Census has a single discourse, which is about ethnic groups and, typically, minority ethnic groups. Thus the British Census shares with the USA the idea of classifying 'minorities', but it calls them ethnic.

However, when in the UK 'ethnic group' was recorded in 1990, a system of classification was devised which was clearly predicated on a distinction between white and non-white, white comprising 94 per cent of the population. Precisely as in the USA, the interest in finer-tuned differentiation is confined to groups perceived as minorities, and as non-whites. In the UK, former Commonwealth countries, especially India, Pakistan, parts of Africa and the British Caribbean, are the substantial 'senders' of so-called non-whites. Others came to Britain from the Far East such as Hong Kong Chinese and Vietnamese refugees. If the question was about ethnic groups in the American sense, where it is often used to mean ancestry differences in the white population, then other groups would be recorded as 'ethnic groups', such as people with Irish, Polish, Italian, Australian, US-American background and more recently arrived East Europeans. There were two main changes for the 2001 Census: the inclusion of an Irish category under the 'white' heading and the inclusion of a mixed-origin category. The inclusion of the Irish category was the first break in the monolithic nature of the 'white' grouping, and an acknowledgement that whites might experience discrimination and social disadvantage. Like the USA, by the end of the twentieth century, use of the data to counter social disadvantage on ethnic lines has become the principal stated purpose of the collection of ethnically defined data (Fenton 1996). In the UK, the term 'ethnic' has become the dominant one in the official discourse of the population, but the group names listed in the Census are a curious mixture of race (colour) categories and national origin categories.

In popular and media discourse, 'race' survives. But there is no final permanent meaning given to the terms 'race' and 'ethnicity'; clearly, where both are used – as in the USA – the distinction is not clear. The distinctions that are made, in the UK or the USA, are different from each other and do not conform to any single logic of how the distinction should be made. In Britain, South Asian Indians have been described as 'coloured', 'black' and 'Indian' in different contexts, or at different times. The inescapable conclusion is that both the language used ('races', 'ethnic groups') and the actual classifications which are deemed to be important are a consequence of historical and embedded social practice. These categories are contested both by activist members of the groups and by more (or less) neutral academics and intellectuals, staggered at the inconsistency of it all or acting as advocates for 'their' group.

Discourse of races in postcolonial Malaysia

British colonial rule had a profound effect on the emergence of ethnic awareness in Malaysia (Hirschman 1986, 1987) and for three related reasons. The first is that it was responsible for stimulating the migration into Malaysia of large numbers of Chinese and Indians, many of whom remained in discrete work areas and areas of residence which marked them off from the Malays. The second is that British ideas of racial difference took on a public and official form when racial or ethnic categories were used to classify the population in, for example, the matter of the Census. Third, the British had a big hand in provoking Malay consciousness by proposing an independence constitution based on a non-ethnic or 'universalist' citizenship which threatened any idea of Malay special rights. Subsequently, they acceded to a constitution which *did* guarantee Malay special rights and thus built a definition of a 'Malay' into the constitution itself.

In an English-language Malaysian discourse, the word 'race' is the one most frequently used to denote these large group categories – Malays, Chinese and Indians. The *New Straits Times* is published in English (as well as Malay). The reporting of politicians' speeches, which may have been made in Malay or English, about 'racial conflict' almost always uses this terminology, speaking about the need to build 'racial harmony' or foster a society in which 'races may live side by side in peace and mutual respect'.

New Straits Times 19 April 2001
Chinese seek knowledge earnestly, Malays don't
. . . values and cultural practices hindering development must be eradicated. This was to ensure the progress of the various races in the country was balanced . . . different races with different cultures achieve varying degrees of success.

New Straits Times 17 April 2001
Bumiputera traders must be bold and emulate other races to succeed

New Straits Times 1 December 2000
BN [Barisan Nasional/National Front] committed to ethnic co-operation despite loss
. . . the electorate in Lunas had voted along religious and racial lines . . . there was no place for racial and religious sentiments.

In the above quotations, the terms 'races' and 'racial' are common. But the third headline refers to the commitment of the Barisan Nasional (the National Front, the party alliance in power) to 'ethnic co-operation' which certainly does not appear to convey anything different from 'racial co-operation'. The emphasis on religion stems from the fact that one of the challenges to the UMNO (United Malay National Organization) comes from the Islamic party. This party (the PAS, or Parti SeIslam Malaysia) is seen by the UMNO as a serious threat because of its potential to split the Malay vote. In the first story, Malays and Chinese are described as 'races' but it is clearly the perceived *cultural* difference which is at issue.

The use of the term 'race' in Malaysia stems from English usage in the colonial period but there is no evidence that it has the same resonance as when used in the UK or the USA. Leaving aside the complexity of Malaysian classifications (Hirschman 1987), the three broad groupings, Malay, Chinese and Indian, are seen primarily as different in two respects: first, in *political status*, with the Malays representing themselves as indigenous and the true heirs of the land, and second, in *culture*, with a boundary between Muslims and non-Muslims being the most important in marking the Malay–Chinese boundary. The Malay word *ras*, meaning race or racial, is not in such common use as a number of other words which convey a sense of 'people' or 'common origin'.

The word *rakyat* means folk or people but with a sense of 'common people' or 'folk'. It also has a secondary sense of nationality or citizenship, with *rakyat Malasia* meaning the Malaysian people or nation. *Warga* also means 'family' and 'people' and the phrase *warga negara* ('people of the state') means citizens and with the Malay suffix and prefix makes *kewarganegaraan*, to mean 'citizenship'. Probably more commonly used than either of these is the word *kaum*, which has an explicit sense of 'lineage group' but has also come to have a much broader sense of 'community' or even simply 'group'. Indicating its precise sense of lineage, Judith Nagata suggests that Malays may place value on a claim to Arab descent:

> Thus some 'Malays' who have been overseas for a number of years have returned with the new titles of Shah or Khan that demonstrates descent from a Middle Eastern lineage or *qu'om*. This is translated into Malay as *kaum* and has a comparable

meaning of 'lineage' or a 'people' but with a definite implication of shared descent. (Nagata 1974, p. 98)

Also in common usage is the word *orang* meaning people. The *Hippocrene Standard Dictionary* gives its first meanings as 'a human being; a man or woman; people generally (especially in the sense of other people)'. It may be combined with national or ethnic names to give phrases such as *orang Melayu*, a Malay; *orang Cina*, a Chinese person. (A Bidayuh man talking about his family told me his daughter had married *orang Canada*, a Canadian.) Through the colonial period and right up to today, *orang puteh* means a white person and at least in the colonial period meant primarily 'British'. *Orang* is also the word most used to refer to peoples indigenous to Malaysia who are not Malays and usually not Muslims. Of these the most frequently used is *orang asli*, 'native or indigenous people', and this is reproduced in government statements and documents when referring to 'development' programmes and state policy towards native peoples. *Orang asing* means foreigner and *orang bukit* (literally 'hill people') means aboriginal tribes people. Equally important, in the Malaysian politics of ethnicity, are the phrases *orang pendatang*, immigrants; *orang bukan-Melayu*, non-Malays; and *pendatang haram*, 'forbidden' or illegal immigrants, which in the 1990s and new millennium would often refer to Indonesians, Bangladeshis and Filipinos (see Coope 1993).

But at least as common as all of these, and most common of all in political discourse, is the word *bangsa* and its derivatives. Again it has a core meaning of 'descent' but Nagata has suggested that it combines meanings of descent and culture:

> The term *bangsa* conveys the double ideas of a people sharing both a common origin and a common culture. Etymologically it is derived from the Sanskrit *vamsa*, 'line of descent'. Emically it has a primordial quality, for it implies that the cultural traits are inalienably and inextricably associated with a particular people . . . carried by a community whose ultimate unity derives from a single origin. (Nagata 1981, p. 98)

Thus Malays are a *bangsa* – *bangsa Melayu* – although within that single *bangsa*, several sub-groupings could be defined, on the basis of territorial origin including regions of what is now Indonesia (see Hirschman 1987). It may be found in combination with *suku* meaning initially 'limb' or 'part', but also 'tribe' as part of a people; hence *sukubangsa* means sub-group within a population. And it may be used in combination with group names to indicate an 'ethnic' or 'national' group, hence *bangsa Cina* and *bangsa India* meaning Chinese and Indians. In this sense and context, *bangsa* comes close to a UK or US and English-language sense of ethnic group. But importantly it is also used in combination with Malaysia, the term used to describe the whole country, just as Malaysian refers to all people of Malaysia irrespective of 'ethnic' or 'racial' origin. Thus *bangsa Malasia* means the nation or the Malaysian people. Similarly, *Bangsa Bangsa Bersatu* ('unified') means United Nations. In derived forms it can take on the meaning of 'national', although there is an English borrowed word, *nasional*, which is used in some contexts. *Bahasa kebangsaan* (or *bahasa nasional*) means 'national language' and *lagu kebangsan* means 'national anthem'.

As well as the neutral 'national', it can also take on a meaning of 'nationalist' as in Parti Kebangsaan Melayu or Malay Nationalist Party; and the *Hippocrene Standard Dictionary* gives *gila kebangsaan* as ultra-nationalist, literally 'madly nationalist'. In Malaysia and other postcolonial societies, the word 'communalism' has described (in English) political groupings or sentiments which are rooted in ethno-national groups such as Malays or Chinese; no doubt *kebangsaan* would be one of the words which could translate 'communalist'. We may conclude that *bangsa* has the original meaning of descent and community of common origin but has broadened out to usages which would translate into English *as both 'ethnic' and 'national' depending on the context*. Furthermore, the discourse of *bangsa* in Malaysia is predicated both on the wish to secure a sense of identity of all Malaysians – as in *bangsa Malasia* – and on the differences between groups such as *bangsa Cina* and *bangsa Melayu*. These differences, as we said above, are largely arranged along two principles – the principle of indigenousness which Malays claim and which makes Chinese *keturunan pendatang* ('descendants of immigrants'), and the principle of culture, especially in the form of Islam and non-Islamic and language differences.

The importance of indigenousness resides in the claim made by Malays to be the people of the region and specifically the territory that is now Malaysia. During the independence negotiations, Malay political leaders feared that a 'universalist' citizenship that ignored the special position of Malays as indigenes would threaten to submerge their cultural survival and their material position (Andaya and Andaya 2001). This was based on their lower participation in the 'modern' economy compared to the Chinese and Indians and their over-representation among the rural poor. Thus the opposite of indigenousness – *pendatang* and *keturunan pendatang*, immigrants and their descendants – is also an important 'status' since the repetition of the history of migration tends to undermine the non-Malays' claim to equal rights. On the Malaysian peninsula there are a small number of *orang asli* (who are indigenes but neither Malays nor Muslims) but it was the entry into Malaysia of Sarawak and Sabah, in East Malaysia or North Borneo, which propelled further the idea of indigenes who were not Malays. In East Malaysia, non-Malay native peoples are more numerous than Malays and most are not Muslims. Since the logic of the recognition of the special rights of Malays was 'indigenousness', then *orang asli* and the East Malaysian native peoples had to be included. This led to the creation of the term *bumiputera*, translatable as 'sons or princes of the soil', that is native peoples comprising Malays, the great majority, and all other *orang asli*.

Nagata (1981) also refers to this 'newer, administratively created ethnic category, the *bumiputera* [or] "sons of the soil", a category contrasted with *kaum pendatang* – immigrant community, applied to the Chinese and Indians collectively'. She saw it as 'artificial' and unlikely to gain popular currency (see Nagata 1981, p. 109). But *bumis* and *non-bumis* have entered popular usage at least in press coverage of the special rights policies (see the press headlines above). The idea that one looks at, say, numbers of students entering higher education and simultaneously compares *bumi* and *non-bumi* entry is well established in Malaysian public discourse.

Asia and Latin America

Malaysia's history of racial or ethnic classification has been influenced by British colonial rule, but in large parts of Asia this has not been the case. Japan, far from being colonized, was in the twentieth century a colonial power. For much of the first half of the twentieth century, both Korea and Taiwan came under Japanese imperial rule, as did other countries during the Second World War. As one consequence of this colonization, many Koreans were brought to live and work in Japan with the result that Japan now has a substantial Korean-ancestry population, more than half a million people. Some have become naturalized Japanese as well as inter-married with Japanese citizens, so the total number of people with some Korean ancestry will be over 1 million, or about 1 per cent of Japan's population.

A powerful influence in Japan has been the development of a strong concept of 'Japanese-ness', what Siddle has referred to as '*Yamato minzoku*, the Japanese race/nation' (Siddle 2003). As Japan modernized through the late nineteenth and early twentieth centuries, it strengthened Japanese national identity, and was at the same time influenced by European racial ideology. This Japanese identity combined elements of racial particularism, posing Japan as a united family of people, with a strong sense of cultural uniqueness. The idea of kinship has made it difficult for non-Japanese (especially Koreans) to become naturalized Japanese, despite pressure on Koreans to 'Japanize', notably by changing their names. Other internal minorities, for example Ainu and Okinawans, have been subjected to pressures to assimilate. In addition to these minorities, Japan has a lower caste, Burakumin, who are much discriminated against and largely confined to undesired and 'polluting' work as well as to seg-regated living areas. Only through recent recognition of minority rights in Japan are Burakumin beginning to articu-late their claims for full social participation and civil rights.

The dominant idea in Japan has been the idea of nation, the idea of a 'pure' Japanese national family backed by a cultural sense of Japanese-ness (see Matsumoto 2008). So other categories are understood in Japan (Koreans, Ainu,

Okinawans, Burakumin) but are not as recognized in public spheres, nor is there a developed idea of a multicultural or multi-ethnic Japan. New migration to Japan, especially returning Japanese from Brazil, has an influence on how people see Japanese-ness. Japan's economic, social and cultural 'internationalization', and its political acceptance of some human rights conventions, may change the public climate, as Lu et al. (2005) observe.

Singapore is an interesting case since it only became a nation-state relatively recently, after having been a trading *entrepôt* of the British empire from the nineteenth century and briefly part of post-independence Malaysia (1963–5). It had been an independent state just before joining the Malaysian federation (1963) and 1965 marks the date of the independent present state of Singapore. The earlier inhabitants of the island were Malays but they are now a minority (about 14 per cent of the 4.7 million population of 2007) having been joined by Chinese, many of them traders, who are now the majority (77 per cent) population, and Indians (8 per cent). A Chinese population, which would have been a minority within a Malay- and Muslim-dominated Malaysia, is now a large majority in a multi-ethnic and basically secular and multi-religious (Buddhist, Taoist, Christian, Muslim) state.

The three main groups – Chinese, Malay, Indian – along with a small (2.4 per cent) 'Eurasian and other' group, are described as 'races' locally, as in Malaysia. In addition, Morning (2008) reports the Singapore Census as recording 'ethnic-dialect groups', with many of the dialect groups being Chinese dialects such as Hakka and Hokkien. Other groups listed reflect local migrations of, for example, Javanese, Thais and Filipinos. Singapore's identification cards indicate 'race' such as Javanese or Malay, along with country of birth. From its independence, Singapore has sought to promote 'multi-racialism', which features as one of the five central values of state ideology (Tan 2005). This was intended to ensure that 'no race is privileged or disadvantaged by state laws, institutions or policies' (Tan 2005, p. 413). In this sense, Singapore as a state promotes a universal non-ethnic citizenship. At the same time, cultural and language differences are recognized. For example, in state education policies, members of these groups are permitted to have part of their education taught in their mother tongue and part taught in English. Ethnic quotas also operate in the allocation of public housing, and since 1988 modified electoral laws have sought 'to ensure the representation in parliament of members from Malay, Indian and other communities' (Tan 2005, p. 416).

Many people regard Singapore as a case of the successful management of ethnic diversity (see Vasil 1995). The tensions in Malaysia are a constant reminder to guard against disaffected minorities and to ensure that the Chinese majority status does not become 'assertive' as an expression of national Chinese-ness. On the contrary, in Singapore the aim is to promote a Singaporean identity even if its majority character is Chinese. For the Chinese and the minority ethnic groups in Singapore the ideal is the retention of cultural identity consistent with national allegiance to Singapore.

We have already seen that Hispanic/Latino immigrants to the USA may be perplexed by the US racial classification system and this is because the US system is unlike the classificatory systems of most of Central and South America; indeed the US system is unusual compared to much of the rest of the world. The case of Brazil has attracted the attention of American scholars for just this reason. Because Brazil is a former European (Portuguese) colony and is a former slaveholding society, it has two structural similarities to the USA. If the hallmarks of the USA are the black/white binary, the one-drop rule and the distinct racial blocs (white, black, Asian, Native American and others), what distinguishes the Brazilian system are the indistinctness of group boundaries, the absence of a one-drop rule and a series of graduated colour differences. The Brazilian Census asks people to note their *cor ou raça*, their 'colour or race', and offers five categories: *branca*, *preta*, *parda*, *amarela*, *indigena* ('white', 'black', 'brown', 'yellow', 'native people'). But people's estimation of where they stand in this system is subject to significant change (Carvalho 2004) from one Census to the next. This is partly because, outside the Census, popular understanding of 'colour' differences is highly flexible and nuanced, depending in part on the social situation. Thus higher status may be viewed as 'lightening' a person. Although European and US racist ideas influenced Brazil at the turn of the twentieth century, it also has a tradition of 'racial democracy' and the celebration of diversity (see Freyre 1959). Undoubtedly, white and lighter-skinned people are on average more socially advantaged and the Brazilian government has recently adopted affirmative action to increase the number of black Brazilians in universities. US observers tend to regard the Brazilian idea of racial democracy as a form of national blindness to racism. However, despite their shared histories of slavery, Brazil and the USA have markedly different ideas about racial classification.

Ethnic classification across the world

There are many more 'discourses of race and ethnicity' across the world, varying by country, region and continent, too many to discuss here (but for the former Soviet Union and Russia, see Tishkov 1997; for China, see Dikotter 1992; for Africa, see Posner 2004). One way of discovering how 'ethnicity' is understood across the world is to examine worldwide systems of Census enumeration by 'ethnic group' or 'nationalities' or 'races', a task undertaken by Ann Morning in her analysis of information provided by the United Nations Statistical Division (UNSD) (Morning 2008). Not all countries yielded information, but the UNSD had records of the Census questionnaires of 141 countries, and it is these that Morning studied. Of the Censuses studied, 63 per cent incorporated some form of ethnic enumeration. The interesting question then becomes 'how do different Censuses classify groups?', for example as 'nationality' groups, 'tribal' groups, as well as 'ethnic groups'? A key finding is that regions of the world differ as to whether they enumerate at all: *absence of enumeration* was most likely in Europe and Africa, Asian countries were close to the norm and countries in the Americas were most likely to have ethnic enumeration (Morning 2008, p. 245). The author cites Rallu et al. (2004), who propose a typology of reasons for enumeration, or political purposes of enumeration. These are 'political control', 'non-enumeration in the name of national integration', a 'discourse of national hybridity' and 'enumeration for anti-discrimination'. *Political control* lay behind colonial administrations such as the one we have described during the colonial period in Malaysia. Until relatively recently, the same could be said of the USA, and throughout the Apartheid era, the strict classification of individuals in South Africa. In Europe, France is a good example of non-enumeration, where racial or ethnic designations are seen to be infringing individual rights and trespassing upon the concept of the universal citizen. Brazil (see above) and other Latin American countries (Wade 1997) are examples of socially and politically recognized hybridity. And today in the USA, and in the UK, anti-discrimination and the explanation of social disadvantage are the declared purposes of ethnic enumeration.

This review of the UNSD reports, from participating countries, showed that 'ethnicity' is the most universal language within which group identities are described, with almost 50 per cent of all classifications using 'ethnic' or a corresponding term (e.g. *grupo étnico*). Recording populations by 'nationality' and by 'indigenous' are the two next most common. 'Nationality' was most common in European countries, and 'indigenous' groups were commonly recorded in North and South America. The most striking finding is that of all countries (eighty-seven) recording population in this way, *only three used a race terminology as the primary term*. A further ten used race as a secondary term. A race terminology was, of course, most common in North America, and more generally 'in New World, former slave societies (e.g. US, Brazil, Jamaica) and/or their territories (e.g. American Samoa, Guam)' (Morning 2008, p. 247).

There are other complexities. Terms were often combined (e.g. ethnicity/nationality), and the populations described as 'ethnic' or 'racial' may in practice be similar across two or more examples. Some Censuses permitted respondents to name more than one category. They also differed in how voluntary or fixed the categories were. In a few cases, the country is an option: New Zealand, for example, uses the term 'ethnic groups' and reports the population as 'European', 'Maori', 'Asian', 'Pacific peoples', 'Middle Eastern, Latin American and African' and, for the first time in 2006, 'New Zealander'. Nepal is a good example of a particular discourse sensitive to regional social conditions: 'caste/ethnicity' is the Census terminology. Local conditions are significant but regional and continental patterns are clear. The language of race is deployed in North and South America and the language of race is an inheritance of slavery.

Summary: ethnicity and nation in their place

By looking at these cases in some detail, we can demonstrate that there is no single discourse of 'race, ethnicity and nation' but a series of such discourses attuned to the historical demands of specific countries, regions and internal social and political dynamics. These 'demands' include the search for social dominance as some people (colonists, early settlers, majorities) seek to exercise power over others. In the USA, racial definitions have been central to the idea of the American nation from its inception. The formally non-racial period after the Civil War was short-lived (about eleven years) and shallow rooted. Ethnic or racial categories are now revitalized by the distribution of public resources according to Census ethnic or racial enumerations and by minority mobilization. Furthermore, three changes, the emergence of 'Hispanic', the explicit construction of whiteness (see, for example, Frankenberg 1993; Jacobson 1998) and the importance of the Asian category, have begun to modify the socio-scape of ethnicity in the USA (see Hirschman et al. 2000).

In the UK, a 'simple' distinction between black and white did not have the same social force as in the USA. Britain's slaves were several thousand miles away. The debates about abolition of slavery involved racist arguments but race was initially not a domestic issue in the way that it was in America. In the early development of English ideas of nationhood in the sixteenth century, religious loyalties were more important than any 'ethnic' ideas (Greenfeld 1992). When England united with Wales and, much later, Scotland and Ireland, Britain's identity was again rooted in religion. The country viewed itself as Protestant and in hostility with France and the French (Colley 1992), who were Catholic. But Britain's position by the mid- and late nineteenth century as the head of a world empire gave force to a view of (white) Britons as natural masters of (non-white) 'less civilized' peoples. Racist and imperial concepts reappeared when immigrants from colonies and former colonies came to Britain in the 1950s.

However, by the time race became an issue in British politics in the late 1950s the word 'race' itself was already under suspicion as a spurious scientific term. The fourth national survey of ethnic groups in Britain was titled *Ethnic Minorities in Britain* (Modood et al. 1997), whilst its predecessor had been called *Black and White Britain* (Brown 1984). Academic writers are inclined to place 'race' in inverted commas and to hedge their bets by writing of 'race and ethnicity', often without specifying why they are using two terms and what the difference between them is intended to be.

Malaysia provided a crucial example because it is a society where 'race' is a public issue but the discourse is in both English and Malay – and no doubt in Malaysia's many other languages too. Having been part of the British empire, Malaysia had inherited some elements of a British discourse of races. An inspection of the words used for 'nation', 'race' and 'ethnicity' in Malaysia shows the emphasis on 'descent'. In Malaysia the overriding concern of the Malay majority was to reduce their fear of being submerged by the wealth, power and success of the Chinese. The political term *bumi* has taken on a quasi-ethnic meaning, and marks a boundary between people who regard themselves as indigenous and people who are tacitly regarded as 'in-comers' and their descendants.

Finally, references to Japan, Singapore, Brazil and New Zealand and Morning's (2008) survey of world usages again show that classification systems are rooted in local histories. In Japan, the history of modernization and the concept of the Japanese national family have shaped how Japanese have viewed 'others'. Morning's world survey showed that an 'ethnicity' language is the most common way of framing the measurement of the social origins of parts of the population, whilst in some countries 'nationality' and 'indigenous groups' were important. Most strikingly, Morning was able to show that an explicit language of race was confined largely to North and South America, a practice that is rooted in slavery and its abolition.

3

The Demise of Race: The Emergence of 'Ethnic'

The exploration of the word origins, of *ethnos* from the Greek and *natio* from Latin, shows that the ideas of ancestry, common origin or descent, and more generally 'peoplehood', are at the core of modern usages of the words 'ethnic' and 'nation' which are derived from these classical sources. The word 'race' too, as chapter 1 showed, shares many of the same meanings, and 'common descent' is a core meaning of race just as it is of the other two words. The three words converge around a single theme, descent and common origin. They differ in that 'race' has had a spurious 'scientific' sense of a universal classificatory system; 'ethnic' has a specific connotation of minority and alien status; and 'nation' implies a claim to self-rule.

So although 'race' has often had a sense very close to nation (Banton 1987), it also acquired a very special sense of division of humankind in a physical anthropological sense. 'American Negroes' were a historically specific group in American society; the use of the word 'Negroes' also implies a group which is a 'local' example of a universal racial category. 'Ethnic group' entirely lacks this association of abstract universal categories.

Ethnic group (ethnie) and nation

'Ethnie' shares much with 'nation' but lacks the sense of self-governing entity; if an ethnic group (ethnie) wishes to rule itself it needs to start calling itself a *nation*, as French Canadians have demonstrated. The existence of multinational states shows that 'state' and 'nation' are not *always* equated. But where several nations are recognized within a multinational state there are always pressures towards self-rule for the smaller nations. There may be claims to more or less limited autonomy, or a demand for independence (Ghai 2000); Scotland and Catalonia are two good examples. If ethnie are sometimes would-be nations, it is also in principle possible for nations to strip themselves of all but the loosest ethnic meanings, that is to stress the *civic* rather than *ethnic* criteria for membership of a nation. The USA is a classic example of a 'civic' nation; Israel one of the few surviving *explicitly* ethnic nations.

Our aim here is to single out some important themes and turning points in the history of these terms (for particular histories, see Banks 1996; Banton 1987; Fenton 2006; Gossett 1965; Greenfeld 1992; Hall 1998; Malik 1996). In anthropology and sociology the term 'ethnic groups' (or 'ethnie') has partly but not wholly replaced 'race and races'; in social anthropology 'ethnic groups' came to be used where once 'tribes' would have been used (see especially Banks 1996); and in political science and sociology the attention to ethnicity has been allied to an interest in nations and nationalism, especially in the distinction between civic and ethnic nationalism (Brown 2000; Brubaker 1996; Greenfeld 1992). This is a distinction which views the idea of nation as primarily 'civic' in which the 'people' are defined as citizens with a legal status rather than as a people who share ancestry and origins. This is contrary to nationalist themes which stress the shared ethnic origins of the people (Fenton and May 2003).

The demise of race

When we speak of the demise of race it is important to understand what is being discarded. There is no dispute that appearance types based on skin colour, hair type and facial features are in some rough and broad-based way distributed and clustered geographically. Nor is there any dispute that typical appearance may be associated with national groupings – most Swedish nationals are light-skinned. The idea that has been in retreat in academic usage for more than a century is the proposition that there are a quite small number of 'stocks' of the human race who share physical features, are genuinely members of an ancestral 'family' grouping and, in race theory, are predicted to have common *non-physical* characteristics such as temperament and ability. Five landmarks may be discerned in the demise of this idea. The first is the effect of Darwinian ideas of evolutionary change which, in scholarship and science but not in the popular imagination, put paid to the idea of 'fixed types'. This meaning of fixed type (see Banton 1977, 1987) replaced an older use of 'race' as synonymous with 'nation'; in scholarship and science the Darwinian idea of change was quite contrary to the idea of fixed type. A second is Durkheim's argument that 'races', which he appeared to treat almost as if they were equivalent to nations, was not a meaningful sociological category and could not be the basis of the explanation of social difference (Fenton 1980). The third was the attack on racial determinism – that is on the idea that racial characteristics were the basis of social difference and unequal abilities – by social anthropologists like Franz Boas, who effectively argued that social difference was explainable by reference to 'the environment' and culture (Boas 1982). Fourth came the concerted attack on the use of the word 'race' at all, by Huxley and Haddon (1935), who notably suggested its replacement by the term 'ethnic groups'. Fifth came the post-Second World War UNESCO-organized group who determined that the idea of races was imprecise and of limited value and laid the groundwork for the conclusion that the 'problem' to be studied was not 'races' but racism (Rex 1973).

Scholarly, popular and political ideas

The timing of the Huxley and Haddon essay reflected the fact that scholarly ideas and popular and political ideas may not run in tandem. A calculated demolition of the idea of race, it was published in the mid-1930s coinciding with the ascendant political philosophy of racial difference in Germany and the genocide that accompanied it. Their thesis shows, they claim, 'the relative unimportance of purely biological factors' (Huxley and Haddon 1935, p. 8). They attack racial ideas as mistaken science. This mistake gets in the way of humanity's task of acquiring 'scientific control of the forces operative in society' (p. 8). The front pages of the book are adorned with sixteen pictures of 'European men' with an invitation to readers to match them to national names such as British and Austrian. No doubt the intention was that most readers would fail, illustrating the unreliability of the idea of physical types matching national groups.

They accept that what they call 'group sentiment' is a powerful force, citing the evidence of admonitions in the Bible to avoid inter-group suspicions. 'The stranger that dwelleth with you shall be unto you as one born among you and thou shalt love him as thyself' (The Book of Leviticus, cited in Huxley and Haddon, p. 12). Humankind is scarcely able to overcome small group mentalities:

> Mankind has shown itself to be still unprepared to accept the idea of universal human brotherhood. Tribal, religious and national sentiment has time and again overruled the sentiment for humanity. (p. 14)

Much of their thesis is designed to undermine the idea of truly shared ancestry. They recognize that 'common descent' is the core idea of 'race' but argue that the claim of common descent is barely tenable except in the very loosest sense. 'Physical kinship', they say, 'which is frequently suggested as the basis of group consciousness culminating in so-called "race feeling" must be fictitious' (p. 22). They then cite examples of complex mixing and untraceable and uncertain ancestry as evidence of the folly of the idea of real shared descent. Group sentiment is really based on things quite different from the fiction of 'blood'; it is based on occupations, social institutions, religion and custom. The idea of the 'stock' of a nation is a biological fallacy. And the idea of a characteristic physical type is mocked by reference to the very German leaders who were advocating it:

> Our German neighbours have ascribed to themselves a Teutonic type that is fair, longheaded, tall and virile. Let us make a composite picture of a typical Teuton. . . . Let him be as blond as Hitler, as dolichocephalic as Rosenberg, as tall as Goebbels, as slender as Goering, and as manly as Streicher. (p. 26)

This, of course, was ironical since Hitler was certainly not blond – and the other Nazi leaders did not have the characteristics given to them in this passage.

They note the use by Herodotus, the Greek historian, of the word *ethnos* (sing.) and *ethnea* (pl.) as national regional and language groupings, including the Hellenic *ethnos* itself. 'Herodotus', they say, 'comes to the sensible conclusion that a group such as the Greeks is marked off from other groups by factors of which kinship is one, but that at least as important are language, religion, culture or tradition' (p. 31).

The more Huxley and Haddon examine the attempts to apply the concept of race the more they assert that it is hopelessly confused and indeterminate. They conclude that 'We can thus no longer think of common ancestry, a single original stock, as the essential badge of a "race"' (p. 106). This quotation is quite possibly the beginning of a long career of 'race' in inverted commas. There is, they suggest, 'a lamentable confusion between the ideas of race, culture and nation' and 'in the circumstances, it is very desirable that the term race as applied to human groups should be dropped from the vocabulary of science' (p. 107). Thenceforth 'the word race will be deliberately avoided and the term (ethnic) group or people employed for all general purposes' (p. 108).

Huxley and Haddon, whilst rejecting the idea of race, were still very much concerned with the range and occurrence of physical characteristics, which they regard as a series of statistical distributions. It was the social anthropologists (like

Franz Boas) and sociologists such as Robert Park in America who began to steer the idea of race away from physically differentiated groups towards a definition by social position and culture. Boas certainly took the idea of physical race seriously and the 1988 collection of his essays from the 1930s is full of discussions of anthropometric measures. But he also entertained the idea that culture and environment were important in shaping 'racial difference', a real departure from others writing at the time. Robert Park retained the idea of *racial temperament*, thus suggesting that he took the idea of fixed racial difference seriously as a determinant of behaviour. But he also developed a theory of 'race relations', largely predicated on *social* processes of migration and an ecological model of the city (Park 1950). In their work, Park and Boas either gave new meanings to the idea of 'race' or replaced it with 'ethnic group'. Broadly speaking, from this period – Boas, Park, Huxley and Haddon covered the pre-world war I era, 1920s and 1930s – up until the 1960s, the terms 'races' and 'ethnic groups' continued to be used, in large measure interchangeably. But the attacks on certainty and determinacy of the idea of race had begun, and in the world of science and scholarship the concept continued to be in retreat never to retain its former eminence in the social and anthropological sciences.

Park's work shows how the concept of race, and in particular the idea of racially inherited attributes, persisted despite his own advances in viewing 'races' in their social and historical situations. Thus he speaks of 'the individual man as the bearer of a double inheritance. As a member of a race he transmits, by interbreeding, a biological inheritance. As a member of society or a social group . . . he transmits by communication a social inheritance. The . . . inheritable character . . . constitutes the racial temperament' (Park and Burgess 1921, p. 140; see the discussion in Banton 1977, p. 102). The individual is therefore seen as not just inheriting physical features – such as skin colour – but also a 'racial temperament'. As an individual he or she is the bearer of a (racial) group characteristic. On the other hand, Park's work also shows a global understanding of social change, colonization and the social effects of European political and economic expansions, within which 'race relations' are worked out (see

Fenton 1981). Competition and conflict between racial groups are to be found at the points where capital expands into frontier areas and where Europeans expand their political domains. If the 'racial temperament' discussion gives Park an older ring, the theme of 'global capitalism' makes him sound a good deal more modern.

Lloyd Warner and American ethnic groups

In the USA, the 1930s were a notable period for the production of studies of 'race relations', among them classics such as Dollard's *Caste and Class in a Southern Town* (1937) and Davis et al.'s *Deep South* (1941) (see Banton 1977). Lloyd Warner's argument that the American pattern of racial segregation and subordination could be characterized as a colour-caste system came from this period of study. At the time, Warner (with Leo Srole) was leading a study of a New England town, part of which was subsequently published as *The Social Systems of American Ethnic Groups* (1945). This is of particular interest for our present purposes because it combines an interest in what were seen as two different but closely related issues of social research – racial groups and ethnic groups. It is interesting because of the distinction between 'racial' and 'ethnic'. But it also gives us a view of how white 'mainstream' America was perceived; it introduces an analysis of caste and class; and the book makes a prediction of how the American racial and ethnic system would evolve.

It is clear that ethnicity is, in Warner's view of things, something that 'foreigners' have rather than mainstream Americans; and foreigners are largely people who migrated in the nineteenth and early twentieth centuries from Europe. Although he acknowledges that 'the so-called "old-American" culture is itself new and ultimately "immigrant"', for the most part Warner speaks of 'old' white Americans as just that – Americans – *without 'ethnic' characteristics*. They are the mainstream which others will eventually join. Although he mainly speaks of ethnic groups as more or less recent immigrants to America from Europe, when he comes to define them he combines what he sees as racial and ethnic characteristics. He speaks of five racial types: Light and Dark Caucasoids, two Mongoloid and Caucasoid mixtures (one largely Caucasoid in appearance, the other largely Mongoloid) and Negroes and Negroid mixtures. He does not call them 'races' and only occasionally uses the phrase 'racial groups'. Rather he sees them as racial characteristics which combine with cultural characteristics, language and religion, to give a greater or lesser ease of acceptance in American society. Three types of groups, he says, are ranked as inferior, 'the ethnic group, the racial group, and the ethno-racial group'. The most likely to be accepted are those with racial and cultural characteristics most like 'old Americans', that is white, English-speaking and Protestant. The least likely to be readily accepted into the mainstream are those with racial and cultural characteristics most distant from the mainstream. But since 'American Negroes' are like old Americans in 'culture' being English-speaking and Protestant, to say nothing of length of settlement in America, it is clearly their racial characteristics which are seen as causing their exclusion.

Warner pays a lot of attention to three racial types and his use of the words 'Caucasoid', 'Mongoloid' and 'Negroid' has a solid ring of classical race science – that is of the classificatory and typologizing style of writing about 'races' which was so standard in much of the nineteenth century (Banton 1977). But unlike Park, who speaks of racial attraction and the inheritance of racial temperament, Warner sees the significance of racial types as lying not in the physical characteristics, that is in what could have been viewed as 'race itself', but in the social meaning attributed to racial difference:

> The racial groups are divergent biologically rather than culturally divergent from the old American white population. These traits have been evaluated as inferior. Such physical attributes as dark skin, the epicanthic fold, or kinky hair become symbols of status. . . . The cultural traits of the ethnic group, which have become symbols of inferior status, can be and are changed in time; but the physical traits which have become symbols of inferior status are permanent. *Unless the*

host society changes its methods of evaluation these racial groups are doomed to a permanent inferior ranking. (Warner and Srole 1945, p. 285; my emphasis)

In Warner's view, the destiny of all white or light-skinned ethnic groups is to join the white American mainstream. This is because the force of American equalitarianism, 'which attempts to make all men American and alike' (p. 295), combines with social mobility, which eventually produces class differentiation among ethnic groups and thus undermines their solidarity. The class order, he says, 'dissolves our ethnic groups'. By this he means that if immigrants are, in early years of settlement, concentrated in poorer paid work they will also be in the same neighbourhoods, their children attend the same schools and their experience of America will be similar. Social mobility will break up these solidarities and similarities and ethnic group cohesion diminishes.

In Warner's discourse, then, 'ethnic' means foreign and, through low evaluation of cultural difference, inferior; 'most ethnics are in lower social levels', he writes, using 'ethnics' as a noun. But this ethnic differentiation will fade, an epoch will have ended and the epoch of race will begin (see Warner and Srole 1945, pp. 284, 285). The 'host society' in the quotation above ('unless the host society changes its . . . evaluation') must mean white society; after all most black Americans would have been there much longer than many European Americans. Warner views the status evaluation of racial traits as being unlikely to change. The racial order rests upon, in a later language, the pervasive effect of white racism (i.e. the 'host society evaluation'). Whites appear to be unlikely to change; the possibility that black Americans may take destiny in their own hands and force change is not considered.

Warner's work not only provides an insight into a mid-twentieth-century American view of race and ethnicity, it is also interesting as a benchmark from which to view subsequent events. Fewer than ten years after the publication of this work, the Supreme Court ended legal justification of racial segregation by renouncing the doctrine of separate but equal in the legal case *Brown* v. *the Board of Education of Kansas*. Not long after that, the pressure of the civil rights movement was bringing even more fundamental changes.

The scholarly tradition: Max Weber and ethnic groups

Max Weber, writing at the beginning of the twentieth century (he died in 1920), is out of chronological order with the American writers mentioned above but then his writings were not widely known in the English-speaking social sciences until after the Second World War. Even then, it was frequently his analysis of capitalism and bureaucratic organization for which he was best known; only recently have contemporary writers interested in ethnicity taken a look back to Weber. A passage from *Economy and Society* (1978) is the most often cited – appearing as a selection in three recent readers (see Guiberneau and Rex 1997; Hughey 1998; Hutchinson and Smith 1996). The idea of 'racial differences' as objective, as constituted through heredity and as capable of systematic study is clearly present in Weber. He writes that 'the degree of objective racial difference can be determined . . . purely physiologically, by establishing whether hybrids reproduce themselves at approximately normal rates' (cited in Hughey 1998, p. 17). This is a statement which takes racial differences as real and worthy of study, consistent with a science of races. His work is therefore another example of the question of 'race' and 'ethnicity' existing side by side, concerned with much the same kind of questions, but with the presumption that 'race' has something to do with physical difference, and sometimes with heritable characteristics.

However, there can be little doubt that the main trend of Weber's argument is sociological, that is to see ethnicity as a *belief in* common descent and then to examine the origins and the consequences of this belief for individual and collective action. Racial or ethnic identities are frequently portrayed as depending on the social perception of difference, and in most cases within the context of political action. This places Weber's ideas close to those who, more than fifty years later, spoke of 'political ethnicity' and the sense of common origin being mobilized for political objectives (cf. for example Cohen 1974). Race, he says, 'creates a group only when it is subjectively perceived as a common trait' and becomes the basis of political action when 'common experience of members of the same race are linked to some antagonism against members of an obviously different group' (Weber, cited in Hughey 1998, p. 17).

Three arguments then dominate much of Weber's discussion in this frequently cited passage. One is that common descent is a key element of ethnic identity but it is the *belief* in common origin, not any objective common ancestry, which is socially persuasive. The second is that differences, both cultural and physical, are the reference points around which group identities are formed. Cultural differences may be especially important if they are readily detectable, such as language, or visible, such as dress and aspects of everyday behaviour. These differences are frequently organized into a system of honour such that ethnic honour and status honour are closely related. His example of the 'poor white' in the American South is one such case. The third is the fact that he several times reiterates the idea of an ethnic group as the basis of political action. In this it is closely tied to the idea of 'nation' whose distinctiveness is its orientation to the 'autonomous polity' (Weber, cited in Hughey 1998, p. 28).

The relationships first of ethnicity to political action and second of ethnicity to status have remained as enduring concerns in the study of ethnic groups or 'ethnicity'. In more recent writing (see for example Brass 1985, 1991), ethnically organized groups are regarded as political actors. That is to say, groups are constituted ethnically outside politics but enter the political arena in order to lobby for their collective interests or even to stake out claims for autonomy. In Weber, the emphasis is rather different. He concedes that ethnic groups may pre-date political organization and may then become loosely represented in the organization of a state. But equally he argues that political groups are formed which *then* attribute to themselves an ethnic character:

> The tribe is clearly delimited when it is a sub-division of a polity which, in fact, often establishes it. . . . When a political community was newly established or reorganised, the population was newly divided. Hence the tribe here is a political artefact, even though it soon adopts the whole symbolism of blood symbolism and particularly a tribal cult. Even today it is not rare that political artefacts develop a sense of affinity

akin to that of a blood relationship. Very schematic constructs, such as those states of the United States, that were
made into squares according to their latitude have a strong
sense of identity; it is also not rare that families travel
from New York to Richmond to make an expected child a
'Virginian'. (Weber, cited in Hughey 1998, p. 26)

This is part of a general tendency for political communities
to be seen or to see themselves as having common descent.
'All history', he writes, 'shows how easily political action can
give rise to the belief in blood relationship, unless gross differences of anthropological type impede it' (p. 25). Weber's
sociological methodology distinguished three types of action:
action guided by rationality, affect and tradition (Weber
1978). This was to distinguish action as based on three different guiding principles: rational calculation; sentiment and
feeling; and the wish to follow tradition. There are hints, in
these passages about political communities and the belief in
common ethnic origin, that he is regarding 'ethnically oriented action' as an example of action guided by affect and
tradition. In this way the 'ethnicization' of political organization or action could be regarded as an instance of the intru-
sion of non-rational action into rationally organized spheres.
In other words, states may be organized on rational-legal
principles but are, or come to be, influenced by personal or
communal sentiments and loyalties. But he concludes by indicating that the category 'ethnically determined social action'
(i.e. action guided by the belief in common origin) is too
diffuse to be very helpful. This is because it would fail to
distinguish so many different aspects of custom and tradition,
including those associated with common language, religion,
political action, attraction and repulsion and sexual
relations.

The association of ethnic sentiments with the organization
of social honour and status is even more central to Weber's
argument:

Next to pronounced differences in the economic way of life,
the belief in ethnic affinity has at all times been affected by
outward differences in clothes, in the style of housing, food
and eating habits, the division of labour between the sexes
and between the free and the unfree . . . that is . . . all of what

affects the individual's sense of honour and dignity. All those things we shall find later on as objects of specific differences between status groups. The conviction of the excellence of one's own customs and the inferiority of alien ones, a conviction which sustains the sense of ethnic honour, is actually quite analogous to the sense of honour of distinctive status groups. (Weber, cited in Hughey 1998, p. 23)

From this point Weber turns his attention to the concepts of nation and nationality. Common descent, or belief in common descent, is again the central idea:

The concept of 'nationality' shares with that of the 'people' – in the 'ethnic' sense – the vague connotation that whatever is felt to be distinctively common must derive from common descent. (Weber, cited in Hughey 1998, p. 27)

Although Weber is quite sure that the belief in common origin is important in political life, and that ethnic evaluations are analogous to status evaluations, he is not sure whether we should take the concept of ethnic groups or 'ethnically determined action' too seriously (on Weber and ethnic communities, see Banton 2007). That ambivalence has persisted in social anthropology and sociology ever since.

Anthropology and social anthropology

If sociology gradually emancipated itself from the term 'race' and at very least adopted a language of 'race' and 'ethnicity' existing side by side, social anthropology adopted the terms 'ethnic group' and 'ethnicity' as a means of escaping some unwanted implications of the term 'tribe'. Students wishing to follow the development of an anthropological construction of ethnicity are very well advised to read Marcus Banks' *Ethnicity: Anthropological Constructions* (1996) for an excellent history and theoretical discussion. Importantly, he shows how 'ethnic group' came to replace 'tribe' under the influence of the members of the Manchester School. These were a group of anthropologists writing in the 1960s and early 1970s and associated with Max Gluckman and

Manchester University (see Banks 1996, p. 25; Cohen 1974; Epstein 1978). They recognized the need to see 'tribal' or ethnic identities and behaviour within the explicit context of white colonial power and of urbanization which disrupted 'traditional' behaviour which had been described as 'tribal'. In this way, they departed from a convention of viewing a people or tribe as a unitary or self-contained community. Tribal*ism* – the persistence in some form of group identities with rural roots in the new urban context – was a problem for colonial administrators and for a modernizing independence project. But it could not simply be understood as non-rational loyalties and adherence to custom which the word 'tribal' had come to express. Thus began the notion of 'political ethnicity', the instrumental uses of ethnic identity which were relevant or irrelevant according to circumstance (see Banks 1996, pp. 24ff).

Banks is also an excellent source on the evolution of the specific term *ethnos* in Soviet anthropological theory. In the 1970s, Soviet anthropologists, led by Yulian Bromley, began to write about ethnic groups, for which they used the term 'ethnos' borrowed from the Greek. As post-Stalinist Russia and the Soviet Union as a whole moved into a more liberal period, it became possible to discuss ethnic groups (or ethnos-es) as collectivities surviving from pre-socialist into socialist society. Earlier, any recognition of the 'reality' of ethnic identities, of peoples defined by language, culture and a belief in common origin, was suspect since it either ran contrary to Marxist theory, which saw modern socialism as transcending ethnicity, or it smacked of 'national' identities which threatened Soviet citizenship. It was clear to Bromley and his colleagues that ethnos-es had nonetheless survived, despite the fearful examples of the persecution of national minorities. They had to be described and analysed with their claws removed. The solution was to see them as real groupings with 'stable cultural features, certain distinctive psychological traits, and consciousness of unity' (Banks 1996, p. 19) which survived through the stages of social evolution but in a causally subordinate position in relation to economic change. Ethnos-es lived on, material history marched on. In this way, Soviet anthropologists were able to acknowledge 'ethnic groups' without damaging the materialist theory of history, and without advancing 'ethnic identities' as any kind of threat to the Soviet state.

The Soviet episode illustrates two points which we have referred to previously. The first is that 'ethnos theory' was subject to local (in this case Soviet) anthropological discourses, the most important being the Marxist materialist historical paradigm. The second is that the political framework, in the Soviet instance the subordination of any 'local' national or ethnic identity to Soviet citizenship, shaped the way in which the Soviet academicians were able to address the question at all. To accord with a materialist theory of history, the ethnos was seen as a real and substantive entity in society and history; any undue emphasis on a people's self-definition and collective consciousness was to give too much ground to subjective factors, or even to give anthropological credence to 'nationalist' (non-Soviet) sentiments.

By the end of the Soviet era, another leading academician published a classic study of nations and nationalism in the former Soviet zones. Tishkov by this time is pronouncing *a reversal of the theory of ethnicity and nationalism* (Tishkov 1997; see also Tishkov 2000). Ethnic identities and national identities are *not* naturally occurring social facts grounded in the existence of substantive ethnos-es. Rather they are the identities built, shaped and reshaped out of a variety of historical materials, and meet the needs, political exigencies or opportunities of the time. In short they are 'socially constructed' and in great measure a product of circumstance.

Real groups

The Russian ethnos example not only illustrates how national and regional political agendas frame the way ethnicity and nation are conceived. This example is also a prompt for considering a question about ethnicity which is raised repeatedly. This is the question of whether 'ethnic groups' can be considered as real, organic and substantive groups. This could be regarded as a philosophical question but that is not what I have in mind; the meanings that can be given to the word 'group' can also be tested against observation and evidence.

So the question 'are ethnic groups real?' is a *sociological question* and not just an *epistemological* one. As a general rule, the further one goes back in sociological and anthropological writing, the more the 'reality' of ethnic groups is assumed or asserted. The further 'forward' we come, the less substantive the idea of ethnicity becomes. The problem here, as I have argued elsewhere (Fenton 1999), is not the word 'ethnic' but the word 'group'. The word 'group' implies some measure of collective organization although the organization may be only loosely articulated. If we look back to Lloyd Warner's ethnic groups, he clearly saw them as definable, relatively distinct and bounded – they were the immigrants from Europe and their descendants, who were culturally different and *sustained some forms of group life*. Among the latter would be greater or lesser control of marriage choices (initially disapproving of exogamy), associations to organize welfare such as insurance and burial societies, residential concentrations, which made possible collective action in neighbourhoods, schools and churches, and in some instances, associations of political defence (Handlin 1973; Yinger 1994). In Warner's account the 'strength of the ethnic sub-system' is indexed by spatial distribution, economic life and the class system, the family, church, language and the ethnic associations (Warner and Srole 1945). The stronger each of these is in sustaining ethnic culture and group ties, the more the group survives as a real ethnic community, which provides a framework for living for its members.

Somewhat later, Morris (1968) also gives a substantive definition: 'An ethnic group is a distinct category of the population in a larger society whose culture is usually different from its own. The members of such a group are, or feel themselves, or are thought to be, bound together by common ties of race or nationality or culture.' But in the same piece he suggests that 'group-ness' ought not to be taken for granted. We should, he writes,

> make the distinction between a social group and a social category. By a group sociologists usually mean an aggregation of people recruited on clear principles, who are bound to one another by formal, institutionalised rules and characteristic, informal behaviour . . . it must be organised for cohesion and

persistence; that is to say, the rights and duties of membership must regulate internal order and relations with other groups. Members usually identify themselves with a group and give it a name. (Morris 1968, p. 168)

All of this suggests what I have been referring to as a 'real groups' conceptualization of ethnicity. But Morris himself recognizes that such a portrayal is problematic, or at least may need to be qualified. 'In practice', he says, 'social groups vary in the degree to which they are corporate' and may sometimes be a 'mere category of the population' lacking any of the attributes of corporate life. Judith Nagata makes a similar distinction. Summarizing the 'etic' (approximately speaking, the observer's rather than participant's) view of ethnic groups, she writes:

Our etic summary of ethnicity as a distinctive social phe-nomenon runs as follows: a category or group with some perception of shared culture, one or more aspects of which will be used primordially as a charter for membership (and for excluding non-members). It has the capacity for an institutionally self-supporting and self-sustaining existence. Consciousness, mobilisation, and formal organisation may vary from the diffuse identity of a mere category to the militant activism of a political movement, and this will be determined by the external social circumstances. (Nagata 1981, p. 96)

Just before this passage she has shown how 'ethnic groups' should be considered as conceptually different from say kinship groups or gender groups:

The final factor seems to lie in the institutional self-sufficiency and self-reproducing capacity of the ethnic community. Hence the common association, on the political level at least, with irredentism, secession, and threats to national integration. (Nagata 1981, p. 95)

Here Nagata is following some of the arguments of Clifford Geertz (indeed she cites his famous work, Geertz 1973) in suggesting that *because* an ethnic group is capable of a kind of self-sufficiency it poses a threat to 'national integration', since it may command the loyalty of its members more than or 'ahead of' the nation. In referring to institutional self-sufficiency and self-reproducing capacity, she is setting quite a high test for qualification as an ethnic group. This would mean that such groups were not only culturally distinctive but also institutionally distinctive by having a range of organizations which met many of the needs of the 'members'. Indeed the very word 'members' suggests something quite substantial about ethnicity or ethnic groups. But since ethnic groups are almost always conceived as sections of a larger population in a nation-state, it is rarely if ever the case that such institutional separateness is complete. The same is true when groups straddle state boundaries, as do the Basques of France and Spain. In segregated America, for example, there were two sets of institutions for white and black Americans: schools, churches, areas of residence, universities, hospitals, even cemeteries were divided by fences marking black from white.

But in Malaysia (where, incidentally, cemeteries are usually ethnically separate – by choice), which will have been the country in Nagata's mind, the degree of institutional 'self-sufficiency' is a matter of degree, and subject to changes in government policy.

Nagata is recognizing this variable degree of organization in the latter part of the first quotation above: 'consciousness, mobilisation, and formal organisation may vary'. In the next phrase is the suggestion that ethnicity may be 'the diffuse identity of a mere category', a phrase which captures almost the opposite of the 'corporate group' idea. But the sting comes in the seemingly harmless and imprecise tail. She says that this variation in political consciousness and organization will depend on 'external social circumstances'. In other words, the level of consciousness and political organization of an ethnic group or category will depend less on internal social and cultural features and more on external political and economic circumstances. This would certainly offer an explanation of why ethnic identities may be socially 'quiet' for long periods of time but burst into action when there is a critical change in circumstances. When they do, people close to the ethnic conflict reflect on how 'we had always got along perfectly well' with our ethnically different neighbours. This was the case in the eruption of ethnic violence in the collapse of Yugoslavia.

The lesson of this discussion, then, is that we should be alert to the possibility that the phrase 'ethnic groups' may carry different meanings in the word 'groups', the apparently innocuous half of the phrase. The variation extends from groups with a real corporate existence to, in Nagata's phrase, *the diffuse identity of a mere category*. If, for example, we think of the public recording of ethnic origins, the people who nominate 'Pakistani' in the British Census are just that: all those people who checked 'Pakistani' on a form. In what sense they constitute the Pakistani ethnic group or 'ethnic community' as sometimes described, is a matter for sociological investigation. This distinction between the corporate group and the diffuse identity should be kept in mind whenever we are considering ethnicity; it frequently is not.

Summary

In the early twentieth century, race thinking was widespread and the idea that the world's population could be classified into unequal races was very much accepted. It was also the time when theoretical critiques of this form of thinking were initiated. Émile Durkheim and Franz Boas, one a French sociologist, the other a German-born anthropologist, led the way in substituting social and cultural explanations for 'racial' ones. The work of the American sociologist Robert Park led in much the same direction. A book by Huxley and Haddon formally proposed the abolition of the term 'race'.

We also addressed the work of Max Weber, the late nineteenth- and early twentieth-century German sociologist who has been possibly the leading classical figure in the founding of sociology. A long excerpt from his essays has been widely cited in contemporary books of readings. Weber remained largely unenthusiastic about the concept of 'ethnic group' but did suggest that its principal meaning lay in a frequently fictitious claim to common ancestry and in its significance in political organization. We examined the work of Lloyd Warner, the American anthropologist who wrote a detailed empirical study of American ethnic groups. He mostly viewed ethnic groups as groups who had immigrated to the USA from European states: hence Polish Americans and Irish Americans. He combined his definition of ethnic groups with an idea of racial difference; physically different – in particular black – populations would remain distinct and disadvantaged as long as the white majority treated blackness as low in status. We discussed the question of how 'real' or 'substantive' ethnic groups are: should they be regarded as vague and loosely defined identities, or as corporate groups or naturally occurring and distinct segments of a population (see also chapter 5). We referred to Marcus Banks' account of the Soviet concept of 'ethnos' to illustrate this discussion. This leads us into the next important question concerning 'ethnicity' or 'ethnic groups' – the long-running primordialism debate.

4
The Primordialism Debate

Primordialism

In his book on ethnicity and nationalism in Russia, Valery Tishkov (1997) was anxious to make clear, right at the beginning of the book, that 'primordialism has been definitively discarded in the West'. The Russian social science tradition had failed to learn, 'being heavily dominated by the primordial approach'. They had failed to recognize that identities are socially constructed by ethnic actors themselves and by states, like the Soviet state. Constructivism is opposed to primordialism since:

> For primordialists there exist objective entities with inherent features such as territory, language, recognisable membership, and even a common mentality. (Tishkov 1997, p. 1)

For its own reasons (see chapter 3) the Soviet state had treated ethnos-es as objective entities; a post-Soviet turn towards 'constructionism' is understandable enough. The Soviet state sought to objectivize ethnicities so as to make them acceptable divisions of the population as 'naturally occurring', but non-political, communities of language and culture. In short, these groups were real, but not very important. But in a post-Soviet Russia, the idea that ethnos-es are real is a dangerous one that threatens the new Russian state by posing divisive ethnic nationalisms. Hence the discovery by liberals of 'constructionism'. This methodology tells us that not only do nationalist doctrines elevate the nation to the highest value, but that they also create the very idea of the ethnos or nation itself. Now the groups are not so 'real', but highly dangerous.

But the problem of primordialism is not so simple or so easily solved as Tishkov would have us believe. In this chapter, we shall see how the idea of primordial groups emerged. First we must be clear about some potentially different meanings of the primordial and the non-primordial. For it is clear that the concept 'primordial' has brought to the surface more than just a discussion of 'objectivist social science' and 'constructionism'. (This is a debate, to be found throughout the history of sociology, about how much observers simply give names to social facts which have an objective existence; how much they see the social facts and the categories as construed by 'actors' or people in everyday life; and how much they themselves are devising intellectual constructs.) There is at least one other question lying on or just below the surface and that is 'are ethnic identities the subject of calculation and reflection or are they more defined by sentiment and affect than by rationality and calculation?' The difficulties in the 'primordialism' debate are heightened by the elision of two questions:

1   Are groups real (or socially constructed)?
2   Are group attachments affective (guided by sentiment) or instrumental (guided by rational calculation)?

We have already made our answer to the first question clear. The understanding of groups as corporate entities and as natural divisions of the population was in need of substantial revision. It was necessary to make way for the argument that identities are in some measure created, sustained and made relevant in political action by ethnically oriented actors and by the state. But the constructionist language of 'invention' and 'imagination' goes too far; for all the invention and re-invention of identities, there are some social realities – of, for example, religious difference, regional concentration, corporate organization and language – which form a substantive base for the construction – and mobilization – of ethnic identities. It may be possible to make and to appeal to sharp lines of ethnic difference, but in the absence of any substantive sociocultural differences, it is hard to imagine how many potentially ethnic actors will answer the call.

'Emotional attachments'

Throughout the whole history of the discipline of sociology there has been a conceptual opposition between an idea of rationality and calculation and an idea of affect, sentiment and emotion. In, for example, the work of Durkheim there is, on the one hand, an idea of behaviour motivated by interest and, on the other, the power of a sense of attachment to a community or 'society' (Durkheim 1933; Fenton 1984). Rational and affective action were central to Weber's ideal types of 'orientations to action'. A similar dichotomy is evident in the Parsonian distinction between instrumental and expressive values (Parsons 1968; Weber 1978). Now this long-standing analytical distinction makes a new appearance in the debates about what kind of social action, social attachment and identity is comprehended by the term 'ethnic'. In popular discourse there is little doubt that ethnic attachments and identities are seen as belonging to the realm of sentiment and 'belonging' as a psychosocial bond. Ethnic sentiments may be seen as not only non-rational but also as defying rationality – that is, despite the gains to be made by acting in a non-ethnic way, people choose to act ethnically. For example, despite their shared interests, workers are seen as being deflected from collective class action by ethnic sentiments. Despite an employer's interest in hiring the most able staff, recruiters discriminate on ethnic grounds.

Although social science in some respects prefers a model of rational action, a discourse of emotion or 'sentiment' is undoubtedly diffused throughout the discipline of sociology. Men, in the popular phrase, 'behave badly' because they are guided by an unreasoned sense of masculinity, and behave even worse when that sense of masculinity is threatened.

People respond to political slogans because their status is undermined, with a resultant sense of diffuse anger or anxiety. Many examples could be given, enough for us to be sure that a language of emotion and sentiment is an explicit or tacit part of sociological thinking. In the field of ethnicity, both models are applied: people are seen to be responding to 'blind' group loyalties, or they are seen to be calculating their individual or collective interest. If behaviour in accordance with ethnic attachments could be seen to be serving some individual or collective political or economic end, then the ethnic action could be reinterpreted as *instrumental*. The instrumental character of ethnic attachment was seen as 'calculating' and therefore incompatible with the idea of an unreasoned and affective tie. The latter was described as 'primordial'. Again, the solution to this conceptual problem will turn out to be more complex than a simple shift from 'real/natural and affective' to 'constructed and instrumental'. Before we return to a summative consideration we should examine how the term 'primordial' found its way into the literature.

'Primordial' as a sociological concept

The sociological term 'primordial' has no special connection to the problem of ethnicity. Some commentators have failed to recognize this. It has often been discussed as if the concept 'primordial' were invented or elaborated in order to explicate a dimension of 'ethnicity' (Eller and Coughlan 1993). In other words, it has been assumed that the debate has been about the question 'is ethnicity a primordial phenomenon?' rather than a quite different question, 'what does the term "primordial" mean and what assistance, if any, can it provide in explaining ethnic ties and identities?' The first is not a sensible question, the second is. The concept 'primordial' is mostly concerned with the nature and quality of social obligations, a question of 'what kind of society do we live in?' And the question 'what kind of society?' could be rephrased as 'what is the basis of social cohesion?' This is just about the most persistent and long-standing question in the history of sociology. If we are to understand 'societies' or 'social action', we must understand the way in which people are related to, obligated to and identified with each other. This meaning of 'primordial' as one of many attempts to capture the nature of social ties in different kinds of societies – and not as an attempt to define ethnicity – can be traced to a 1950s article by Edward Shils (Shils 1957).

Edward Shils and primordial, personal, sacred and civil ties

Shils first addresses himself to the problem of moral integration in a modern social order. He begins by arguing that the highest ideals, which would include civic or civil values, 'can be lived up to only partially, fragmentarily, intermittently and only in an approximate way' (1957, p. 130). This proposition about civic values is a very important argument, to which we return in chapter 9. Shils probably intends this distinction, between the ideal value system and everyday practice, as a feature of all organized societies. But it is particularly interesting as a feature of societies aspiring to civic status, that is of societies who seek to implement some universalistic values about citizenship and duties to 'the whole' which are expected to 'rise above' the ordinary – hence Shils' reference to the sacred as against the purely routine and mundane. Great occasions, national crises or important events such as elections remind us of civil and sacred ties. At other times our concerns are much more immediate:

> for the rest of the time, the ultimate values of the society, what is sacred to its members, are suspended amidst the distractions of concrete tasks, which makes the values ambiguous and thus gives freedom for individual innovation, creation and adaptation. (Shils 1957, p. 131)

The ideologist (meaning here the advocate of the civic ideals) is affronted by people's attachment to 'their mates, family and wish for improvement' (p. 131), but it is the routines of work, family and leisure which generate the sense of obligation and purpose which are the functioning fundamentals of a society as a 'going concern'. Thus modern society is neither merely a market place in which individuals engage with each other only in limited transactions, nor does it replicate the moral uniformity of small communities or so-called 'traditional societies'. It has certain grand moral elements, its supreme values and its civic morality, and on great occasions the sacredness of these moral ideas are re-celebrated. But the moral integrity of modern societies is also realized through a multiplicity of obligations and sentiments at a much 'lower order' of social organization. This in fact is Shils' formulation of the 'problem of integration' posed classically by Durkheim (1893), Tönnies (1963) and others, who were concerned to understand how the modern social order could be free, individualistic, open and contractual without becoming hopelessly impersonal and fragmented. Shils' answer is quite explicit:

> As I see it modern society is no lonely crowd, no horde of refugees fleeing from freedom. It is no *Gesellschaft* [a reference to Tönnies' concept of a modern society], soulless, egotistical, loveless, faithless, utterly impersonal and lacking any integrative forces other than interest or coercion. It is held together by an infinity of personal attachments, moral obligations in concrete contexts, professional and creative pride, individual ambition, primordial affinities and a civil sense which is low in many, high in some and moderate in most persons. (p. 131)

From this beginning – which contains the first reference to the word 'primordial' – Shils proceeds to review a series of researches which were relevant to the consideration of the role of small groups in large societies. Time and again, he argues, people's attachment to the immediate group within which they are engaged is the main focus of loyalty. This was particularly striking in the case of military units, where membership of something bigger – the army in service of the *country* – may have been thought to provoke a wider and higher loyalty. This was not true of either the American army (p. 138) or the Soviet army. The Soviet army was 'a very powerful organisation which had a great deal of coherence, yet very little of that coherence seemed to come from attachment to ideological or political symbols, or even intense patriotism' (p. 143).

In the context of small groups, quite intense feelings of loyalty and obligation are generated. This is particularly so within the family because of the significance which is attached to kin obligations. We are not attached to another family member only as a person ('I do like my Uncle Harold') 'but as a possessor of certain "significant relational" qualities, which could only be described as primordial' ('Uncles are important people about whom you must care'). Shils is dismissing a (then) recent argument by George Homans that kin attachments simply flowed from interaction. Rather he says that the quality of attachment arises 'because a certain ineffable significance is attributed to the tie of blood' (p. 142).

The main burden of Shils' argument is that *primary and civil ties co-exist* in the same social order. The former arise from experience within the small group, as in the loyalties developed in army units, or are part of the definition of the relationship as in 'primordial' ties of kin. The latter, civil ties, are more abstract and called upon and saluted from time to time but not fervently acted out on a daily basis. All in all, Shils is articulating a basis for understanding modern societies and their 'coherence' or 'integration', the fundamental problem as envisaged by the classical sociological tradition (see Nisbet 1967). His own answer is that modern societies are not hopelessly fragmented and 'soulless'; people are not alarmingly detached from each other and lacking in any kind of bonding ties to others; nor are they obligated to the society as a whole because of adherence to some compelling and sacred-like public moral ethos. Rather, they have real ties of a 'first-order' type within their networks of kin, they have binding ties and sentiments of loyalty within small groups of, for example, the workplace, area of residence, or leisure. And beyond this, they have an intermittent sense of obligation to higher-order values, more abstract symbols and a broader civic sense of duty. The argument corresponds to some elements of Durkheim's sociology of cohesion in modern societies (Fenton 1984). It is certainly an outline theory of the nature of moral and social attachment within a contemporary social order. A good deal of subsequent sociology has been about a parallel question: under what conditions does this routine array of attachments and occasionally enthusiastic commitment to the civil order break down?

We should note that there are two curiosities, possibly contradictions, in what Shils writes. The first is that the term 'primordial' is used in the article but much of his discussion is more properly described as being about *'primary* groups', a much more general reference to face-to-face groups, with whom we are said to feel some strong sense of attachment (i.e. soldiers die for their mates). This is a significant confusion since primary groups are *acquired* in everyday life as well as being 'given' (i.e. not chosen), as in our families. Primordiality is often portrayed as essentially 'given', not acquired. Second, Shils is arguing that these primary attachments are routine and secular, again rather in contrast to the idea that some group memberships, at least in the primordialist view, have a sacredness about them.

Clifford Geertz and the integrative revolution

A second source of the term 'primordial' can be found in the anthropologist Clifford Geertz's essay, first published in 1973, in his book *The Interpretation of Cultures*. As I have argued in my earlier book (Fenton 1999), Geertz is mainly concerned, in the relevant chapter 'The Integrative Revolution', with the conditions of social and political stability in 'new states', in the immediately postcolonial era of the 1960s. He argues that, in many of the new states, people's primary attachment is to others who are seen to be of the same 'race', who are kinsmen and women, who speak the same language, or whose sense of collective past and future is based on shared experience of people of a region, of the same religion, or on a community of culture and custom. These communities of custom, kin ties, religion and region are the basis of people's sense of self. These are the real and immediate communities to which people feel that they belong:

> The multi-ethnic populations of the new states tend to regard the immediate, concrete, and . . . meaningful sorting implicit in such 'natural' diversity as the substantial content of their individuality. (Geertz 1973, p. 258)

Two features of this quotation are especially interesting. The first is that the reference to 'immediate' and 'concrete' social attachments almost exactly mirrors Shils' argument as we have set it out above. The second vitally important feature is the quotation marks around the word *natural*. This may not seem much but it is crucial. It is a direct indication that Geertz is regarding these sources of diversity as something other than organic or biological or unchanging human divisions which command the loyalty of their members in a pre-social way. Rather the quotation marks suggest this: people may think of these divisions as natural, but we know that they are culturally and socially moulded, as well as being grounded in place, language and shared historic experience.

In the next passage, Geertz's argument diverges significantly from that of Shils. Whilst Shils had argued that these primordial attachments existed *side by side* with intermittent commitment to higher-order values, Geertz appears to argue that the strength of the first *interferes with* the flourishing of the latter. Thus he writes that people in new states may find it difficult and risky to 'subordinate these specific and familiar identifications in favour of a generalised commitment to an overarching and somewhat alien civil order'. As a consequence, he argues, new states are *'abnormally susceptible to serious disaffection based on primordial attachments'* (p. 259; my emphasis). There then follows the passage which has been cited more than any other as the basis for outlining the use of the term 'primordial':

> By a primordial attachment is meant one that stems from the 'givens' – or more precisely, *as culture is inevitably involved in such matters, the assumed 'givens' of social existence*: immediate contiguity and kin connection mainly, but beyond them the given-ness that stems from being born into a particular religious community, speaking a particular language . . . and following particular practices. These congruities of blood, speech, custom, and so on *are seen to have* an ineffable, and at times overpowering coerciveness in and of themselves. One is bound to one's kinsman, one's neighbour, one's fellow believer, *ipso facto*; as the result not merely of personal affection, practical necessity, common interest, or incurred obligation, but at least in great part by virtue of some unaccountable absolute import *attributed* to the very tie itself. The general strength of such primordial bonds, and the types of them that

are important, differ from person to person, from society to society, and from time to time. (pp. 259–60; my emphasis)

This goes a good deal further than Shils in trying to flesh out what a primordial attachment is: there is a sense of obligation to others which is rather taken for granted, and is not a matter of calculation, nor is it the kind of obligation upon which we reflect very much – it is a kind of given, just there. The sentiments surrounding these ties (social attachments, obligations) are not easily put into words (i.e. they are ineffable) but we certainly feel that these are obligations which we can scarcely escape. This deep sense of obligation is not the same thing as the obligation arising from practical relationships, from 'merely personal' affection, or from the reciprocity of exchanges. It is something we feel bound by because of the kind of obligation that it is – like the more or less unquestioned sense of duty we usually feel towards members of our family.

This immediately preceding paragraph, written in my words, is clearly a paraphrase of the Geertz quotation. The only difference is that the second version omits some of the linguistic flourishes of the former – 'congruities of blood', 'absolute import' and the like. Three central ideas come from this passage, in either version. One is that primordial ties are not reflected upon, they are not for the most part a matter of calculation. Second, they are deeply felt; we feel that the obligations or sense of attachment are of a kind that are not easily renounced or evaded. Both the first and second features are evidenced by the fact that they are not easily put into words. Third, 'primordial' describes a kind of attachment which has an importance attached to the tie itself – the 'absolute import' as Geertz describes it. This third part is exactly what the original Shils article describes as 'significant relational qualities'. Shils is arguing that we regard some relationships as different in kind from others. In Shils' case the model type is the kin relationship. As we observed from Shils before, 'The attachment to another member of one's kinship group is not just a function of interaction . . . it is because a certain ineffable significance is attributed to the tie of blood'.

There are other quite important things to notice from the Geertz quotation. The most notable, given the nature of subsequent discussion of 'primordiality', are the phrases wherein he is clearly indicating that this kind of attachment and sentiment flows from social attributions and not from any non-social nature of the group. This is signalled in the phrases '*assumed* givens', and '*are seen to* have . . . [a] coerciveness' and the 'import *attributed* to the very tie itself'. Each of these phrases is indicating a social and cultural process through which a particular meaning is given to these kinds of relationships. This meaning is not, so to speak, there in the first place, or in the nature of the group. It is there because people learn to regard some kind of relationships as different in quality from others. Nor is primordiality a fixed and universal quality of certain relationships – just how deeply these ties are felt varies from society to society and 'from time to time'.

Equally important as a feature of the elaboration of the term 'primordial' is the list of examples which Geertz provides of the kinds of circumstances which may give rise to this sense of obligation and attachment. There is, in this passage, *no mention of racial or ethnic group*. Geertz is thinking of the sense of place and family, of the sense of belonging deriving from religious identity, from speaking the same language and from custom. Geertz has in mind parts of the world where such identities are particularly important, and where groups of this kind live precisely side by side. Throughout much of South East Asia we find peoples with different languages (e.g. Malay, Javanese, dialects of Chinese), with different religious identities (Muslim, Christian, Buddhist) and visibly different in custom such as dress and eating habits (pork-eating Chinese, as against Muslims).

After Geertz

Despite the fact that the core of the Shils and Geertz argument was that there could be detected relationships which had a distinctive quality – primordial – marking them off from, say, contractual relationships, much subsequent discussion has proceeded on the false premise that *they were defining ethnicity* rather than elaborating an ideal type of relationship. In addition to this, the Geertz view has been misrepresented as conceptualizing 'ethnic ties' as almost pre-social, fixed, biological, purely 'emotional' and unreasoning (Eller and Coughlan 1993). This conceptual misrepresentation of what 'primordial' means – and of its association with ethnicity – has been the basis of an enduring debate within the sociological literature about the distinction between 'primordial' and (variously) 'circumstantialist', 'situational', 'instrumental' or other models of ethnicity (Scott 1990). There are, of course, two distinctive analytical questions: the first asks about the nature of the ethnic tie itself, and the second, whether or when the ethnic tie is important. These have been conflated so that an 'instrumental' view is seen as non-primordial since it involves calculation as against affect. These different models could be defined as follows:

- *Circumstantial:* that ethnic identity is important in some contexts and not others: the identity is constant but circumstances determine whether it matters.
- *Situational:* that the actual identity deployed or made relevant changes according to the social situations of the individual: the situation changes, the relevant identity changes.
- *Instrumental:* that the deployment of the identity can be seen to serve a material or political end and is calculated thus.

None of these actually runs counter to a primordial view of the nature of ethnicity. To make this clear we can say that someone may have an ascribed ethnic identity which is embedded in their personality and life experience, yet still perceive the circumstances under which it may be instrumental to deploy it.

Judith Nagata and mobilized identities

The reference to these divergent views can be found in the work of Judith Nagata, writing not long after the original Geertz work (Nagata 1981). Nagata puts her finger rather neatly on a reason why critics of a 'primordialist' view are so eager to replace it with a so-called 'circumstantialist' view. 'The primordial viewpoint', she observes, 'leaves some social scientists academically uneasy, for they feel poorly equipped to handle such loyalties and sentiments, which seem to slip dangerously out of the world of tangible interests and groups into a half-world of emotion and unreason' (p. 89). By contrast, we may think of 'ethnic identity and *particularly ethnic mobilisation*' as 'relatively flexible and amenable to change as dictated by external exigencies' (p. 89).

The distinction here between ethnic *identity* and ethnic *mobilization* is interesting. In the first instance, it is a question of explaining how an identity is formed. Why for example do people come to regard the language they speak as some kind of mark of group membership, and furthermore as an attachment which is not easily given up or disregarded? This is a question of how social identities are formed. A second question is: under what circumstances do these identities become the basis for a social movement, for concerted political action or for any kind of collective organization which goes beyond the routine daily familiarity of the identity itself? That is to say, there is a move from 'I am a Malay speaker, I feel at home speaking Malay' to 'We Malay speakers must stick together, organize, defend what we have got', or 'Sometimes being a Malay is important, sometimes it isn't'.

Nagata's article itself illustrates how circumstances influence how a person will present him- or herself. Someone may be significantly a 'Malay' in one context, where for example, as Nagata suggests, there are many non-Malays in the same region. In other circumstances, distinctions *among* Malays may become relevant, as among Malays who identify as such but have their origins in neighbouring Sumatra (an island close to Malaysia and part of Indonesia). Again, depending on circumstances, people may see their place of origin, their ancestry and aspects of custom and culture as fundamental to their being. In these circumstances, she suggests, people attach a 'primordial' meaning to these attributes; they are seen as fundamental, even biological, certainly grounded in place (of birth) and similar in nature to ties of kinship. When 'cultural attributes' are viewed in this way, they may be regarded, Nagata suggests, as being 'primordialized', thus making it clearer than Geertz does that 'primordiality' is bestowed on a relationship and not simply inherent to it.

Much more recently, the debate has tended to descend into a rather futile exercise principally based upon an entirely 'straw man' portrayal of 'primordial' attachments. Eller and Coughlan (1993) set out to show that ethnic ties cannot be regarded as primordial by portraying the 'primordial' as something pre-social, or biological or indefinably grounded in emotion. They comment on Shils without acknowledging that Shils was not writing about ethnic groups and, indeed, never uses the word 'ethnic'. They are particularly concerned about the use of the word 'ineffable', finding that it means 'incapable of being expressed in words' or even, in other contexts, 'not to be uttered, taboo'. Only one page later, they write: 'It is well known that social actors are often unable to explain their feelings and behaviours . . . but sociologists ought not to be satisfied with this layman's view of the world' (pp. 189–90). It is not, however, clear that Geertz is accepting the layperson's view as much as describing the nature of the attachment. At this point, Eller and Coughlan concede that the errors may not have been so much those of Shils and Geertz but errors of 'subsequent analysts' who saw 'primordial attachments as ineffable and hence un-analysable for sociologists' (p. 190). Of course there is nothing in either of the earlier writers to suggest that 'primordial' ties were 'un-analysable', rather that they may be associated with the kind of sentiments which are taken for granted, assumed as 'givens' and, by and large, not reflected upon or calculated by actors (rather than observers).

It is not easy to say who these subsequent analysts were in Eller and Coughlan's account since virtually all the further literature they cite is in support of a 'circumstantialist' view of ethnicity. The exception (which they do cite) is the work of Van Den Berghe who has attempted to ground an understanding of ethnic sentiments in socio-biology, a proposition that individual action in accordance with ethnic membership is a group-level extension of a self-preservation principle (Van Den Berghe 1981). The repeated misunderstanding in Eller and Coughlan is their view that Geertz speaks of 'primordial' (ties, obligations, identities) as 'natural' and 'pre-social' rather than socially grounded (compare here the excellent discussion in Gil-White 1999). They appear to think of 'primordial' as meaning prior to all social experience (p. 196); indeed, if that were what was meant they would be right in attacking the idea as profoundly un-sociological. If 'primordial' can only mean 'natural', 'biological', 'pre-social', uninfluenced by culture, then Eller and Coughlan are right. In a contest between natural and social, or between nature and society, for sociologists only 'the social' can win. It is difficult to imagine that as distinguished an anthropologist as Geertz would think of human attributes as pre-social or pre-cultural.

Indeed, this is the main lesson which students of sociology should take from this confused and confusing debate. However much *actors* (in sociology this means 'people in everyday life' as against *observers*) may think of their attachment to a particular ethnic identity as mystically grounded in 'blood', sociologists and anthropologists are almost bound to think otherwise (cf. Gil-White 1999). They will observe that ethnic identities change, the way in which they are formed is not fixed and the ends which such identities serve – for example, as rallying points in a struggle – may be manipulated by 'ethnic leaders'. This is simply good sociology – there are no pre-social realities. Thus the emphasis on what has been called 'constructionism' in the sociology of ethnicity is nothing more than the good application of a standard sociological theorem: what is seen to be natural by actors is understood by sociologists as socially construed. No doubt there are many actors who also are not deceived.

On this argument, what are described as 'givens' of human existence are precisely the very basic ties, sentiments and cultural attributes acquired through socialization. As John Rex has put it, 'as a matter of empirical fact, there is a set of social ties which is an inevitable part of the human condition' (1996, p. 189). In this sense 'all of us have ethnicity'. Rex is here tying the idea of ethnicity quite closely to family or, more analytically, to socialization. Ethnicity is thus something we are socialized into. Equally important, it is something we can grow out of. In arguing this, Rex has put the question in a manner very similar to the way I have been posing it in this book:

If all this [about socialization] is conceded, there is nothing mysterious about the ties involved. They can be comprehended and described sociologically. What is questionable is the suggestion that these ties bind us together with particular others in an unalterable way for life. We do not in fact remain infants all our lives. We may replace the ties which are given to us in our families of birth by others which we choose. In doing so we may identify with an increasingly wide range of chosen others, ties with whom may supplement and may displace those with our immediate community of birth . . . what has to be explained is the extension of the feeling of original ethnic bonded-ness to a wider range of persons and into adult life . . . the task of the sociologist should be to describe and explain the process by which it happens. (p. 189)

At least *some* people in *some* circumstances continue to feel a strong sense of attachment to a wider group, linked in personal history to socialization. This might explain why, in an inventive study, Gil-White suggested that evidence indicates that many people do indeed see their ethnic identities as 'primordial' (Gil-White 1999).

Summary: primordial ethnic groups

The term 'primordial' was in its original formulation a perfectly intelligible distinction between civic and non-civic ties, the civic being those ties associated with citizenship and citizen-like obligations in a modern state. By contrast, primordial ties were those deriving from birth into a particular family, community, religious or language group. Birth into and experience of living in these primary groups brings with it a complex of attitudes and cultural dispositions. In this sense, the primordial–civic distinction was similar to a familiar range of sociological distinctions such as 'universalistic' and 'particularistic' (see Parsons 1968) or between *Gemeinschaft* and *Gesellschaft* (Tönnies 1963). These distinctions are highly schematic; but few would deny that there is being discerned a real distinction between relationships which have a certain 'given' or ascribed quality and relationships which are ordered by contractual considerations, by 'interest', or by the regulatory principles of states and formal organizations.

In the field of ethnicity, the difficulty began when some writers began speaking as if 'primordiality' was viewed as a characteristic of ethnic ties. This was then translated into a 'primordial' conceptualization of ethnic groups (or ethnicity) as against other conceptualizations, mostly characterized as 'instrumental' and 'circumstantial'. This is a wholly mistaken debate and its protagonists – above all Eller and Coughlan – appear to have seriously 'missed the point' or addressed something quite different from those they claim to criticize. In the end, Eller and Coughlan appear to want to deny, not the existence of primordiality as a quality of ethnic groups, but the existence of primordiality at all (Eller and Coughlan 1993). That is, to 'think out of existence' primordiality is somehow to turn one's back on affect, the powerful influence of familiarity and customariness in social life and the diffuse sense of attachment that flows from circumstances of birth and socialization, use of language and ingrained habits of thought and social practice.

To speak of this kind of 'customariness', 'familiarity', 'conventions of language and thought' and the like is not to invoke an unexplored and unexplorable realm of irrationality in human behaviour, and certainly not to imply that 'irrationality and affect' are dominant forces in social life (cf. Bourdieu 1990). It is simply to acknowledge that this kind of familiarity exists, that habits of thought do become ingrained and are often associated with early life, place, the family and wider groupings or regions. Those who originally made the distinction between civic and primordial ties were making precisely this point – and not describing ethnic groups as 'primordial'. It is perfectly possible to have a conception of ethnic groups which allows us to see them – or more abstractly, to see ethnic ties or ethnicity – as being constituted by elements which are civic, instrumental, circumstantial and primordial. In plain terms, the question of the primordiality of ethnic ties is one for exploration not definition. A model of ethnicity which pre-ordains ethnically oriented action (or ethnic group membership, ethnic politics) as instrumental (circumstantial, situational) or as affective will be escaping the difficulties.

5
How Real are Groups? Political Ethnicity, Symbolic Ethnicity and Competition Theory

It was usually assumed in the 1940s and 1950s in the USA that ethnic identities gradually faded in a steady path of assimilation into an American mainstream. This was the view of Lloyd Warner and others writing at this time, as we saw in chapter 3. Two factors contributed to a reconsideration of immigration and ethnicity in the 1960s. First, the 1965 immigration reforms instigated renewed large-scale migration to the USA, with increased proportions from non-European sources. Second, the 1960s civil rights legislation highlighted the postwar drive for racial equality. It was preceded by black-led mass movements and followed by further protest and urban demonstrations. At the same time, throughout Africa, countries which had been subjected to colonial rule by European powers were gaining independence. All of this seemed to indicate a revival of ethnic awareness and nationalism. These events prompted, in the USA, a renewed interest in 'ethnicity' marked by the publication of works such as those by Glazer and Moynihan (1963, 1975). The question of the survival or revival of ethnic identities was thoroughly reopened. These debates, about assimilation, the entrenchment of ethnic disadvantage and the political deployment of ethnic identities, were to continue to the end of the twentieth century and beyond, as we shall see in chapters 6 and 7.

If some argued that ethnic identities had reappeared, it was also acknowledged that the motive force of ethnic identification might be 'instrumental' rather than affective or cultural. In other words, whilst emotional attachment to an ethnic group might decline along with the loss of cultural distinctiveness, there were nonetheless social circumstances in which people saw certain (political or economic) gains in claiming an ethnic identity. The same model may be applied to nationalist identities and actions (for an excellent discussion, see Brubaker and Laitin 1998). In the US sociology of ethnicity, Gans argued that ethnic names, and maybe a sentimental attachment, survived after the cultural distinctiveness and social solidarity of the groups had declined or disappeared altogether – this he called 'symbolic ethnicity' (Gans 1979).

Four theoretical orientations which bear on this question of the nature of ethnic groups are discussed in this chapter. The first is the landmark essay of Barth (1969), in which he suggested that the critical dimension of ethnicity was the demarcation of people in social transactions. His work introduced the concept of 'ethnic boundaries'. The second is a large body of writing, principally in the USA, grounded in the idea that it is inter group contexts, especially contexts of *competition and threat*, which account for heightened awareness of ethnic boundaries and explain violence across these boundaries. Third, we discuss the work of Edna Bonacich (1972, 1973, 1975), who placed the explanation of ethnic antagonism within a framework of *class analysis*. Fourth, in the last part of the chapter, we discuss the work of Brubaker (2004), who has led the way in a critique of the concept of ethnic groups.

Cultures and boundaries

The work of Norwegian anthropologist Fredrik Barth has been singularly influential in the study of ethnicity. Barth's landmark essay, published in 1969, was written as the introductory essay in a volume of collected essays deriving from a conference at Bergen in 1967 (Barth ed. 1969). Two of the contributors wrote about peasant or nomadic communities in Norway; the others were concerned with ethnic identities in Sudan, Ethiopia, Mexico, Pakistan, Afghanistan and Laos. The central proposition coming out of Barth's work was that ethnic identities are sustained by the maintenance of what he calls 'boundaries', the lines which mark off one group from another. These lines are not drawn by simple cultural difference, e.g. the As are the people who speak 'A-language'. Rather, the boundaries are drawn by social behaviour which is relevant to the recognition of membership, and to the drawing of distinctions; the cultural 'items' which are used to make these distinctions vary, and may be only a small part of the cultural repertoire of a particular group. This could be stated as the proposition that (1) the As are the people who are not Bs and (2) speaking 'A-language' is a way of knowing this and showing this. Language is a major cultural marker – and Barth argued that quite *small* markers can be decisive in distinguishing one group from another.

Barth's central proposition has general application. The kinds of segmentary societies – societies and collectivities with a distinctive way of life which are largely self-reproducing but lack a formal central authority – that Barth is discussing are often found in postcolonial societies straddling the geography of neighbouring states, such as Pakistan and Afghanistan. As these postcolonial states attempt to secure their power and command over diverse populations, these segments are at risk. If they do not constitute part of a majority population or a politically dominant elite, minorities distinguishable by a feature of language or religion find themselves under suspicion. Furthermore, where new states are weak, both economically and in the command of their territory, rivalries between contiguous groups or groups side by side in the same region may prove beyond the capacity of the state to control and restrain. Such groups, many of them in parts of Africa and Asia, are of the kind traditionally studied by anthropologists, such as Evans Pritchard (1962) in the colonial era, by Edmund Leach (1982) rather later and by Barth and his colleagues at the point of de-colonization and beyond. For Barth, the Pathans of Pakistan and Afghanistan are an 'ethnic group', compared to the USA where the term was applied mostly to immigrant communities and their descendants. Barth begins by outlining how anthropologists typically define ethnic groups, citing four lines of definition:

1 A group which is largely self-perpetuating.
2 A group which shares fundamental cultural values.
3 A group which makes up a field of communication and interaction.
4 A group which has a membership which identifies itself and is identified by others as constituting a category distinguishable from other categories of the same order.

Barth does not dismiss any of the conventional meanings of the above but he is at pains to make clear that it is not possible to define an ethnic group as the 'possessor' of a distinctive culture which functions to make it distinctive. The more he pursues his case, the more he inclines to identifying 'social organization' as the definitive feature, and feature '4' above as the decisive one:

> We can assume no one-to-one relationship between ethnic units and cultural similarities and differences. The features that are taken into account are not the sum of 'objective' differences but only those which the actors themselves regard as significant – some cultural features are used by actors as signals and emblems of difference, others are ignored. (Barth 1969, p. 14)

It is not that culture is unimportant or that there cannot be found real patterns of cultural difference. He speaks of overt signals or signs, including dress, language, house construction and lifestyle as well as moral values and standards. But the critical thing in defining the ethnic group is the 'maintenance of the boundary' between one group and another. The culture of a group may 'be transformed' (p. 14) and the cultural item which marks As from Bs may be changed. Nonetheless, the As and Bs persist. This leads Barth to his most succinct definition of this approach, the one subsequently most repeated:

> The critical focus of investigation from this point of view becomes the ethnic boundary that defines the group, not the cultural stuff which it encloses. (p. 15)

Having established a way of thinking about ethnic groups, Barth proceeds to examine how members of ethnic groups may behave both individually and collectively. Within an ethnic group, behaviours are construed differently from behaviour which crosses ethnic boundaries. With other members with whom identity is shared there is, as Barth puts it, an 'acceptance that both are playing the same game'. When this is so it makes it possible for their relationship 'to cover all different sectors and domains of activity'. Their relationship is not, in another sociological way of describing relationships, single-stranded. A relationship, for example a trading relationship in which As exchange things with Bs, is single-stranded if outside the trading exchange; the As have little or nothing to do with the Bs. Thus, as Barth puts it, 'a dichotomization of others as strangers implies a recognition of limitations on shared understandings and a restriction of interaction to sectors of common understanding and mutual interest' (p. 15).

Barth's emphasis on identification of members and strangers, on the system of classification, on 'boundaries' and on the common understandings which govern relationships has been taken up by subsequent anthropologists (cf. Banks 1996; and particularly Eriksen 1993). These common understandings govern relationships between members, between members and strangers and the scope of the relationships between members and strangers (i.e. do they for example just trade with each other, or do they engage with each other in many ways?). But the most striking consequence of Barth's (quite short) essay has been to detach 'culture' from ethnic group in the sense that ethnic groups are not described by the sum of their cultural characteristics but by their deployment of markers of difference in relation with other 'marked' groups.

Competition theory

The Barthian conceptualization of ethnic groups as the social definition of boundaries which are 'guarded', 'porous' or 'reinforced' has been very influential. His thinking has inspired

an important strand of ethnicity theory particularly prominent in US sociology, namely 'competition theory' or 'group
threat' theory. Cunningham and Phillips (2007) suggest that
'ethnic competition theory builds on Barth's emphasis on the
socially constructed boundaries through which ethnic groups
ascribe difference' (p. 783). When, in US society, group
boundaries are defined – including some primary categories,
'white', 'black', 'Asian' and 'Hispanic' – people, it is argued,
see their fates bound up with the future of the population so
defined. In residential areas, in the workplace, in community
politics and more broadly in public symbolic representations,
these populations are seen to be groups in competition with
each other. In this situation, 'competition . . . becomes a key
mechanism through which particular boundaries are reinforced' (p. 3).

The critical components of the theory are: (1) that (ethnic)
groups are defined as different collectivities and 'members' of
a group see their fates as bound up with co-ethnics; (2) that
advances made by one group may be at the expense of
another; (3) that competition creates or reinforces prejudices
at the points where group boundaries are defended; and (4)
that a wide range of social attitudes or types of mobilization
and acts of violence may be viewed as a response to a 'group
threat'. Much of the literature has focused on the dominant
population category 'whites' and the defence of their prerogatives and privileged position in the face of competition from
minorities. American 'ethnic history' has been about the constant reassertion of the black/white boundary, including its
enshrinement in law, politics and public policy, and the ethnic
majority's persistent defence of its dominance or racialized
privilege. The defining of 'whiteness' and the black/white
binary division are the critical features of the system of ethnicity in the USA. But group competition between minorities,
such as between African Americans and Hispanics, can also
be important.

Sociologists have built on this 'competition model' (Nagel
1995) over the last three decades, but the antecedents are
older. We could even go as far back as the classic 1930s study
of the Jim Crow South, *Caste and Class in a Southern Town*
(1937), in which Dollard viewed white prejudice and discrimination as producing certain gains. As long as the fixed

boundary between black and white was enforced, over jobs, sexual relations and symbolic power, then whites preserved their 'gains' in class, status and sexual competition. Prejudice could be explained by psychological and other theoretical approaches, but Dollard emphasized the material and symbolic rewards it produced. This has remained a feature of competition theory: behaviour and attitudes are explained in relation to a *group context*, rather than in relation to individual characteristics, such as personality traits or factors like age and level of education. These individual facts may partly help us understand why some individuals are more likely than others to act (including in aggressive and violent ways) in defence of group privileges; but 'boundary-maintaining' action and the defence of the group is about the inter-group situation. This 'group context' dimension is the strength of competition theory. Its several weaknesses, such as assuming the permanence of groups and identification with them, are discussed later in this chapter and in chapter 7.

These elements of competition theory are present in the two sources that have been most cited as originators of this theoretical model: Blumer and Blalock. In a 1958 article Blumer argued that 'race prejudice' could be understood, as his title read, 'as a sense of group position' and the attitudes or behaviour of the dominant group could be seen as a response to threats to its 'established group privileges'. In a similar vein, Blalock (1967), in his *Theory of Minority-Group Relations*, argued that the size of a minority group was perceived as a threat by the dominant group. As a minority presence grows, as in a 'residential transition', so the perceived threat grows. People can feel more threatened in a precarious economic situation. In a worsening economy, as resources become scarcer (e.g. access to jobs, housing) the sense of threat is heightened. The majority dominant group 'ethnicizes' this sense of threat – perceives it to be along the lines of ethnic boundaries. Even in a relatively stable and prosperous society, one group with historical privileges may see itself as threatened by any advance of a less privileged group. These ideas can be illustrated further by taking a look at subsequent work framed by this model.

Jacobs and Tope (2007) set out to explain how members of the US House of Representatives voted, on 'roll call' votes, especially in relation to measures which could be deemed 'liberal', i.e. in some way redistributive and designed to use public funds to assist low-income and disadvantaged populations. They deployed many variables in a complex methodology, but their main argument was that *perceived group threat* led to conservative voting. They focused on 'the threat from large minority populations that is likely to produce greater support for conservative legislation' or non-support for liberal measures. Response to perceived group threat was measured by the voting records of state representatives in the House; the likelihood of threat was measured by the size of minority populations in the states they represented. As minority presence grows and minority aims are articulated, they are seen as a 'threat to majority group dominance'.

A key argument (or assumption) is that policies designed to assist poor and working-class families are viewed as beneficial to minorities. In short, class politics are racialized or ethnicized. 'Ethnic others' are perceived (including by poor and working-class whites) as the targets of the redistributive policy so that 'policies that help the least prosperous are less likely [to gain support] if underclass minorities are seen as the primary beneficiaries' (Jacobs and Tope 2007, p. 1459). In particular, they are less likely to receive support from the ethnic majority. These are 'the politics of resentment' based on the resentful attitudes of 'dominant group members' even where they, as white, working-class and even poor, may themselves benefit from redistributive measures. This is indeed another version of the politics of 'class and race' in US history – the very great difficulty in forging class alliances across ethnic lines, despite the vast areas of shared interest. With some very important exceptions, such as some black and white labour unions working together (Worthman 1969), the white working class has perceived its 'future' in ethnic terms. The ruling and political classes, at least some amongst them, have understood this and have been ready to exploit this persistent social fact.

Thus Jacobs and Tope suggest that (1) dominant group voters are likely to see a growing minority presence as a threat; (2) this is turned into support for conservative measures or opposition to 'liberal' measures; and (3) conservative politicians are *conscious* of the political gains of deploying fears, resentments and antipathies. The evidence they draw on is from memoirs of those involved in Nixon's 'Southern strategy', quoting a Nixon aide as saying 'the whole secret of politics is knowing who hates who'. These and similar documented items suggest that indirect but readily understood appeals to public fears and resentments are consciously made. As Erlichmann, counsel to the President, was reported to have said: 'We'll go after the racists'. He indicated that this 'subliminal appeal to anti-black voters was always present in Nixon's statements and speeches' (Jacobs and Tope 2000, p. 1490).

The authors are able to demonstrate clear empirical support for their 'group threat' hypothesis, i.e. that a larger minority presence in a state translates into ideological anti-liberal voting. They know that this is not the only factor in explaining 'conservative' roll call votes. High unemployment and strong unions are *positively* related to liberal voting. But what they also refer to as 'racial threat' is consistently related to conservative votes. The relationship only diminishes, and reverses, when the minority presence itself is sufficient in numbers to influence political representation in a liberal direction. The conclusions are rather pessimistic, partly because the voting pattern is described as 'ideological'. By this they mean that it is not restricted to votes on items which directly affect minorities, but is 'generalized' to a wider range of anti-liberal votes. They conclude that coalitions of disadvantaged populations across ethnic groups, as in the New Deal era, were temporary and atypical. More typical, they argue, is a political pattern which reflects that the USA remains 'divided between majority whites and dis-privileged minorities' (p. 1488).

A second illuminating case is the study by Cunningham and Phillips (2007) of Klan[1] mobilization in North Carolina in 1964–6, the period immediately following new civil rights legislation and the outlawing of segregated facilities such as schools. The researchers benefited from a US government inquiry into Klan activity in this period, which provided them with a detailed database of the location of 'klaverns' – local Klan chapters. The inquiry findings were detailed enough to leave behind a precise description of the location of klaverns county by county in North Carolina, a place where Klan activity was very much in evidence. They based their theoretical approach in 'ethnic competition theory', which they describe as a 'powerful explanation for a range of political action, from riots to voting behaviour to the rise of ethnic collective identity' (p. 781). The structure of their argument is similar to that outlined above: that a dominant population (whites) perceives increased minority presence and mobilization as threats to the prerogatives of the dominant group; and that the dominant group responds by a collective ethnic response.

The authors conceptualize competition or threat in three modes: demographic threat, economic threat and political threat. *Demographic* threat is defined by the percentage of non-white residents in a county; *economic* threat as (1) the median white family income, since lower-income households could be expected to be more vulnerable to competition than others and (2) the ratio of white to non-white workers in the manufacturing sector, where, again, de-segregation would threaten whites' primary position in manufacturing employment; and *political* threat was defined as the presence of black political mobilization in the county, especially the presence of a chapter of the National Association for the Advancement of Colored People (NAACP). All these *threat variables* are measured at the county level, matching the records of Klan presence in 1964–6.

The findings overwhelmingly confirm the competition model hypotheses. Percentage black presence is related to Klan activity, and the finding is particularly strong where there is an increase in black presence in an area where historically few non-whites have resided. No doubt, in those areas, whites see the new non-white presence as an 'invasion' into previously 'protected' ethnic territory. The relationship only weakens when white presence becomes small, presumably reflecting decreased capacity to organize. Low-income white households and the proportion of non-white manufacturing workers are also related to Klan activity, confirming the economic threat hypothesis: low-income white households were more vulnerable to economic competition, and 'non-whites in manufacturing' was taken as evidence of competition in an area which had been largely or exclusively white. Entrenched NAACP presence was not related to Klan activity but *new* NAACP presence was. This they interpret as meaning that long-standing NAACP chapters had been 'accepted' as non-threatening, whereas new chapters in a county where there had previously been none could be seen as a threat in the new de-segregationist climate. In addition to these findings, they sketch a 'contagion' hypothesis and a 'historical' hypothesis. The first was to suggest that Klan activity was more likely in a given county when there was Klan activity in a neighbouring county and good communications (e.g. connecting highways) between the two; this was shown to be the case. The second was to argue that historical incidence of violence towards blacks would have an effect on future white organization, constituting a local 'tradition' of violent racist action. They found that counties where lynching had taken place earlier in the century were more likely to have Klan activity in the civil rights period.

The authors are taking indicators of increased competition between ethnically marked populations as independent variables explaining the incidence of white defensive organization, or organization to protect dominant group positions. This theoretical strategy is a successful one. As well as the two examples above (explaining votes against 'liberal' measures and explaining Klan activity in North Carolina), the competition or group threat model has been applied to other areas, such as the incidence of lynchings (Creech et al. 1989; Olzak 1990; Tolnay et al. 1989), racial violence more broadly (Olzak 1990), white protest against 'bussing' as a means of school de-segregation (Olzak et al. 1994) and prejudice towards immigrants and minorities in European countries (Quillian 1995). For the last, Quillian found that average levels of prejudice were higher in countries with higher proportions of immigrants in the population.

Olzak stands out as one of the leading exponents of competition theory and (with Shanahan and West) provided an explanation of white mobilization against 'bussing' (moving schoolchildren by bus across residential areas in order to de-segregate schools) in the 1960s when segregated institutions were required by law to change. Olzak et al. (1994) find that anti-bussing protests were greatest where there were increases in 'exposure' of whites to blacks, and where there had been most school de-segregation. They also show that protests were greatest in white working-class areas, confirming Wilson's (1980) argument that inter-racial conflict was a consequence of competition between 'have-nots', i.e. less advantaged blacks and whites. Working-class whites, they suggest, both experienced greater inter-racial contact and had fewer resources to 'flee', compared with middle- and upper-class whites' ability to send their children to private schools.

> Poor white communities generate more anti-bussing activity not because they hold more racist attitudes but because they have fewer alternatives. (Olzak et al. 1994, p. 204)

Olzak's (1989) analysis of labour unrest and anti-black activity in the period 1880–1914 is even more ambitious in deploying historical data. In this period of US history, black–white relations were tensely contested. Some black workers were moving northwards or out of Southern rural areas into Southern towns; whites were organizing into (usually) all-white labour unions. At the same time, the economy of the South was sensitive to world cotton prices and Southern elites were anxious to protect their land, investments and supply of manageable labour. Olzak is able to show that the founding of unions by whites is related both to strike activity and ethnic conflict. Immigration and poor economic conditions sharpened competition in labour markets, both in northern cities where immigrants mostly arrived, and in the South where European immigrants joined black workers in competition for jobs. In Olzak's words: 'The rising supply of low wage labour increased levels of ethnic competition in urban labour markets, thus raising rates of ethnic conflict' (1989, p. 1303).

In her further analysis of violence against black people (Olzak 1990), she shows that both economic competition and political competition represented threats to white dominance, which are causally linked to acts of violence (including lynchings) against black people; these acts of violence are interpreted as reinforcing the boundary between white and black *and* enforcing whites' privileged position. The political threat came from the Populist movement which developed in the South, in the latter part of the nineteenth century, as a challenge to landowner and capitalist interests, and for a period managed to unite black and white workers and farmers into a single political cause (Vann Woodward 1963). Increases in labour market competition linked to immigration and black migration intensified racial conflict, as others have shown. But Olzak was able to show that '*political* threat' was also related to violence against black people. She cites economic historians and sociologists who 'have claimed that the political challenge of Populism was met with swift and violent resistance by the white power structure' (1990, p. 415). She notes Populist party challenges and shows that 'indicators of political challenges to one-party rule are associated significantly with levels of lynching' (p. 415).

Competition or group threat theory has much to offer as a basis for explanation of dominant group responses to minority group threat (or response to being exposed to competition) and of inter-group conflicts more generally (for example, competition between minorities where a 'new' minority threatens an older one, such as the case of Hispanics and African Americans). It is an advance on explanations which depend on individual characteristics of actors (e.g. explaining prejudice by reference to age, education) because it offers a view of a total context, a social situation in which one group sees its privileges and taken-for-granted primacy as under threat. The competition model is also presented as superior to 'structural breakdown' theory, which argues that 'modernization' and 'urbanization' disrupts accepted ways of living, thus leading to 'stress' or 'anxiety' which are translated into aggressive or irrational responses. But the competition/threat model is not without difficulties and some serious disagreements.

One difficulty is the tendency to pose a 'group' (which in most cases is after all only a large population category, namely 'whites') as a collective actor. The theorists in this field (see for example Banton 1983; Bélanger and Pinard 1991; Blalock 1967; Blumer 1958; Cunningham and Phillips 2007; Jacobs and Tope 2007; Nagel 1995; Olzak 1990; Quillian 1995) typically recognize that this is not the case, but there is, nonetheless, a core conception of group A posing a threat to group B, a threat to which group B responds with violence, discrimination and opposition. In the case of lynchings, the subject of several papers, it is clear that a particular lynching is carried out by a relatively small number of people in the group whose dominance is threatened or seen to be so. We can of course observe that during the 'high period' of lynching (1880–1910) in the USA not much was done by other whites to prevent it. The general (white) population, the police, the courts or state and federal government by and large 'stood by'. But if there was perceived to be a *general* threat, the response came from a *small* number.

So, if the competition/threat model has the virtue of posing a situation in which group A perceives a competitive threat from group B, it will almost always be the case that *some members* of group A are, or see themselves to be, much more threatened than others (but see Quillian 1995, p. 587). We saw in the Olzak case that the white working class were viewed as more 'threatened', more vulnerable to threat/ competition and having fewer resources to deal with the 'threat'. In several of the studies (see Olzak 1990; Quillian 1995) increased immigration is seen to be posing a possible threat to an 'established' group. But our sociological sense tells us that some members of the US dominant group ('whites') are more 'threatened' by competition from immi- grants than others; by and large, political and economic elites favour open immigration policies. Olzak (1990) argues that it is precisely increased labour market competition flowing from immigration that poses a competitive threat. This competition is felt by those white workers directly engaged in the same competitive labour market. We know that working-class opinion is frequently against immigration, whilst political and economic elites favour it, even if they remain publicly neutral. Governments may take action to restrain immigration because they fear public opinion, not because they share the fears of the most affected workers. So we can scarcely help concluding that the people affected by competition are not 'a group' but some particular members of a group.

There are some further puzzles in the papers cited above. Olzak, in writing about lynchings and violence against blacks, argues that Populism (a *political* threat) was 'met with swift and violent resistance by the white power struc- ture' (1990, p. 415). Now here is a curiosity: the political threat (Populism) came, for much of the period studied by

Olzak (the earlier part), from a political movement which had considerable success in *uniting* black and white in shared *class* interest. Yet all this is seen as a threat to white dominance. But it could be seen equally as a threat to political and economic *elites* in the US South in particular, who had expended considerable effort after the Civil War in creating the Jim Crow system of white supremacy. The threat, as described by Olzak, was to *the white power structure*, a different description from describing an ethnic group (i.e. whites). And resistance (presumably *by* the white power structure) was 'to impose widespread terror through lynchings' (p. 415). Now we are faced with the very difficult question of who instigated lynchings: was it 'freelance' gangs of white thugs? Or agents of the wealthy and powerful? Or gangs who were secretly working in alliance with the political establishment? The notion of *economic* threat, where immigration raises competition in the labour market, threatening the low-income and vulnerable members of the 'dominant group', follows a relatively simple logic. By contrast, the notion of 'political threat' is usually more complex, since 'taking sides' in politics is (usually) more multifaceted. But both depend on the notion of a 'dominant group' threatened by a 'subordinate group' in a game in which one group's gain is the other's loss.

Some difficulties are posed by the considerable breadth of type of responses to threat (lynching, conservative voting, anti-bussing protest, anti-immigrant prejudice, for example). Lynching was nominally unlawful (although usually unpunished) and required brutal violence; conservative voting was indirect, being based on political representatives 'reading' the suspicions and prejudices of their constituencies; anti-bussing protests were 'lawful' action in the main but required a level of community organization; and prejudice (see Quillian 1995) is a rather diffuse sentiment expressed in answer to survey questions. It might be argued that these differing outcomes require different logics of explanation; on the other hand, it could be a mark of the power of competition/threat theory that in each case the theoretical approach gains confirmation. The methodologies adopted in all these studies required measurement and quantifying of events – number of lynchings, number of anti-liberal votes, number of protests: Quillian's prejudice indicator (see below) is an exception. But the number of events might be subject to errors in measurement, as Tolnay et al. (1989) argue with respect to the analysis of lynching *per county*.

Quillian's analysis is different in another key respect. Because it focuses on a survey-based measure of prejudice, he has no action (act of violence, vote, protest) to which to refer. He also treats prejudice as 'antipathy with a faulty generalisation' (p. 587) and thus treats it as 'irrationality' or mistaken judgement or both. This appears to place his case outside a 'rational choice' model, which has a close relationship to competition models (Banton 1983) in that people are seen as acting in defence of an interest-group dominance. At the very least, it raises the question as to whether people, responding to competition, can properly be seen as taking action to defend their threatened privileges. If they are seen in this way, then they are not treated as 'irrational' but as 'reasonable actors' defending their position. Some competition/threat theorists write of '*perceived* group threat' (Blumer 1958), thus bypassing the question of whether they are seeing a *genuine* threat. The test need not be the test of a 'real threat', although Bobo (1983) argues for what he calls 'realistic threat theory'; a threat is where members of group A could *reasonably see themselves* threatened by group B. This raises questions which are not easily answered within the framework of sociology, such as are native workers' jobs really threatened by new immigrants or migrants? Are, for example, African American workers really under threat of being replaced by Hispanic immigrants, as some accounts suggest (Johnson et al. 1997)? Were white workers right to fear that black and immigrant workers would be used as strike-breakers (which they were) thus threatening their (white) collective position? Even if competition/threat is *reasonably perceived*, it is equally difficult to judge whether *response* x is a reasonable one. We could ask whether white and black workers in the South of the 1880s, looking to occupy the same areas of economic activity, were 'reasonable', for example whites, to fight against black competition (which they did) or to unite in unions and political movements to fight for their shared class interests (which they also did, if less often).

Across competition/threat theorists there is variation too in what the *context of threat* is – from the most local, in the case of county by county analysis of lynchings in the USA, to country comparisons as in the case of Quillian's multi-country analysis of prejudice against immigrants in European countries. In the latter case, where 'level of threat' is measured by percentage immigrant presence per country and response is measured by per country levels of prejudice, the assumption must be that the ethnic majority in a country has a *nationwide* perception of the presence of immigrants, and that a greater presence is perceived as a greater competitive threat. This is quite different from a *localized* analysis, where local measures of immigrant or minority presence would certainly be reflected in local perceptions of that presence. The locally based popular estimates (of numbers of immigrants) may not be accurate when set against Census figures, but they will reflect experience in the community. At the level of a country, it is probable that most people have no realistic idea of the number of immigrants in that country. Again, this does not invalidate competition theory but it does raise the question: how does actual minority presence in a local, regional or national context translate into a perception of that presence, as well as a perception of that presence *as a threat*?

Indeed, two commentators, Bélanger and Pinard (1991), have pointed out that, in the USA and many other countries, 'competition' is viewed as entirely legitimate, and even revered as a principle of social action. So, they suggest, the argument needs to be further specified, to include the proposition that, for competition to lead to ethnic conflict, the competition *'must be perceived to be unfair'* (p. 448). And competition will be seen as unfair if it 'violates norms' in a situation where discrimination is routine, when it is 'seen as involving unjustified threats to claimed rights and possessions', or when 'the rules of competition are contested'. This principle ('competition must be perceived to be unfair') makes open and explicit what is implicit in the idea of a 'dominant group', which in the USA means 'majority whites'. That is, the dominant group perceives a threat because they see themselves as having certain prerogatives and prior claims, and as having a 'turf' which they are protecting. So long as competition/threat theory is applied to whites and blacks in the USA, then the very idea of entrenched superordination and subordination is necessary to the concept of threat.

In this respect, competition theory assumptions and findings restate a long reiterated theorem of ethnicity and status in US society: that blacks are not seen as rightful competitors with majority whites and thus that the ethnic majority will do as much as, or more than, is necessary to protect their privileges against minority aspirations. In the analysis applied to pre-civil rights America, the idea of threat reflects the social order and mentalities of a caste society, especially where the caste lines are in any danger of being breached. But the same theoretical approach works outside this time period. To that extent, it indicates that *the ethnic majority (whites) do not regard competition from minorities or new migrants as fair or legitimate.* In simple terms, it is continuing evidence of a racist society, indicated by persistent and wide inequalities between ethnic groups, and of the majoritarian assumptions found in public and private discourse. Insofar as competition/ threat theory is applied to black white relations it is an analysis which is often stated, in much starker terms: the continuing story of inequality, racism and the persistent white defence of prerogatives. In other words, competition/threat theory assumes something (the white sense of prerogative) which others place at the centre of their analysis – and call it racism (see Feagin 1991; Omi and Winant 1986; Winant 2000).

This is the most dispiriting and pessimistic aspect of competition theory applied to white–black relations in the US because, in theory, the only 'solution' to 'unfair' competition is the absence of competition. This would only be possible in a system of complementarity where people remained in differentiated sectors of economy and society. In the plural colonial society of apartheid and segregation, competition is – in theory – avoided by separation (Bélanger and Pinard 1991). A more optimistic view would be this: ethnic antagonisms stemming from competition/threat would be reduced by maximizing situations in which two or more ethnic groups can see their interests as shared. Then trans-ethnic collaboration would be more rewarding than co-ethnic defence against perceived ethnic threat.

Class as a complicating factor in ethnic competition analysis; ethnicity as a complicating factor in class analysis

In several of these studies, the concept of class interests has formed part of the analysis. A dominant group (meaning US whites) and a 'subordinate group' (meaning US blacks) are portrayed as groups in competition, with one defending a privileged position, the other posing a 'threat' to that privileged position: a short but plausible account of US history. So, the key elements of the equation are 'ethnic groups', whilst classes are referred to when necessary. We saw that Olzak et al. argued that *working-class* whites were *most* 'threatened' by de-segregation. In this sense, class is viewed as a complicating factor in ethnic competition analysis. It is possible – and entirely plausible – to reverse this proposition: then, we treat ethnicity as a complicating factor in class analysis. This is closer to what, in a landmark series of articles, Bonacich (1972, 1973, 1975) has done.

Although some of the writers cited above have treated Bonacich as a 'competition theorist' (but see Banton 1987), it would be more accurate to see her as presenting a class analysis of a highly racialized or ethnicized society (the USA) where class competition and class conflict commonly has an ethnic profile. She draws a picture of class analysis, and, so to speak, fills in some of the gaps with 'ethnic colours'. This is a quite radical difference and why we should not treat Bonacich as a competition theorist. Bonacich's basic idea is not that ethnic groups compete, but that in a capitalist society, the business class (capitalists, employers) is in a constant struggle with labour, since labour constitutes a production cost which affects the competitiveness and profitability of capital. The business class seeks both to assert control over labour and to obtain labour at a low cost (for other examples of class analysis see also Gottlieb et al. 2005; Johnson et al. 1997; and chapter 7). The element of 'control' is found in the struggle over labour unions which seek to protect workers in *strategic* ways with a long-term view. This would include trying to influence legislation (such as the right to strike), protecting workers' safety and bargaining for long-term benefits like health care and pensions. Unions also seek to protect *immediate* interests of workers in defending levels of pay. These are the highly simplified 'bare bones' of the structure and dynamics of a capitalist society. For much of US history, these struggles have largely been acted out within the US itself, notwithstanding the fact that newly available labour (i.e. immigrants) has constantly replenished the US population. In recent decades, these struggles have to be understood within the framework of a global economy. If car production in Detroit becomes unprofitable it shifts elsewhere or is replaced by production elsewhere (e.g. Japan). Bonacich's contribution is to develop an understanding of how this system of competition and struggle in the US has become complicated by the deployment of racial categories. These categories are embedded in US history, especially the history of the enslavement of Africans as a source of hyper-exploited labour in the plantation and other economies (Wilson 1980).

Much of what Bonacich wrote centred on four classes: the business class (employers), high-paid labour, low-paid labour and what she called 'middleman minorities', the last being a special case to which we shall return. Typically, high-paid labour is labour which has acquired a measure of organization, social prestige, political influence and bargaining power. The reasons for these advantages, or their opposite, in the labour market are historical. Labour without these advantages are typically immigrants, and especially low-skill migrants and forced migrants. In the USA, the most important forced migrants are those Africans who were brought into slavery. Herein lies the origin of the category 'black' in American society and the overarching centrality of the black/white boundary in US ethnic classification.

Because of its historical advantages, white labour has been able to acquire a certain 'privileged' position in the labour market, especially in relation to black labour. Until 1865, the system of slavery, and the high degree of control asserted over 'free blacks', ensured white privileges in the labour market in what Van Den Berghe has called a 'paternalistic system' (see Kinloch 1981). The end of slavery initiated, in Van Den Berghe's terms, 'competitive race relations' (see Van Den Berghe 1978), and the efforts of whites to protect their 'privileges' in the labour market against new competitors were a big part of this competition. Workers without any social privileges (i.e. organization, prestige, political influence) are vulnerable to becoming low-paid labour. This initiates what Bonacich describes as a three-way struggle:

> When the price of labour for the same work differs by ethnic group, a three-way conflict develops among business, high priced labour and cheaper labour. (Bonacich 1975, p. 603)

It is important to be clear about two things. First, the critical terms of the theory are 'business', 'high-paid labour' and 'low-paid labour'. Second, the position of lower-paid workers is not a consequence of prejudice. As Bonacich puts it

> The prejudices of business do not determine the price of labour, darker skinned or culturally different persons being paid less because of them. Rather business tries to pay as little as possible for labour, regardless of ethnicity, and is held in check by the resources and motives of labour groups. Since these often vary by ethnicity, it is common to find ethnically split labour markets. (Bonacich 1972, p. 553)

In this three-class situation, business seeks low-paid labour, high-paid labour 'fears being reduced to the level of low paid labour' (p. 553) and low-paid labour is constrained by its lack of bargaining power in the labour market. White capitalists are not motivated by 'ethnic solidarity' (i.e. a shared interest and sense of common cause with all whites) but by the interests of capital. Bonacich describes the instance of 'Okies' (poor workers migrating westwards in the Depression) who were stigmatized as 'undesirable' and seen by other workers as dragging down pay levels. And Okies were white (p. 557). Capital is itself multi-ethnic (and now global), and has typically no regard for non-relevant (e.g. ethnic) features of workers, but in the right circumstances will hyper-exploit vulnerable workers, and acquiesce in the demands for protection by high-paid workers.

High-paid labour, Bonacich argues, will seek to protect itself from low-paid labour by two methods. One is *exclusion*, where workers who have some advantages seek to prevent competition with workers who might work for less pay – typically immigrants and internal migrants. Examples would be the exclusion of Chinese workers by preventing their entry or by barring them from jobs once in the country.

In the USA, attempts by white workers to protect themselves against competition have had mixed results. Where their great political power has been critical they have been successful. But employers have undercut white workers by turning to immigrants and internal migrants. The second method is what Bonacich calls 'caste' and means that the subordinate group is weakened by its low status. Workers of the superordinate caste organize to protect certain occupations for themselves, or, where they work in the same occupations, the privileged group protects its advantaged position *within* the occupation (holding the best jobs, supervisory jobs or higher pay for the same work). This is, in broad outline, the set of relationships which developed in the US in the Jim Crow period; that is, from the last decades of the nineteenth century through the early decades of the twentieth. The privileges of white workers are never secure, so there are likely to be periodic conflicts over new instances of apparent competitive threat. White workers do have another option: to work together with black workers in defence of their shared interest as workers, and undoubtedly this has happened and does happen. Historically, the dominant trend has been the defence of ethnic privilege.

Using the same kind of logic, Bonacich generates what she calls a theory of 'middleman minorities'. These are populations marked by some cultural or phenotypical difference, who find a place as 'sojourners' (non permanent settlers) in a society and seek to make their way by deploying 'portable' assets, i.e. cash crops, professional skills and capital. They too are subject to ethnic hatreds because they compete with 'local' business, pre-empt some business activities (e.g. wholesale, retail business), or are seen to gain at the expense of local workers as consumers. They are also politically vulnerable because they are non-permanent, viewed as 'clannish' because of their absence of social ties with the local majority and regarded as having a primary allegiance to a 'home' state (Bonacich 1973). All these factors make them vulnerable to political attack by a populist government or physical attack by the local majority. This whole profile of the middleman minority would fit many situations around the world. Two well-known instances are Asian business and professional classes in East Africa and Chinese entrepreneurs in Indonesia.

Both of these groups have experienced political attacks, as in the expulsion of Asians by Idi Amin in Uganda 1972, and/or popular violence, such as attacks on Chinese entrepreneurs in Indonesia (Mann 2005).

Critiques of groupism

The difference, we have argued, between an 'ethnic groups' analysis and a 'class analysis' is crucial. Class analysis does not seek to make 'ethnicity' a simple product of class relations; rather it sets ethnic sentiments and solidarities *within a context* of class analysis. But sociology (and not just class analysis) should certainly be cautious about over-concretizing ethnic groups (or 'races') and should be sceptical about treating ethnic groups as actors. By this we mean that there are theoretical and methodological flaws in treating ethnically defined populations (i.e. populations described by a single fact of ancestry or migration history, e.g. Polish Americans) as if they were groups with an assumed collective 'will' and an assumed shared culture. Equally, there are flaws in treating individual actors as simply 'ethnic actors'. Indeed, researchers and writers in the field are increasingly recognizing the mistakes of over-stating the concreteness of ethnic groups. Rogers Brubaker has stated the critique of 'groupism' more elegantly than anyone. Originally published as an article (2002), restated in his book *Ethnicity without Groups* (2004), he has recently set out the argument again in a debate with other scholars (Brubaker 2003: see also 2002). The clarification of the problem of 'groupism' has become a landmark in the history of the field. The theoretical mistake, Brubaker argues, is:

> The tendency to take sharply bounded putatively homogeneous groups as basic constituents of social life, chief protagonists of social conflict, and fundamental units of social analysis. (Brubaker 2003, p. 553)

The phrase 'sharply bounded' indicates that an uncritical use of the term 'ethnic groups' treats them as readily definable groups (or 'populations' or 'communities') where membership and non-membership are clear; in practice, this is rarely the case. Indeed, 'membership' is the wrong concept: rather

we need to think of *categories* of people, which actors embrace
or reject or modify; categories which are voluntary, or
enforced in an unequal relationship; and categories which are
themselves subject to change. Even in the case of a category
which has long been fixed historically, and enforced as well
as chosen, i.e. 'black' or 'black American', we can see significant shifts over recent decades. In the 2000 Census, for the
first time, people were able to indicate 'more than one race',
opening the way for 'mixed-race' identities. And in the UK,
the 2001 Census recognized 'mixed-race' as a separate category, which was chosen by a large number of people. Second,
'black American' has gradually been replaced by 'African
American'. And third, as a consequence of the civil rights and
black power movements, African American has become much
more a 'voluntary' term as an element of political and cultural
confidence and assertiveness.

The phrase 'putatively homogeneous' points to a false
tendency in 'ethnicity' analysis: that is where sociologists
assume that culture and identity are shared across all those
designated as belonging to a group. Ethnic groups are portrayed as 'sharing a culture' and 'identity' and these are then
assumed to be the explanation of some shared pattern
(success, failure in social mobility). This kind of thinking has
been exposed by Steinberg and many others by showing both
that ethnic groups are far from homogeneous and that the
researcher has to *demonstrate* the values held in a population
(Steinberg 1981). If, for example, a population, defined by
an ethnic term, has lower average educational results than
another population, we should not assume that this population places a low value on educational success, and that this
'low value' explains relative educational failure. Educational
values will almost certainly vary across the population. And
even those who value education highly will face other obstacles to success, obstacles over which they have little control.

In the final phrase in the above quotation from Brubaker
he refers to the error of seeing ethnic groups as 'basic
constituents of social life, chief protagonists of social conflict,
and fundamental units of social analysis'. Here we have not
just a challenge to some assumptions about 'ethnic groups'
but a challenge to the whole enterprise of placing 'ethnic
groups' at the centre of our view of society, our framework
of analysis and our mode of explanation (cf. Fenton 2004).

Summary

The question which underlies most of this chapter is this: how seriously do we take 'ethnic groups'? Mode 1 is to take ethnic groups as constituted by shared culture and ancestry, as the key components of individual identity and social structure, and as the source of explanation of social action. Mode 2 is to view ethnic 'names' or categories as part of a historically contingent social system of classification; the task for sociology is to understood how and when these categories are deployed, especially within relations of power and inequality.

In this chapter, and indeed this book, we are mostly making the case for Mode 2.

Earlier US sociologists (Glazer and Moynihan 1963) raised the question of a revival of ethnic groups – or ethnic identities – in a period when they were expected to decline in the face of the social trends favouring assimilation. If ethnic identities had survived, then was this because of the persistence of group cohesion and cultural difference? Evidence was largely against this (see Alba and Nee 1997; Gans 1979). Gans, in two important papers (1979, 1994), used the phrases 'symbolic ethnicity' and 'symbolic religiosity' to express this notion that identities may survive even if much of the cultural content has been stripped away. This is a crucial step in conceptualization; Gans detaches, or semi-detaches, the idea of culture from the idea of ethnic group.

Barth (1969) had opened the argument about 'culture' and 'groups' by his use of the term 'ethnic boundaries'. The equation of 'ethnic group' with 'culture difference' has to be qualified. It may seem like common sense to say that ethnic groups are the 'envelopes' containing cultural difference but the Barthian emphasis on 'group boundaries' rather than 'cultural content' reverses this argument. The idea of cultural difference tends towards a classificatory idea of ethnic groups (the As are the people who do this, believe that, speak 'A-language'). The group boundary concept points towards a relational concept of ethnic groups (how do the As know who the As are and who the Bs are, and how do they 'draw a line' between each other?). This Barthian emphasis does not discount the importance of cultural difference itself. People do attach importance to customary dress and a familiar language; in multilingual societies, the defence of language rights comes to be seen as very important to group members. But the Barthian analysis starts in a different place: in the relations or 'boundaries' between groups and the ways those boundaries are protected or breached (for an excellent discussion see Cornell, 1996).

Competition theory has built on the Barthian analysis of ethnicity. In the competition model, people who identify themselves with an ethnic group, let us say group A, view possible competition with group B as a threat. The situation of competition and threat explains the antagonism of A towards B. This is what Blumer (1958) referred to as 'group position' as an explanation of prejudice; and what Bonacich (1972) referred to as a 'theory of ethnic antagonism'. Competition theory has all the gains of a Barthian approach. The emphasis is not on groups as distinct populations constituted by shared cultural characteristics, but on a *set of relationships* and a *context of action*. Once we understand this context of action, we predict the actions of people who are likely to be associated with a named ethnic category (e.g. white Americans), by asking what people might do when faced with a competitive threat. In the cases we examined, this, supported in most cases by large data sets, proved to be a highly successful model.

The competition/threat theory nonetheless presented us with some difficulties. For all the emphasis on 'context', there is still a tendency towards concretizing 'groups'; for the purposes of analysis, especially when using recorded data (in which people are simply classified as being members of group A or group B), people are seen as being primarily 'members of ethnic groups'. The difficulty is best exemplified by reference to the description of white Americans as the 'dominant group'. But white Americans are a hugely differentiated population and whilst on average non-Hispanic whites are better off than other Census population categories (except Asians), 8.2 per cent (in 2007) were deemed to be living in poverty. Some are clearly more 'dominant' than others. In practice, competition theorists recognize this and describe some group members as more vulnerable to threat than others. At this point, we depart from a conception of populations as members of 'groups', to a conception of *differentiated* groups, unequally vulnerable to competitive threat. Bonacich by contrast takes class differentiation and class analysis as her starting point: this was class analysis complicated by ethnic groups, as against ethnic competition complicated by class differentiation.

Competition/threat theory, whilst here applied to the USA, could be applied to any comparable contexts and to different combinations of groups. In practice, at least in the examples we have discussed, the model was usually applied to 'black–white' relations, in which the minority black population was posed as a threat. White behaviour was explained as a response to this threat. It would have been more satisfying if the competition logic were also applied to the minority: how do minority group members behave when they know they face competitive disadvantages, and when they also know that the more they realistically compete with the 'dominant group' the more likely they are to produce an antagonistic response. In other words, if we apply rational choice theory (see Banton 1995) to the logic of choice for minority actors, what might they do in competition situations? The same question applies to minority groups as to a majority: how does the behaviour of relatively privileged minority group members differ from that of the more disadvantaged? This question of the nature of 'group-ness' continues to 'worry' the sociology of ethnicity. No one has addressed this more lucidly than Brubaker, whose work we addressed in the later part of the chapter.

Note

1   The Ku Klux Klan, a segregationist organization, was founded after the US Civil War, and dedicated to the preservation of 'white Christian civilization'. Having been active post-Civil War, and in the early decades of the twentieth century, it revived again in the wake of civil rights legislation in the 1960s.

6
Migration and Ethnicity

Migration is a primary social context for the formation of ethnic identities and for this reason alone students of ethnicity should have a basic appreciation of world migration and its consequences. In this chapter we establish some of the main features of migration, examine the links between migration and the emergence of ethnic communities and identities, and review the key debates in this field in the case of the USA. There is no single pattern of migration and equally there is no single pattern of the incorporation of immigrants into the new society. We first address the main features of immigration: who migrates, what are typical labour market demands and what are the variant conditions surrounding entry?

Forced migrations

An estimated 20 million Africans were seized and transported into slavery from the sixteenth century onwards (Walvin 2007). They made up the manual labour force for plantations and mines through North, Central and South America and the Caribbean, with by far the greatest number destined for Brazil. Subsequent migrations of Indian and Chinese workers, into plantation labour in Trinidad, Fiji and Guyana, were hardly less forced, their conditions similar to slavery. The same was true of Chinese and Japanese labourers brought to work in sugar plantations in Hawaii (Lind 1968). The length of time and the intensity of the oppression was such that post-slavery populations have struggled to recover, frequently in the face of racism and renewed exclusion (Fredrickson 1988; Wilson 1980). Former slaves faced violence and discrimination after the abolition of slavery, when they were potentially in direct competition with poorer whites. As well as the post-slavery formations in the USA and Brazil (see chapter 2), the exploitation of immigrant workers under colonial governments led to what have been referred to as 'plural societies'.

Migrants and plural societies

The term 'plural societies' came to be applied (Smith 1965) to colonized and formerly colonized societies where migrant workers had been imported by the colonizing power (Fenton 1999; Rex 1973, 1996). The term 'plural' was applied to societies composed of culturally different segments where the segments lived largely separate existences. These separate communities would be different from the majority in one or more major cultural attribute, typically language and religion. Indians in Malaysia would be a good example, having been rubber plantation workers imported in the early twentieth century, as were Indian sugar plantation workers in Fiji. Most of Malaysia's Indians were Tamil-speaking Hindus who lived in plantation communities. The decisive change in the significance of ethnicity came with political independence, in the 1960s. The sense of ownership of new nations was tensely contested in postcolonial societies such as Sri Lanka, Fiji, Guyana, Trinidad and Malaysia (Horowitz 1989). People now recognized that the newly independent state could greatly influence their individual and communal lives. In newly democratic states people could influence – or try to influence – major political decisions. The colonial order had largely insulated members of different groups from each other, encapsulated in different niches in the economy, and only meeting in impersonal economic relations. In the colonial state, different people had different rights; in this sense, the colonial rulers created the ethnic groups which became the basis of postcolonial conflicts (Hirschmann 1987). With the advent of democratic politics and greater individual mobility within the economy, the process of individuation or detachment from group allegiances may begin. The question then becomes, how far does this process of individuation go? Can people be detached from collective obligations and collective identities which have been the basis of security in the recent past? In most cases, on the opening up of a democratic political space, the early consequences were to harden ethnic identities. In democratic contest politics, tacit identities become politically explicit and in competition (Horowitz 1989; Little 1994; Mann 2005; Wimmer 1997). These plural societies, along with the key post-slavery societies, are major examples of forced migration and the social formation of ethnic identities.

World migration

In the nineteenth century, the USA became a target of immigrants mostly from Europe and a large proportion from Britain:

> The greatest era for recorded voluntary mass migration was the century after 1815. Around 60 million people left Europe for the Americas, Oceania and South and East Africa. An estimated 10 million voluntarily migrated from Russia to Central Asia and Siberia. A million went from Southern Europe to North Africa. About 12 million Chinese and 6 million Japanese left their homelands and emigrated to East and South Asia. One and a half million left India for South East Asia and South and West Africa. (Hirst and Thompson 1999, p. 23)

In the most recent decades, more countries than ever before have become senders and receivers, and more people move, more quickly, than ever before. We live in the age of the globalization of migration. The Global Commission on Migration reported in 2005 that '200 million people are living outside their countries of birth or citizenship' (Martin and Martin 2006). This is a large *absolute* growth on a decade before, but as a percentage, this remains at about 2–3 per cent of the world's population (Martin and Martin 2006; see also Castles and Miller 1993). Although the traditional immigrant-receiving countries such as Canada, New Zealand, Australia and the USA accepted many millions for settlement, and continue to do so, Martin and Martin (2006) argue that the 'old paradigm of permanent migrant settlement is giving way to temporary and circular migration' (p. 6). The more this is so, the more it can be expected to influence the persistence of post-migration ethnic identities. Even in relatively settled communities, people can communicate or travel between new country and home country, giving rise to the idea of *transnational* communities and transnational transfers. The concept of 'transnationalism' suggests people 'living across' borders, or *transactions* across borders, of people, goods and cultural attributes (Vertovec 1999).

More countries have become immigrant senders and receivers. Oil-rich Middle Eastern countries are now large in-migrant societies; the countries of Southern Europe, particularly Greece, Italy, Spain and Portugal, historically exporters of people, have become receivers of in-migrants; Malaysia has a large part of its agricultural labour force, documented and un-documented, from neighbouring Indonesia. Japan has a growing immigrant population, with people coming from neighbouring countries and from South Asia, including Nepal (Yamanaka 2000). Many of Japan's immigrants are also undocumented, possibly as many as 200,000 by an estimate for the early 1990s (Yamanaka 2000), and they typically work in construction and manufacturing. The oil wealth of the Middle East, specifically the Arab Gulf states, has drawn in migrant workers, usually in service occupations, unskilled work and construction. The Middle East 'accounts for more than 10 per cent of the world's total migrants and the oil-rich countries of the Arab Gulf have the highest concentration of migrant workers in the world' (Calandruccio 2005, p. 268). The new paradigm of temporary and circular migration (Martin and Martin 2006) is exemplified here. Typically, migrants to the Arab Gulf have 'no expectations of permanent settlement or citizenship rights' (Calandruccio 2005, p. 268), despite forming up to 'one fourth of the total population'. Many countries contribute workers to the Middle East labour force, with India (3.2 million), Egypt (1.8 million) and Pakistan (1.2 million) contributing most (p. 269). As in much of the rest of the world, these states also import women, both as workers and as women who are trafficked for commercial sexual exploitation. Women 'from Moldova, Russia, Ukraine' and other former Soviet countries (p. 270) are, for example, imported into Israel where they live in 'involuntary servitude'.

Internal migrants

Governments and international agencies record migrants as people who have 'crossed a border' and live in a country other than their home country. But many migrant workers have not crossed a state border even though they may have travelled large distances. These are internal migrants, and in the two most populous countries in the world, China and India, these internal migrants are hugely important to the national economy. They are also likely to be in a structural position similar to international migrants. They lack full rights in their new location, they are distinguishable by being engaged in low-paid work, living in concentrated zones of poor housing, sharing cultural markers of difference (language, style, dress) and being the target of xenophobic abuse and violence by a local majority. China's internal migrant population 'in the 1990s is generally reported to be at 80 to 100 million' (Feng et al. 2002, p. 521). Until the 1980s, when internal migration began to grow, rural workers had been restrained from moving. The system of household registration (*hukou*) means that people moving outside their registration location are disadvantaged; these workers, like rural workers living in Shanghai, are segregated and worse off than other workers with regard to living conditions and access to social benefits (Feng et al. 2002, p. 522). In India too, migrant workers travel large distances from poorer states to centres of commercial growth. In 2008, local xenophobic agitators, demonstrating against internal in-migrants, caused mayhem in Mumbai, attacking migrant workers and advocating violence (*International Herald Tribune* 21 October 2008). The leader of the anti-immigrant party, taking the position of defending 'local rights' and the Marathi language, was arrested. The *International Herald Tribune* report refers to migrants to the city comprising '37 per cent of Mumbai's 18 million people'. China and India, as two of the world's largest and fastest-growing economies, both have huge rural hinter-lands, on which they draw for internal migrant workers.

Professional migrations

The migrations described above are often from developing societies to rich industrialized societies or from rural to fast-growing urban areas of developing economies; some are between developing societies, and often between neighbour-ing countries. Not all movements follow the poor-to-rich pattern; some indeed follow a rich-to-rich route, such as contemporary movements of people between European countries, the USA, Canada and Australia. And not all migrations are destined for poorly or lower-paid work in the new country. Professionals, doctors, engineers, accountants, teachers, academics and researchers, corporate employees and information technologists move from developing or emerging economies to developed economies (Indian and African doctors to Britain, Indian software specialists to the US and Germany), from former Soviet and East European countries to western societies (Russian scientists to America) and from developed to developed countries (British research-ers to the US). The migration and circulation of scientists is part of a global knowledge business (Meyer et al. 2001). Typically, the countries of origin bear some or all of the social cost of producing these professionals even though the final leg of training may be in the destination country.

The occupations of foreign-born US residents illustrate how different types of migrations are associated with regions of origin. Among native-born workers, 36.2 per cent were in management and professional occupations, whereas among foreign-born workers, the figure is 26.9 per cent. But this masks large regional disparities. Among foreign-born workers originating in Latin America, 12.7 per cent were in management and professional occupations, and as low as 7.9 per cent among Central Americans; but among those originating from Asia, 47 per cent were in management and professional occupations (US Census Bureau 2004).

Both Germany and the USA have targeted Indian-trained information technology workers, as Indian education in mathematics and technology makes them sought-after workers (Khoser and Salt 1997; OECD 2002). Indian workers are well paid in America by comparison with their potential earnings in India. But in their absence, American employers would have to pay much more for home-trained staff. This is not only because home staff would demand and expect more, but also because in the absence of Indian 'competitors' their market situation would be much stronger:

> For high tech industries dependent on highly-skilled workers, the region's ability to attract or 'drain' highly educated Asian immigrants provides clear competitive advantages. Not only has another country borne the social cost of educating these workers, their degrees will earn them more in the United States than they can at home, yet those workers still cost employers less than their domestic counterparts. The region's low-tech post-Fordist firms have also replicated the advantages of going abroad, or virtual globalisation, by targeting undocumented immigrants, particularly Latinas, as their primary labour source. (Valle and Torres 2000, p. 17)

The high- and low-skilled types of migrant labour reflect the demand for workers in the 'first world' economies where typically the skilled and manufacturing working class has shrunk, whilst there remains demand for less educated and unskilled workers in such employment as field labour, food processing and urban service employment (janitors, cleaners, hotel workers). At the same time, there is strong demand for professional workers in the growing high-skilled service sector.

Undocumented workers

For all the workers with appropriate papers, there are millions of 'undocumented' workers (Castles 2000). Legal status is a singularly crucial question since undocumented workers and those who fear that their legal status as migrants may be brought into question are unable to act as full citizens of their new country and unable even to attempt to use the protections that may be open to them. Of all migrants, undocumented workers are least able to rely on state protection. The question of legality goes much further than the undocumented workers themselves. In a society where, for example, the right to stay and the right to bring in spouses and dependants, and the right to leave and return, are constantly in question for those *without* proper documents, these rights may also become questioned and 'questionable' for all those from the same origin as the undocumented. The uncertainty and anxiety on the one hand (among migrant families) and the suspicion and aggression on the other (among public authorities, immigration officers) becomes 'generalized' well beyond those who may actually have made an illegal entry.

In public and in government statements, receiving societies deplore undocumented immigrants. Ordinary citizens and political pressure groups frequently join in the condemnations of undocumented workers and the 'threat' they pose to the integrity of the receiving society (Cornelius 2005). But the destination societies frequently will tacitly condone the arrival of illegals simply because they constitute necessary labour which can scarcely be recruited from any other source. Employers can make gains from taking undocumented workers. If migrant workers in general are liable to exploitation, undocumented workers are liable to super-exploitation since it only takes one false move for them to be removed by their employer or threatened with exposure. Equally, if documented migrant workers compare their wages with expectations in their home countries, then undocumented migrant workers are likely to accept even lower income and dirty or dangerous work. The USA and Malaysia are two countries who receive large numbers of immigrants from a poorer neighbouring country – Mexico and Indonesia respectively. The numbers of illegal immigrant workers in these two cases constitute necessary labour in, for example, service employment, fruit-picking and oil-palm plantations; it is unlikely that the two states receiving these workers have exhausted their talent for keeping out or rooting out 'illegals'. They arrive because they are needed not because they cannot be stopped. However, it is possible that states may wish to exert more control over undocumented entrants, but find it very difficult to achieve. It has been argued that efforts by the US government to control 'unwanted' immigration along its southwest border have been largely unsuccessful in the face of strong demand for labour (Cornelius 2005). A strong market for immigrant workers in Portugal has meant that a 'weak state' has failed in the face of a 'strong market' (Peixoto 2002); and Castles (2003) has argued that in Britain and other European Union states, migration policies fail.

Migration, gender and family

Whilst migrations have typically been led by men, there are many migrations which are led by women, as in the case of maids and nurses recruited from poor to rich countries (B. Anderson 2000). But where migrations are led by men, especially men travelling alone, there is frequently some disruption of 'traditional' values and practices. Men may break with custom by linking up with women who are not co-ethnics; they may certainly abandon, albeit temporarily, restraints in dress, religious observance and daily practice. Punjabi men in Britain, for example, stopped wearing turbans in order to get jobs (Ballard 1994; Ballard and Ballard 1977). Changes in custom may also be because of the absence of women who, if present, would have had a role in the enforcing of family and ethnic custom. Women, as well as being migrant workers themselves, can be important in the business of enforcing customary practices. They teach their language to their children, play a key role in managing the family and take the lead in 'connecting' – keeping up obligations to others, remembering birthdays and other family celebrations.

Women are also critically implicated in custom itself as, for example, the main focus of marriage arrangements; what are sometimes regarded as traditional attitudes and practice are in fact rules about gender roles and the proper behaviour of women (see Anthias and Yuval-Davis 1992; Bradley 1996; Shaw 1988).

These tensions are implicit both within the histories of migration and in the formation and reformation of ethnic identities and communities (Jacobson 1997a, 1997b). The tension is between the solidarity which is the ideal of family, extended family and ethnic community life, and the individuation and individualism which are implicated in 'success' and mobility in the new environment, a tension which is particularly acute for women. Women whose family origins are in what are called 'traditional communities' may face resistance to mobility from the *majority* population. They can also encounter resistance from the *minority* community, especially the men within it. Within their communities of origin, the 'liberation' – i.e. individuation and individualism – of women can be viewed as a break with traditional values. Thus women of minority ethnic groups are at the forefront in fighting racism and discrimination coming from outside their community, and patriarchy coming from within it (*The Guardian* 14 August 2001). It is not therefore surprising that these women find majority women advancing a kind of feminism which is out of tune or unsympathetic with the dilemmas and interests of minority women (Mirza 1997). Similarly, minority women have two difficult priorities which are hard to reconcile: recognizing and opposing the racism and discrimination that they and their ethnic brothers experience whilst opposing their ethnic brothers in the matter of 'traditional' attitudes to women.

Questions of integration and citizenship

In modern migration, as in colonial migrations, the state is a key actor. The state not only controls in-migration (and in some cases out-migration), but has a role in determining the status of immigrants and minorities, nowhere more so than with regard to the ease of acquiring citizenship. In Germany and Switzerland, for example, it has been very difficult for foreign-born residents, and even their native-born children, to acquire citizenship (Bloemraad 2006). Naturalization rates can be calculated as the annual number of naturalizations over the non-citizen foreign population; by this measure in Europe 'Germany, Ireland, Italy and Switzerland recorded an annual naturalisation rate of less than one percent in the early 1990s' (Bloemraad 2006, p. 674). In the USA, where citizenship is less restrictive, almost half of foreign-born residents entering the country between 1980 and 1989 have become citizens; for those entering before 1970, 80.9 per cent were US citizens by 2003 (US Census Bureau 2004). The importance of ethnic identities in any society is influenced by the activities of the state, and the protection which the state does or does not provide. Citizenship is one key to this security. In many cases, the state barely guarantees security and protection for migrant workers, let alone provides cultural and legal recognition (Calandruccio 2005).

In countries where citizenship is very difficult to acquire (like Germany and Switzerland; Bloemraad 2006), minority identities are likely to persist, not least because the host community perpetuates a discourse of foreign-ness. In other countries, such as the Netherlands, Sweden and Canada, citizenship is more easily acquired. Here migrant populations may be the basis of voluntary mobilization by ethnic and religious groups, in the attempt to promote their interests and secure rights in relation to religious practice (Koopmans et al. 2005). Discrimination and xenophobia are certainly present in these more open societies, but ethnic mobilization and political identities are at least possible, and indeed probable. The 'survival' of immigrant ethnic identities depends on whether migration becomes a permanent settlement, whether new migrations from the same home country augment settled communities and on how state policies shape the experience of new citizens or residents. (For an excellent comparative analysis of citizenship in the USA, Germany and Britain, see Joppke 1996; and for a critique of multicultural citizenship, see Joppke 2001.)

The case of the USA: migration and ethnicity in the late twentieth and early twenty-first centuries

Two migrations have had critical importance for the creation of important social categories in colonial America and the USA: the forced migration of Africans brought as slaves to the English colonies from 1619 until the early nineteenth century (by then the USA), and the long and varied migrations of Europeans as voluntary migrants in search of employment and advancement. Around these migrations the social and political categories 'black' and 'white' have been drawn. As early as the seventeenth century, marriages or 'miscegenation' between white settlers and Africans were being forbidden (see Jordan 1968). Being African or black and being a slave were virtually co-terminous. Over half a million Africans, mostly from West African regions including Ghana, Mali and Benin, were brought to the colonies and the USA and sold into slavery. In 1860, in the US South, *circa* 7 million people were recorded as white and 4 million as black; among blacks, just one-sixteenth, 258,346, were recorded as 'free'. (In the northeast region of the US in the same year, just 156,001 were recorded as black, virtually all of them as 'free'.) Thus, with these exceptions, status as 'black' and status as 'slave' were virtually the same. With the abolition of slavery, 'racial status' had to be founded on a new basis: disfranchisement and Jim Crow (Vann Woodward 1974). Whiteness and racial purity formed the fundamentals of US racial ideology (F. J. Davis 2001; Fredrickson 1988; for an account of US racial categories see chapter 2).

It was not until the US Census of 2000 that it became possible to describe oneself as being of 'more than one race'. By contrast, white European immigrants were seen as eventually 'assimilating' into a 'mainstream' position (Alba and Nee 1997; Gans 1979, 1997; Gordon 1964; Yinger 1994) both in identity and socioeconomic position. African Americans remained disadvantaged and disproportionately poor – in 2004 36 per cent of African American children were living below the poverty line. The black/white division continued to be the main narrative of race in the US. In the last decades of the twentieth century and the early twenty-first century the shape of US ethnicity became significantly more complicated. The change largely resulted from the Immigration and Nationality Act 1965, which abolished national origin quotas and opened up migration from Asian countries and from Mexico, Central and South America.

America's growing Hispanic population

In 1950, 89.5 per cent of the US population were classified as 'white' and 10 per cent as 'black', thus covering the vast majority of the population. By 2000, 75.1 per cent was recorded as 'white', 12.3 per cent as 'black' and 3.6 per cent as Asian, with almost 10 per cent falling into 'other' categories. Until 1980, 'Hispanic' was not recorded except by estimates. It is separate from the 'race' category; the terms 'Hispanic' or 'Latino' refer to persons 'who trace their origin or descent to Mexico, Puerto Rico, Cuba, Spanish speaking Central and South America countries, and other Spanish cultures' (US Census Bureau 2001). By 2000, 12.5 per cent of the US population were recorded as Hispanic. The growth of the Asian and especially the Hispanic populations represents a major shift in America's ethnic profile, and ways of viewing race and ethnicity. After the European sending societies of the nineteenth and twentieth centuries, in 2003 53 per cent of the *foreign-born* population of the US were born in Latin America (Central, South America and the Caribbean) and another 25 per cent in Asia; Europe contributed just 14 per cent (US Census Bureau 2004). The scale of in-migration – and in 2006 12.5 per cent of the US population were foreign-born – shows the continued demand for labour to work in the American capitalist economy.

We should *always* keep in mind the fact that the population described as 'Hispanic' or 'Latino' is heterogeneous both in country of origin and socioeconomic status in the US. Of over 40 million Hispanics (2004) almost 26 million (64 per cent) are Mexican, with Puerto Rican (9.6 per cent) and Cuban (3.6 per cent) constituting other significant groups. The rest are divided between Central and South American countries such as Guatemala (1.7 per cent) and Colombia (1.7 per cent). Just one simple indicator of difference in social advantage – level of education – shows the variation between countries. Among Mexicans (in 2004) 8.6 per cent had a Bachelor's degree or more; among Cubans it was 25.3 per cent, among Peruvians it was 30 per cent. Differences like this have a significant influence on the prospect of seeing a growing middle class in the immigrant generation and second generation (see Portes and Rumbaut 2006; Rumbaut and Portes 2001).

The growth of the Hispanic population is unevenly spread across the USA. The Hispanic population increase has been largely concentrated in California, especially southwest California; in the 2000 Census close to 11 million of the 35 million Hispanics in the US lived in California. Texas accounted for a further 6.7 million. Of California's Hispanics in 2000, almost 8.5 million were Mexicans:

> In California and the South-West, *Mexicanos* and their children are not just another immigrant-based ethnic group. They are instead by far the largest minority and are rapidly becoming the single largest ethnic group, destined to outnumber whites sometime in this century. (López and Stanton-Salazar 2001, p. 58)

Hispanics and Mexican Americans: social profiles

In the black/white model of race relations in the US, two main questions were: could African Americans attain a collective socioeconomic profile closer to the 'mainstream' and would patterns of racial discrimination and racist ideas among whites be changed? New questions are pushing to the front of public policy. Researchers are addressing the question of how deeply entrenched the pattern of Mexicano disadvantage is likely to become (Rumbaut and Portes 2001). They suggest that a critical factor working against Mexican Americans is the historically entrenched racist stereotypes and socioeconomic disadvantage:

Just as Mexican immigrants early in the twentieth century inherited the traditional status of Mexicans in the United States, so today's immigrants and their children are inheriting the inner and outer burdens of Mexican 'color' as it developed throughout the twentieth century. (López and Stanton-Salazar 2001, p. 60)

Earlier commentators on the future of Mexican Americans (Grebler et al. 1970) had suggested that they might follow a 'delayed path of assimilation' like European immigrants, or they might share the 'caste-like fate of African Americans' (López and Stanton-Salazar 2001, p. 60). Speaking of Mexicans, the largest population in the category 'Hispanics', López and Stanton-Salazar argue that key factors affecting the prospects of new Mexican immigrants to the southwest US are 'poverty, sheer numbers, racial ambiguity and negative stereotypes' (p. 59).

Some Hispanic populations are more prosperous, including America's growing Cuban middle class. But most Mexicans and many other Hispanic populations are poor and low-paid working-class immigrants and their families who are subject to unfavourable treatment and racist stereotypes. Their fate, it is argued, has been influenced by what López and Stanton-Salazar call 'historical depth' (p. 59). The twentieth-century history of Mexican in-migration 'laid down' generations in the US whose social location became relatively fixed, as did the racialized view of them. This was the social setting into which new Mexican migrants moved as migration recommenced in large numbers after 1965. Thus 'the fate of the pre-existing Mexican-American population determines the expectations and stereotypes of new Mexican migrants' (p. 59). The debate about 'Hispanic futures' has led to a renewed intellectual dispute about the concept of 'assimilation', to which we turn shortly.

The Latin American source of much new migration means that the proportion of the population (aged over five years) who speak a language other than English at home is rising every decade. In 1990, this figure for the whole of the USA was 14 per cent or almost 32 million people; in 2000, the figure had risen to 18 per cent and almost 47 million. Most of those who speak a language other than English in the home also speak English 'very well' or 'well' (US Census Bureau 2003). The largest non-English language (i.e. Spanish) is widely used in the American southwest, including in television, radio, political campaigns and in schools. Indeed, in California in 1990, 31.5 per cent of over-five year olds spoke a language at home other than English; in 2000, this figure was 39.5 per cent, i.e. two in every five Californians (over the age of five) speaking a language other than English at home.

The survival and persistence of the Spanish language, not just in the home, but as a growing bilingualism in social institutions, has brought controversy. Among conservative whites in the USA, Hispanicization – or Latinization – is viewed as a threat to the hegemonic English-oriented traditions of the country (Califa 1989; Santoro 1999). These examples come from California and the southwest. There are of course migrations to other parts of the USA, but the destinations are highly concentrated: Alba and Nee (1997) report that 80 per cent of new migrants in the 1980s came to just six states: California, New York, Florida, Texas, New Jersey and Illinois (for a case study in Virginia, see chapter 7). The geographical distribution shows that this labour is not simply attracted to the USA in general, but to the regions with rapid urban growth and high economic activity.

Likely futures for new migrants and their families and for American ethnicities

Earlier European immigrants to America, who came in large numbers in the nineteenth and early twentieth centuries, faced opposition and discrimination in the early years of settlement. This was true, for example, of Irish, Jewish and Italian migrants. Irish were portrayed as undesirable: most were Catholics in a predominantly Protestant country, and were viewed as a 'threat to democracy' (Ignatiev 1995). Initially, Italians were almost socially recognized as 'black' (see chapter 2: Jacobson 1998); each of these groups had to work their way towards recognized 'whiteness' (Hartman 2004).

By contrast, the post-1965 Hispanic immigrants continued to be followed by new migrants, and this has reinforced cultural difference – in California, for example, many Mexicans and Latinos generally live in large conurbations with high concentrations of co-ethnics:

> By 2000 Santa Ana, – the ninth most populous city in California . . . – had the seventh highest percentage of Latino residents (76.1 per cent) of any American city with over one hundred thousand people. (Gottlieb et al. 2005, p. 77)

> Latinos occupy almost all of Los Angeles and Orange County's traditional blue-collar housing tracts and suburbs adjacent to the three great corridors of industrially zoned land. (F. J. Davis 2001, p. 53)

There will be very different outcomes for the Hispanic populations, differentiated by class and country. But, as we sketched out above, some suggest a difficult future for Mexicans in particular. López and Stanton-Salazar (2001) argue that (some of) the Mexican American second generation in California and the southwest may not become successfully integrated but make a transition from a 'permanently disadvantaged minority to a permanently disadvantaged majority' (p. 62). Tacitly, these authors (and others) are treating African Americans as a 'model' of a permanently disadvantaged minority. This statement itself could be questioned, or seen as only partially correct. African Americans have made gains in political struggles against racism, and there has been an enlargement of the black middle class. African American achievements against the odds of enduring obstacles have been great (for an account of black–white inequalities, see Waters and Eschbach 1995). But the *overall* profile of African Americans shows large proportions in low pay, poor housing and below the poverty line:

> About 26 per cent of Blacks were living below the poverty level in the 12 months prior to being surveyed, compared with about 9 per cent of Non-Hispanic whites. The poverty rate was generally higher for children (under age 18). About 36 per cent of Black children and about 11 per cent of Non-Hispanic white children lived in poverty. (*American Community Survey Report* 2007)

Furthermore, entrenched class disadvantage to a very great extent reproduces itself: wealth inequality, as Shapiro (2004) and Conley (1999) have argued, is an enduring structural obstacle, as are segregation (Massey and Denton 1993), poor housing and lack of access to health care (in 2006 about 16 per cent of Americans, 11 per cent of non-Hispanic whites and 20 per cent of non-Hispanic blacks had no health insurance). These are symptoms of the depth of class inequalities in the USA which disproportionately affect black Americans. The question addressed with regard to the Mexican American population is whether they face a similar disadvantaged future.

The renewed debate about the concept of assimilation

The post-1965 migrations from Asian countries and from the Caribbean, Mexico and Central and South America have changed the demographic profile of the USA. They have also raised new questions about patterns of incorporation into American society. Many authors have contributed to the debates (see especially Alba 1999; Alba and Nee 1997; DeWind and Kasinitz 1997; Kasinitz et al. 2002, 2008; Neckerman et al. 1999; Portes et al. 2005; Portes and Zhou 1993; Waldinger 2007; Waldinger and Feliciano 2004). One of the main lines of divergence is between broadly optimistic and broadly pessimistic assessments of the future outcomes for the children of the new migrants who have come to the USA in recent decades.

Those taking a more pessimistic view argue that, as an example, (some) Mexican Americans may evolve, as we have noted above, into a 'permanently disadvantaged minority'. Three types of argument are usually deployed to sustain this view: human capital arguments, class and ecological arguments and arguments based on embedded racism in US society. The human capital arguments apply to those immigrants (and their children) who have low education and may be unlikely to steer their children towards better educational outcomes. They are applied to all those labour migrants who come to do low-skilled work typical of the many Mexican immigrants in the American southwest. In the class and ecological arguments, the emphasis is on the patterns of residential concentration which co-exist with other disadvantageous factors, including poor inner-city schools and contiguity with alienated native minorities in deprived neighbourhoods. The class disadvantages of the urban low-paid workers and their families are transmitted to their children. Finally, some new Latino migrant populations, it is argued, face the native racism and discriminatory treatment which have been obstacles for African Americans for many generations. These cumulative disadvantages affecting new minorities create the risk of an enduring 'rainbow underclass'.

Some or all of these arguments can be found in the work of Portes and collaborators, and have been summed up under the concept of 'segmented assimilation'. They argue that new migrants and their children assimilate in different ways depending on their own resources (capital, education) and the social conditions of their insertion into US society. In their terminology, different sections of the migrant and second-generation population (e.g. more and less educated, white and non-white) assimilate into *different segments* of US society. Portes et al. (2005) set out a schema (see p. 1011) which depicts differential paths of social mobility from 'complete integration' and 'marginal working-class communities' to 'downward assimilation to underclass' status.

A contrary view, or at least a critical commentary, comes from the work of Waldinger (2007), Waldinger and Feliciano (2004), Alba and Nee (1997) and Kasinitz et al. (2002, 2008), among others. Kasinitz and colleagues represent the more optimistic view, arguing that the children of new migrants are successful in moving into the mainstream, and acquiring jobs and lifestyles that match those of the native majority. Kasinitz et al. (2002) provide a critique of one crucial element of the segmented assimilation thesis: that settlement in inner-city urban neighbourhoods means contact with alienated native minorities from whom second-generation new minorities learn an 'oppositional culture'. On the contrary, they suggest, 'this model holds a far too negative stereotype of native minorities and the supposed self-defeating role model they provide for second generation immigrants' (p. 1031).

In the decades since the 1960s, the USA has not only had the civil rights legislation in place, but also native minorities have been able to develop social and political skills in combating discrimination. Thus, they argue, 'the struggle for minority empowerment has established new entry points into mainstream institutions and created many minority-run institutions' (p. 1032). The social context for these new minorities – in Kasinitz's case, based in New York – is mostly not 'majority whites', but native minorities and other second-generation new minorities. This society they portray as vibrant and successful, not 'balkanized groups huddled within their own enclaves, but of hybrids and fluid exchanges across boundaries' (p. 1033). This then is a different set of ecology/class arguments from those deployed by Portes et al. Kasinitz and colleagues are arguing that the second generations in New York are living lives contiguous with relatively successful native minorities who know their way around the 'American system' and can provide guidance for new minorities.

These arguments present a double difficulty for segmented assimilation theory, *if* this theory is taken to mean that second-generation minorities will assimilate into the urban underclass. One difficulty lies with the concept of underclass itself, much criticized as not being a class concept at all but being a 'cultural theory' which attributes a culture of failure to native minorities (but see Wilson 1991 for a revised view). This is conveyed by the phrase 'oppositional culture', meaning, among other things, a culture which rejects school authority and values. Second, segmented assimilation theory might be taken to assert that 'native minorities', usually meaning African Americans, are uniformly non-mobile, stuck in the 'underclass' and purveyors of this oppositional culture. In my view this misrepresents segmented assimilation theory, as I shall explain below. Working-class African Americans can, as Kasinitz et al. argue, 'educate' new minorities into their civil rights and opportunities, illustrated by the African American led unions with largely West Indian rank-and-file membership (p. 1032). Furthermore, upwardly mobile members of native minorities provide mobility models for new minorities.

This latter argument has been advanced by Neckerman et al. (1999). They point out that whilst domestic minorities, and in particular African Americans, are disadvantaged, they are neither all 'underclass' nor all part of an 'oppositional culture'. The considerable African American middle class, and other minority middle classes, provide what they call 'minority cultures of mobility'. We should note that 27 per cent of the US black employed population are in 'Management, professional and related occupations' and 17 per cent have a Bachelor's degree or more (*American Community Survey Report* 2007). Those African American and other non-white minorities who have succeeded have faced the problem of relating to others in largely white institutions (that is, where black mobility has been via mainstream majority-white institutions); and have learnt to deal with criticism, of race 'sell-out' or race-class 'sell-out', from less mobile co-ethnics. Learning the minority culture of mobility will be of assistance in living in a middle-class mainstream, especially in work and other public spheres. Mobility and cultural adaptation are also likely, the authors argue, to be achieved within a corresponding ethnic or racial category: 'We expect diffusion of the minority culture of mobility from one group to another to occur mainly within a racial or pan-ethnic category' (Neckerman et al. 1999, p. 961).

Occupational structure: the hourglass labour market

One element of the argument that second generations of the post-1965 immigrants face a difficult path to social mobility is the change in the US occupational structure. We know, for example, that there has been a steep decline in manufacturing employment, from 1950 when 30 per cent of non-farm employment was in manufacturing, to 2006 when this had fallen to 10 per cent (Lee and Mather 2008). This, it is argued, narrows the routes to a step-by-step upward mobility, whereby immigrant and second-generation workers progress from low-paid service work (or, for example, food processing, agricultural labour) to the better paid manufacturing jobs which have been the foundation of the stable working class for decades. Furthermore, the step from menial occupations to professional and managerial occupations is a big one, requiring a large investment in further and higher education, a difficult aim for low-income families. As Portes et al. (2005) put it: 'In this changed labour market, high demand exists at the low end for unskilled and menial workers and at the high end for professionals and technicians' (p. 1007). This 'hourglass' labour market compounds the obstacles facing immigrant workers and their children.

There are questions raised against this argument. Waldinger (2007) has argued that earlier European immigrants did not all benefit from manufacturing jobs on their route to mainstream society. If manufacturing jobs have diminished this does not mean that there are *no* jobs intermediate between unskilled service jobs and professional and managerial employment. Kasinitz et al. (2002) suggest that the manufacturing sector 'continues to play an important role' for the immigrant generation, but that their children diversify in employment (away from the economic niches of their parents) so that 'their occupational distributions resemble each other and those of all New Yorkers their age and gender' (p. 1026).

In the full publication of their New York-based research (Kasinitz et al. 2008), they present their work as evidence against the concept of segmented assimilation and its theoretical predictions. Kasinitz et al. see the 'segmented assimilation' analysis as offering two predictions, both contrary to standard assimilation theory. One prediction is downward assimilation as a result of assimilation into a failing class or racialized underclass. The second is that some second-generation young people may be shielded from this, and assisted towards upward mobility, by life *within* a protective enclave, or non-assimilation. The New York evidence does not support these arguments. 'Few of our respondents' they report, 'followed either of the two . . . predictions of the model' (Kasinitz et al. 2008, p. 347). In their summary, they present an optimistic view:

> Most of the second generation young people with whom we spoke are not affluent professionals, but neither are they perennially unemployed nor part of a 'permanently impoverished' underclass. Instead they are working members of the lower middle class service economy, employed as white collar

clerical or service workers in retail or financial services. Their labor market position resembles that of other New Yorkers their age more than it does that of their parents. They rarely drop out of the labor force to become criminals. Most have achieved real, if modest, progress over their parents' generation. They have more education, earn more money, and work in more 'mainstream' occupations and sectors. (p. 348)

Summary: the opposing views

These opposing analyses cannot either be easily reconciled or arbitrated. Kasinitz and colleagues claim to have captured something new emerging out of New York city, where 'minorities' – native-born, immigrant and the children of immigrants – form the majority of the population, in a city where fewer than 20 per cent of the population are native-born white. Waldinger and Feliciano (2004) also argue against the hypothesis of segmented assimilation and the prediction of 'downward mobility for the children of immigrant garment workers and dishwashers' (p. 379). On the other hand, Portes and colleagues make a strong case for the multiple obstacles facing the children of recent immigrants, and make a vigorous defence of their position in Portes et al. (2005). Yet based on evidence from south Florida, the claims of Portes et al. are actually more modest than has been suggested. Broadly they conclude that 'the new second generation in South Florida is progressing well educationally, and that the majority lead comfortable lives' (2005, p. 1019). Their concerns are directed more towards a minority of the second generation who are vulnerable to entrapment in entrenched inner-city disadvantage. Where they face so many obstacles, including the low education of their parents, life in disorganized neighbourhoods and poor educational prospects for themselves in local schools, then for some, the fears of Portes et al. may be realized. The pessimistic view entertains the possibility of deep-rooted disadvantage; the optimistic view is closer to the long-cherished ideal American story.

There are three other considerations that serious students should bear in mind. One is that Portes and collaborators' work is based on research in south Florida and southern

California, whereas Kasinitz and colleagues have researched New York city. The ethnic composition of the three areas is significantly different and this is bound to be a factor in the emergence of different outcomes. Rather than the Mexicans studied in Florida and California, Kasinitz et al. are studying evidence from Puerto Ricans, native blacks, Dominicans, South Americans, Chinese, Russians and native whites. It is clear that the *most* successful groups are Russians and Chinese. Second, although the Kasinitz work is more recent, both studies are reflecting on outcomes quite early in the 'history' of new migrants. The conclusions about earlier European migrations have the benefit of several generations having passed. Third, the children of the immigrants studied are themselves mostly in their twenties; we simply do not know where they – and their children – will be in thirty years' time. Whilst European migration slowed almost to a halt in the 1930s, the new migrations have to date been continuous, bringing new cohorts in each decade. With the recession of 2008 and on, we cannot be sure how long this will continue. We should, too, continue to keep in mind the distinction between Mexicans as one Hispanic population, and all Hispanics. Students are strongly advised to read the key articles cited in this chapter and to read the recent books: Portes and Rumbaut (2006) and Kasinitz et al. (2008).

7

Social Conditions of Ethnicity: Global Economy and Precarious States

In the previous chapter we took migration as one context for ethnicity. In the present chapter, we shall look at three further, and more abstractly conceived, sets of conditions of ethnicity and social action. The conditions of action are conceived here as: (1) the global and local implications of gross economic inequalities; (2) the degree of security which a state is able to guarantee to its citizens, that is the greater or lesser 'precariousness' of the state; and (3) the influence on state politics, including ethnic politics, of inter-state politics and geopolitical changes. In the recent past, the collapse of the communist world is the most significant geopolitical change; to that we can now add the 2008 financial crisis and the possible weakening of US global power (National Intelligence Council 2008).

Theorizing the conditions of ethnic action

The development of a unitary theory of 'ethnicity' is a mirage, as is the search for an ultimately precise definition of *ethnicity* or *ethnic groups*. Of itself, the term 'ethnicity' has no precise point of reference. The sociological description of 'ethnic

groups' is more of a classification than a system of explanation. As I argued before (Fenton 1999), the *variants* or 'forms'
of 'ethnic groups' are at least as significant as the common
ground between them. And the *contexts* in which they are
found (Eriksen 1993; Fenton 1999) are the source of explanation rather than inherent qualities of ethnicity itself. Land,
dispossession and genocidal violence make the framework
within which indigenous ethnicities are formed; labour
importations, indentured labour and colonial government
make the framework of plural societies; global capitalism,
maximization of profit and demand for flexible labour are
the context of immigrant ethnicities.

In the present chapter we examine in detail two sets of
conditions which are intimately linked to the formation and
political uses of ethnic identities, and to occasions of severe
ethnic conflict and violence. These two sets of conditions are,
broadly, *economic* and *political*: on the one hand, situations
of competition for scarce resources, of inequalities and exploitation; on the other hand, geopolitical stability or instability,
and unstable, factionalized or precarious conditions of the
state.

Features of the contemporary world

Inequalities of a grand scale between the richest and poorest
zones of the world remain a feature of the contemporary
global economy, a feature which has shown no sign of
diminishing since the immediate postcolonial period of the
1960s. These inequalities have increased not only because
material poverty of an absolute kind, coupled with near
poverty and chronic insecurity, continues in the poorest
zones; but also because the enrichment of privileged minorities reaches ever new heights. These inequalities can be
identified by citing nation-states in a simple listing of the
poorest and the richest countries – from the USA, Germany
and Japan to Chad, Bangladesh and Burkina Faso. The
global rich and the global poor are not only identified by
rich and poor zones and countries. Within *both* zones there
are clearly marked rich and poor classes within them. Ankie

Hoogvelt's 'Globalisation and the Postcolonial World' (2000; see also Hirst and Thompson 1999) establishes first of all that economic, social and power relations have been recast to resemble not a pyramid but a three-tier structure of concentric circles. All three circles cut across national and regional boundaries. She then goes on to define the three concentric circles thus:

1 The elites of all continents and nations, albeit in different proportions in relation to their respective geographic hinterlands . . . (this is some 20 per cent of the world's population who are 'bankable').

2 The above are encircled by a fluid larger social layer of between 20 per cent and 30 per cent of the world population (workers and their families) who labour in insecure forms of employment, thrown into cut-throat competition in the global market.

3 The third and largest, concentric circle comprises those who are already effectively excluded from the global system. Performing neither a productive function, nor presenting a potential consumer market in the present stage of high tech information-driven capitalism, there is for the moment neither theory, world view or moral injunction to include them in universal progress. (Hoogvelt 2000, p. 358)

These are not just classifications of groups. They are held together by arguments about how the global system works. The secret of the first group is to be found in the phrase 'bankable'. That is to say they do not simply have 'more' than the others – more yachts, more world travel, more money, more accommodation – but they are able to convert this surplus into social leverage and economic power. With respect to the second, they are chronically vulnerable to the effects of new technologies and the decisions made by corporate managers and political leaders. Under these conditions people may not be able to achieve any economic security; when they do, they are often unable to perpetuate or protect it (Conley 1999; Oliver and Shapiro 1995):

State of the art technology, frenzied capital mobility and neo-liberal policies together ensure both a relentless elimination of jobs by machines, and a driving down of wages and conditions to the lowest global denominator. (Hoogvelt 2000, p. 358)

For the third group, development has virtually passed them by and for them the future promises 'containment and exclusion'. This is not just a classification of the rich, middle and poor, but a theoretical account of world capitalism in which corporate capital and the organized pursuit of profit produces a rich class which owns and manages, a labouring class which produces a surplus for minimum rewards and an excluded poor for whom global capitalism offers virtually nothing beyond the merest survival and frequently not even that.

This scenario is well established in the political economy of the modern world. In the last decades of the twentieth century and into the twenty-first century we have witnessed the intensification of exclusion and poverty, the inclusion of some East Asian economies into the global system, the demise of the state communist project and the Soviet empire, the weakening or abandonment of socialist and welfarist politics in rich western states and the spreading of neoliberal politics in rich, poor and formerly state communist societies. By 2008, the relentless pursuit of neoliberal economics had caused the largest financial crisis for eighty years. Economic power appeared to be shifting from 'the West' and the US in particular, towards China, Russia and the emerging economies of Brazil and India (Goldman Sachs 2007; National Intelligence Council 2008).

These economic and social changes are understood as 'structural': they constitute the external forms of economic organization and the disposition of power. Only with enormous effort can the acts of individuals, even when organized collectively, surmount these structures. But the power of this 'external structure' does not indicate a theory which denies the agency of individuals who live within it. Rather, an 'external structure', of economic and political power, sets the scene for the choices of individuals, however constrained those choices may be. Economic changes affect people's ability to purchase the transport which would get them to a workplace, their ability to hold onto meagre allotments of land upon which their livelihood depends, their ability to purchase a home, afford education and keep their families, in even the most modest way, secure, intact and whole. In other words, this global 'structure' constitutes the stage on which, at the micro-social level, people make decisions about how to sustain a tolerable life, how to improve their prospects, how to resist displacement and dispossession, about what they regard as valuable and about whom to trust. The main character of these situations *is not ethnic* – but in virtually every one we can detect the outlines of action, organization and cultural innovation which have the potential to become *ethnically marked.*

Postcolonial economic conditions

Hoogvelt indicates that she uses the term 'postcolonial' to describe the global social order in which 'the aftermath of colonialism interacts with the forces of globalisation' (2000, p. 359). The first of these postcolonial conditions is 'exclusion and anarchy', which is 'exemplified in sub-Saharan Africa, where the patrimonial state form emerging after independence proved too weak to weld a viable political unity or civil society out of the mosaic of ethnic fragments bequeathed by colonial administrations'. The second is the 'anti-developmentalism of Islam' where 'the failure of the developmentalist project, coupled with the exclusionary effect of . . . globalisation, has interacted with the spirit of renewal ever present within Islam *and* with its long history of confrontation with the West'. The third, typically in East Asia, is where 'the state-led developmentalist project has succeeded in catapulting the economies of a small number of NICs [newly industrialized countries] into the heartland of the reconstructed global capitalist system'. The fourth is typified by the South American 'revolt against Western models of modernity and progress' whilst being a 'testing ground for neo-liberal policies of globalisation and privatisation'.

In the rich world too, as we noted above, the poor and the insecure but employed labouring classes can be found. Thus the socially and economically excluded of the USA's vast degraded urban spaces, America's white, black and Hispanic poor, belong either to the impoverished population or at best to the insecurely employed, perpetually at the mercy of shifts in markets, downsizings, relocations and vast and rapid movements of capital and points of production. These economic insecurities are *in principle* ethnic-blind. International corporations are interested in exploiting workers, not just white or black workers. But the political and social responses, the expressions of social resentment, in a society with a historic racialized discourse, are highly likely to be framed in ethnic and racial terms (e.g. in the use of terms like 'black underclass'). Where racist language is routinely condemned, replacement language – like opposition to 'welfare' – is used (Jacobs and Tope 2007).

William Julius Wilson and the disappearance of work

No one has done more to explain and demystify this situation in the United States than William Julius Wilson. He first argued that the social disadvantages of an excluded African American population could not be fully explained by reference to the racist attitudes of whites. He followed this with an equally compelling analysis of the 'disappearance of work' (Wilson 1999).

It is crucial to Wilson's thesis that not only are African Americans subject to disproportionate exclusion from paid employment but that also many white Americans are similarly excluded. Those who are in work live in a more or less permanent state of anxiety about its continuation. In this situation, (some) white political responses do not reproduce the categorical racism of an earlier period, but do give voice to a new racism which associates black people with welfare, crime and fecklessness. This is coupled with a populist and racist politics which is opposed to welfare spending, especially where this is seen to benefit an 'undeserving' and racialized population. There is a powerful momentum behind anti-welfarist politics. This obstructs the modest ameliorations which state-funded interventions might bring both to identified ethnic minorities, such as affirmative action programmes, and to all the disadvantaged – such as measures to protect employment, improve education and social security (see Jacobs and Tope 2007, ch. 5; also Gilens 1996). The politicization of ethnic difference takes place against a backdrop of massive increases in joblessness. Speaking of three neighbourhoods representing the 'historic core of the Black Belt in the city of Chicago', Wilson writes:

> In 1950 69 per cent of all males aged 14 and over who lived in these neighbourhoods worked in a typical week, and in 1960, 64 per cent of this group were so employed. However by 1990 only 37 per cent of all males aged 16 and over held jobs in a typical week in these three neighbourhoods. (Wilson 1999, p. 480)

This pattern of joblessness is caused or exacerbated by movements within the global economy. Employment in the USA is 'exported' when American capital in, for example, the computer microchip and processor industry relocates to Central America or South East Asia to take advantage of lower wage costs and lighter regulation. Employment in America is undermined when goods are imported (e.g. clothes) which take the place of American employment in the same product area (Wilson 1999). This pattern is complicated by investment in northern Mexico by US-based firms (and by Japanese and Korean corporations) creating the *maquila* economy (see M. Davis 2001) and utilizing low-wage Mexican labour. At the same time, Mexican workers are entering the USA to work in low-wage economies like garment and toy manufacture in Los Angeles (M. Davis 2001).

De-industrialization affects the lives of the traditional African American working class:

> Today, we are experiencing the transformation of American cities from centers of manufacturing to centers of service and high technology. The loss of well-paying manufacturing jobs in the cities as US corporations have sent their low-skill jobs to Third World countries and non-metropolitan areas of this country has devastated the black working class. (E. Anderson 2000, p. 267)

Economic changes affect jobs, neighbourhoods, schooling and housing. The processes of economic change – global movements of capital, flexibilization of labour, new technologies, competitive pressures on production costs – are 'universalistic' or ethnically neutral in principle. But they are, in practice, *ethnically marked*, as Wilson and Anderson both observe.

Economic change and Hispanic migration into the USA

The largest and most recent contribution to the pool of available labour in the US economy has come from Mexico, Central and South America, as we saw in chapter 6. This growth of the Hispanic or Latino population is differentiated by country of origin (Cuba, Mexico, Ecuador, Peru, Puerto Pico and others) but it also has a particular regional and economic profile. We can illustrate this by examining three recently published case studies situated in Virginia (Zarrugh 2008), Compton, a suburb of Los Angeles, (Johnson et al. 1997) and Los Angeles as a whole (Gottlieb et al. 2005).

Food processing in Harrisonburg, Virginia

The southwest, New York and Florida have featured most in studies of the US Hispanic population, but, as the US Census reports (US Census Bureau 2000), parts of the old South are now seeing remarkably high growths in Latino in-migration. As M. Davis observes:

> A decade ago Latinos were a negligible element of the cultural landscape of the New South. Exponential growth of the Latino population in the 1990s – nearly 400 per cent in North Carolina and 300 per cent in Georgia – has changed this. There are now more than 1 million Mexican immigrants in Georgia, Tennessee and the Carolinas. In Northwest Arkansas, where Tyson and other large food-processing firms dominate the economy, (some) rapidly growing cities are 20 per cent Mexican. (2001, p. 4)

Harrisonburg, Virginia is an instructive example of the way in which an industry is affected by global competition and the availability of Hispanic labour. Zarrugh's (2008) intimate account tells us how, in the 1960s, Harrisonburg was describing itself as a town which was '99 per cent US-born and 94 per cent white' (p. 19). It was not until the 1990s that this picture began to change. In that decade the foreign-born and Hispanic population quadrupled. The migrants came, Zarrugh shows, in response to demand for labour in industries which were feeling the effects of global competition: labour costs were a critical part of this competition. The poultry industry in particular was facing stiff competition from China, in an industry that was by nature difficult to mechanize. Workers in the industry had, until the 1980s, been drawn from the local white population, both men and women. Two factors set labour force changes in motion. First, some white workers were attracted to alternative and cleaner employment (like garment factories); second, when workers went on strike to protect a living wage, employers turned towards immigrant – and non union – labour. By 2000, 85 per cent of the workers in the industry were immigrants. The city now has a school enrolment with 'students from 64 countries who speak 44 languages' (p. 19).

The Harrisonburg story illustrates, at a very local level, the ethnic transformation of the USA and specifically what Zarrugh calls 'Latinization'. The population moved via 'chain migrations' where early immigrants contact and direct later ones, so that peoples from the same villages in the home country form communities in the USA:

> The Garcia brothers, who were among the first Mexicans to settle in Harrisonburg, 'invite' family and friends from their hometown in the state of Jalisco [who] now form a community of 300–500 people. (p. 46)

The earliest Latino migrants had worked on a temporary basis in the region's orchards. This made them familiar with the area and 'in the know' when new work became available. The migrations affect the home country towns and villages: they may become ghost towns or they may thrive from immigrants' remittances.

Compton LA: de-unionization and de-industrialization

At the turn of the twenty-first century, Los Angeles (county) had a population of just over 9.5 million of which almost 45 per cent were Latinos. Even in the few years up to 2006 the county's population had grown to over 9.9 million and the Latino share to over 47 per cent. In the area designated by the Census as East Los Angeles, Latinos were (in 2000) 97 per cent of the recorded population (see Gottlieb et al. 2005, p. 78; US Census Bureau 2001). All this is a large demographic shift from a Los Angeles which in 1960 was 82 per cent non-Hispanic whites.

In Los Angeles county there has been a marked change in core economic activity from a traditional industrial and manufacturing basis to new economies in the highly competitive service sector and replacement manufacturing. These shifts 'draw in' migrant workers for whom low-paid employment under hard working conditions nonetheless represents a gain over poor economic prospects in the home country. In the period of the great demographic change, employment has been transformed. Johnson et al. (1997) report that 'the traditional core of the city bore the brunt of the decline [of manufacturing jobs]' (p. 1073). They calculate that 70,000 high-wage stable jobs were lost between 1978 and 1982 and another 200,000 between 1982 and 1989. In this 'restructuring of the Los Angeles economy', traditional high-wage manufacturing virtually disappeared. Many of the new jobs which were created were in industries which 'rely primarily on undocumented migrant labour and pay at best minimum wages' (p. 1073). These changes, as in other regions of the USA, are in response to the demands of global economic competition. Older industries, like auto manufacturing in Los Angeles and Detroit, have had great difficulty in competing with Asian competitors, and the US economy responds in several ways. One is the greater emphasis on high-technology industries, which demand highly trained and professional employees; a second is the relocation of US industries to lower-wage locations; and a third is the emphasis on particular new industries which can be sustained (inside the US) with low-wage migrant labour. In Mexico, part of the North American Free Trade Agreement (NAFTA), US companies relocate as *maquila* industries and they are favoured by US tariff arrangements.

Service employment, for example as janitors and cleaners, is also restructured by sub-contracting and the introduction of non-union labour. These changes – global economic competition, loss of traditional manufacturing, de-unionization, new low-wage economies – are economic, not 'ethnic'. They acquire an ethnic character when they are mapped onto racial and ethnic categories through the association of jobs, residential spaces and institutions with ethnic populations. Hence people speak of 'white police' or 'Mexican field workers' or 'Korean store owners'. Johnson et al. (1997) provide an intriguing example in the case of Compton, a suburb of Los Angeles, formerly predominantly white, then in the 1960s becoming an area with an African American majority. Though many African Americans were poor, with their numerical majority they were gradually able to gain political control and overcome racial discrimination. Then through the 1980s and 1990s, the demography of Compton changed, so 'by 1990 only 55 per cent of the Compton population [were] black' and 42 per cent were Hispanic. In at least three areas of life, the African American residents of Compton have watched the erosion of the gains they had achieved.

In employment, African American workers, who had done well in a unionized industrial economy, find themselves threatened by 'economic restructuring' and the business-class search for efficiencies and cheap labour. In housing, their tenancies are seen to be at risk: as Johnson et al. put it 'blacks claim that landlords are forcing out black [tenants] and replacing them with higher rent multi-wage Hispanics' (p. 1074). And, in education, schooling gradually changes in response to demands for bilingual teaching – and hence bilingual teachers. In these circumstances, monolingual African American teachers are at a market disadvantage. Black political gains from the 1960s onwards had fostered a sense of entitlement among them, all the more so since these gains were among the earliest hard-fought victories after the civil rights legislation. Although the source of the threat to 'black entitlement' lies in economic restructuring and the demand

for migrant workers, it is hardly surprising that some anger
and resentment is directed at the Hispanic incomers.

On the other hand, Hispanic residents begin to view
African Americans almost as African Americans had earlier
viewed whites: as dominating the main social institutions,
including the police force, whose actions are viewed as
oppressing Hispanics. This situation has a similar profile to
the ethnic conflicts described by 'competition theorists' in
chapter 5. The main difference is this: Johnson et al. take
economic change, global economic competition, business
search for new cheap labour and the actions of real estate
agents and landlords as their starting point – rather than
ethnic 'groups' who come into competition. In an increasingly
flexible labour market, employers 'prefer immigrants as
workers' because they are seen as 'compliant and industri-
ous', and they sub-contract labour recruitment to 'firms with
access to immigrant networks'. In service occupations (for
example, janitors) older established workers are replaced by
non-union flexible workers. Again the economic changes are
ethnically marked. None of these ethnic markers are based
on perfect matches: no ethnically named population (whites,
blacks, Latinos, Mexicanos) is a perfect fit with a socioeconomic niche, form of employment or class position. But there
is enough of a match to create a likelihood – or at least a
possibility – that these situations and social relations will be
framed in ethnic terms.

Ethnicity and class in Los Angeles

On a larger canvas, Gottlieb et al. (2005) present a very
similar analysis of ethnicity and class changes in Los Angeles.
Los Angeles had been a key centre of auto production, with
Ford opening a plant there as early as 1914. And after the
Second World War, southern California industrialized at a
great pace:

> In the post war years Southern California became an indus-
> trial powerhouse, as defence contractors and other heavily
> industrial sectors opened factories. These plants were quickly
> unionised . . . after [a] struggle . . . and thus provided decent-

wage jobs that anchored LA's cluster of growing suburbs. (p. 83)

But by the 1980s, this socioeconomic structure began to disintegrate under the pressure of global competition from imports; by the end of the 1980s and early 1990s, 'most auto manufacturers had abandoned the region' and in 1992 General Motors 'shut down its Pontiac and Chevy production factory in Van Nuys in the San Fernando valley' (p. 83). The number of manufacturing jobs fell precipitately in the Los Angeles area, 23 per cent between 1990 and 1994. Gottlieb et al. summarize this dramatic period of change:

> As late as the early 1980s two thirds of LA manufacturing jobs were in higher-paid often unionised industries such as autos, tires, electronics, and aerospace. Even during the 1990s expansion, LA continued to haemorrhage high wage jobs in 'heavy' manufacturing (e.g. durable goods such as cars and airplanes) while adding more low wage jobs in sweatshops and other 'light' factory sectors. By the year 2000, nearly half of regional manufacturing employment was in lower-wage sectors, exemplified by garment, furniture, toy manufacturing, and food processing. (p. 86)

All this was accompanied by declining unionization. In 1945, 35 per cent of the US labour force had been in unions, but by the year 2000, it was only 12 per cent. The authors describe the region as a system of four major classes: a business class of rich and super-rich partly integrated into global capital, and housed in the gleaming office blocks of downtown Los Angeles and supported by corporate professionals; a middle class of better-paid workers and lower professionals; poorly paid and under-protected workers; and an unemployed semi-permanently disadvantaged 'underclass'. The wealth gaps between each of these classes are growing. In Gottlieb et al.'s words, there is a 'widening divide . . . between the working poor, an eroded middle class, and the region's wealthiest professionals, managers, and business elite' (p. 84). Some of the losses of the better-paid workers can be explained by the disappearance of the manufacturing industries. In other cases, reasonably paid and union-protected workers (janitors) are undercut by the conversion of union to non-union jobs and the hiring of replacement (low-pay) workers. Compared to Johnson et al. (1997), Gottlieb et al. (2005) give much more space to the organized struggle against the erosion of living standards, and the political fight for a 'better Los Angeles'. These political lobbies, they argue, were organized across racial or ethnic divides so that a cross-ethnic alliance 'gave the lie to the myth that ethnic groups will always protect their own rather than expanding the circle of justice' (p. 81). The tensions and struggles described in these accounts are seen as arising from actions based on class interests, such as the flight of the rich and super-rich to outside the taxable zones, reducing the tax base for public services. But there is always the possibility of social struggle becoming ethnic conflict, as in the 1992 civil unrest in Los Angeles (Gottlieb et al. 2005, pp. 69–71). Indeed, in all the cases of economic change that we have described, we have also shown how these changes may be *ethnically marked*. By this, we mean that an economic complex (employment, competition for jobs, patterns of residence) can take on an ethnic character both *materially and cognitively*; materially when there is an actual match of an ethnic population and, say, an area of employment, and cognitively when this matching is part of common perception and discourse.

Precarious, factionalized, democratizing states: unstable geopolitical conditions

In the first part of this chapter we have discussed the *economic* situations in which ethnic antagonisms can be formed. Now we turn from the economy to the polity, from economic structures to the critical importance of the state.

It is in the political sphere that ethnic identities can become the basis of mass mobilization or can be the basis of state organization. South Africa in the Apartheid era organized its political system entirely on the basis of the classification of a number of racial groups. The system was so binding that all individuals had to have an official racial identity; where an individual's racial identity was in doubt, the state drew on official tests in order to classify a person in a final way. In present-day Fiji, a person's constitutional position is determined by their racial status as native Fijian, Indian Fijian or Others (Lawson 2004; see also Lawson 1992, 1997). In Malaysia, political parties either bear the name of an ethnic group or they are widely known to be predominantly supported by an ethnic population (Mauzy and Milne 1999). In many other countries, the rights of citizens are not *determined* by racial or ethnic identity, but ethnic identities are commonly mobilized in political organization.

In discussing the state, we will be referring principally to constitutions and institutions of government; closely allied to these are the judiciary, the police and the military. In Fiji, to which we just referred, the constitution defines the civil status of the two main ethnic groups: indigenous Fijians and Indian Fijians. In a series of coups d'état since 1986, the military have intervened to prevent what they regarded as a threat to indigenous Fijian primacy; or they have acted to protect the state against coups which they did not approve. Pakistan, Indonesia, Thailand and Turkey are other countries in which the power of the military places limits on the action of the purely political sphere. Similarly, the police and the judiciary can be expected to support the legal institutions of the country, whilst ideally retaining a measure of independence from the political system. All of these state institutions can be ethnically marked, where for example the state is dominated by an ethnic elite, where the police or military is mono-ethnic in a multi-ethnic state, or where ethnic minorities in democratic societies are effectively excluded from political power if voting follows ethnic contours.

Strong states, weak states, factionalized states

As we saw in chapter 4, Geertz (1973) has argued that, in newly developing state systems, primordial loyalties compete with allegiance to the state. Primordial loyalties would include loyalty to kin and clan groupings, to ethnic and national identities, or to religious affiliations. If these are powerful then it can be difficult for a newly developing state to call on the allegiance of the citizen and for nation-state identity to 'trump' these competing identities. The postcolonial state

of Indonesia had to contain the competing claims of Aceh-
nese, Balinese, Javanese, Madurese and Dayak peoples (and
of course many others); in 1999, the last two groups were
involved in serious outbreaks of violence (Mann 2005). It is
possible to reverse the argument that strong primordial
attachments impede nation-state integration; this would be
to argue that weak states enable or permit alternative communal identities to flourish. This can be the case in so-called
'failed states', where state institutions have not been established or have not commanded the compliance of the population – as is clearly the case in present-day Somalia (Simons
1997). Communal solidarity can also be expected in states
where political power is in the hands of one ethnic group
– or rather the elite of one ethnic group – at the expense of
others.

So Ann Simons (1997) has argued that in Somalia, kinship
groupings are the primary basis of trust. The state cannot be
relied upon to create conditions of security either for material
survival or personal protection. Under those circumstances
people turn to people they know they can trust. The Somali
state, she argues, 'never sufficiently proved itself credible as
the guarantor of a secure future to any of its citizens' (p. 277).
Under these circumstances, 'traditional ties' are all the more
important. Kinship relationships are the focus of what she
calls 'charts of trustworthiness':

> Somalis follow strategies [which are] common among nomadic
> pastoralists around the world and are grounded in the trust
> and obligation encoded in genealogical relationships . . . gene-
> alogies chart links among kin which are only kept if people
> prove worth remaining tied to . . . they are charts of trustwor-
> thiness. (p. 276)

In such a society, kinship groups command the loyalty of an
individual. In Simons' terms, the society is not 'individuated'.
'What I mean by individuation', she argues, 'is that individuals are able to stay apart, construct their own political identities if they so choose, *and deny the claims of others*' (p. 278;
my emphasis). The opposite to this is where the individual
can barely assert an identity separate from the one they are
known to have through their kinship connections. This argu-

ment adds to our understanding of 'situational ethnicity'. The more individuals respond to different and multiple contexts or *situations* of action, the more they are exercising a certain degree of licence over the identity they adopt. When group identities are compelling, the claims of kin groupings *must* be followed. On the other hand:

> Having to be situational also means individuals' identities cannot be unitary. Having to be situational means people have to be allowed to selectively display or hide their multiple allegiances to or from a wide variety of entities: family, party, church, friends, work. (p. 279)

When group identities *are* compelling, this is frequently described in the press and elsewhere as evidence of 'tribalism'. This is an unsatisfactory word, attributing some mysterious power to group loyalty. At least three factors have to be considered. The first is that postcolonial states were, particularly in Africa, formed out of amalgamations of territory conforming to divisions agreed among competing colonial powers; and these borders frequently crossed language, religious and historical national groups. At the same time, culturally distinct regions of colonial states were subjected to differential treatment by the colonial power, as Ejiogu (2001) argues for Nigeria, a 'nation-state' he describes as 'artificial'. Second, postcolonial states face enormous difficulties in creating material security for their citizens. They have suffered as a consequence of the unequal conditions of world trade, particularly the devastating effect of world fluctuations in commodity prices coupled with the rising costs of imported manufactured goods (Held and McGrew 2000). There are, thus, a considerable number of states which can barely pay their way in the world, and can offer neither economic stability nor political security to their citizens. Third, in a number of states – such as Indonesia, the Philippines and Zaire (now the Democratic Republic of Congo) – these conditions have in the past been seriously compounded by corrupt rulers or regimes, often backed by western powers, which have drained any surplus for their private wealth. If states cannot or do not provide for the material security of their citizens then a crucial citizenship bond is either broken or never formed.

Ethnic conflict, violence, insecurity and the state

Most observers now agree on two seemingly contrary arguments: the first that conflicts involving national and ethnic group identities are widespread and can be marked by high degrees of violence; the second that this *cannot* be explained by some inherent power of ethnic attachments, or by the 'inevitable' clash of group loyalties (Fenton 2004; Lake and Rothchild 1996). Indeed, Lake and Rothchild argue that 'most ethnic groups, most of the time, pursue their interests peacefully through established political channels' (p. 43). In regions and countries where we find multiple ethnic identities – and this would apply to almost everywhere in the contemporary world – inter-ethnic harmony is the norm. If harmony is too strong a term, nonetheless a kind of reasonable, compromising, getting along is the norm. This does not just mean that 'ethnic groups' get along, but that ethnic identities are rarely or only sporadically deployed and that group-ness is significantly 'thinned out'.

This suggests that where severe and violent ethnic conflicts are found we need explanations which go well beyond the mere fact of multi-ethnicity. On this subject, there is a large and intriguing literature (see for example Brown 2001; Diamond and Plattner 1994; Esman 2004; Fearon and Laitin 1996; Lake and Rothchild 1996; Mann 2005). In what follows I discuss two critical dimensions which appear in most theoretical approaches: *fear and security* and the *state and democracy*. People may fear for their future in economic and political senses. We have discussed conditions under which people feel threatened by competition and anticipate a loss of a privileged position (see chapter 5). In more extreme economic circumstances, people may fear for their survival. Under these circumstances it is not *inevitable* that people mobilize along ethnic lines; but it is a real possibility. And where material fears are coupled with a sense of defending 'our people', the conflict can be all the more acute (Ruane and Todd 2004).

In the political sphere, the same theorem applies. Conflict and social fragmentation can be expected when 'ethnicity is linked with acute social uncertainty, a history of conflict, and fear of what the future may bring' (see Lake and Rothchild 1996, p. 43). This sense of fear is likely to be linked to, and indeed partially caused by, the weakness of the state. As Lake and Rothchild argue, 'Collective fears arise when states lose their ability to arbitrate between groups or provide credible guarantees of protection for groups' (p. 43). So, with a failure of central authority, people begin to think that they must look after themselves, and at this point 'themselves' can be articulated around ethnic identities, as has occurred in some crucial examples:

> State weakness helps to explain the explosion of ethnic violence that has followed the collapse of communist regimes in Eastern Europe, and the former Soviet Union, and it has also led to violence in Liberia, Somalia, and other African states. (p. 43)

People may anticipate that the state, especially as its central authority begins to fail, will not protect them, and in particular will not protect the community with which they are identified. In making their calculations, people will be influenced by the way in which ethnic groups are incorporated into the state. Three types of regime can be distilled from Rothschild's (1981) classification: one where there is a dominating majority, the second where there is a dominating minority and the third where there are multiple groups which live together in a 'relatively cohesive political system'. Variations on these types include situations where there is no outright majority but a number of small 'groups in balance', or where a multinational or multi-ethnic society has a strong state which accommodates several ethnic or national populations, often through laws which protect minorities and through semi-autonomous regions which protect a historical identity.

States which illustrate some of these variations, in particular the ones most subject to recent conflict, are frequently reported in the world's media. South Africa during the Apartheid era (i.e. from 1948 to 1994) was a state predicated on the power of a dominating minority in white supremacist rule; Tutsis in Rwanda were for a time a dominating minority. Sinhalese in Sri Lanka are a dominating majority but

Tamils continued to struggle for secession as long as they retained hope of success (Little 1994). In Malaysia, Malays are a dominant if not *dominating* majority, but their power is balanced by the size and relative economic strength of the Chinese Malaysians. Prior to the coup of 1986, indigenous Fijians were slightly smaller in population than Indian-origin people in Fiji but since the coup (and subsequent coups), native Fijians have become a majority because of the emigration of Fijians of Indian descent.

The sense of threat is not always confined to minorities: Serbians are an example of a people who have a historical notion of being beleaguered and endangered. It is this kind of majoritarian idea of being under threat that is often associated with the portrayal of a minority as an 'inner enemy'. Taguieff (1990) has written of 'differentialist racism', a modality of racism in which a majority view a minority as entirely 'other'. This 'other' group or people is portrayed as an 'enemy within' and as a presence that, in the end, cannot be tolerated. This mentality can be part of the wider mentality of elimination that was cruelly exemplified in Germany in the Third Reich and the Holocaust (Bauman 1989). In less 'final' but nonetheless severe conflicts, a critical role is played by the degree to which potential combatants can expect external support. In Sri Lanka, Tamils may have looked to India; in Northern Ireland, Protestant Unionists have looked to Britain, Nationalists to Ireland in the South and to the USA; in Rwanda and now the Democratic Republic of Congo, ethnic conflicts are complicated by the co-presence of groups in those two states, plus Uganda and Burundi. Thus a minority in one place can have a reasonable expectation of support from their 'brothers and sisters' in a neighbouring state.

Michael Mann, in his landmark work *The Dark Side of Democracy: Explaining Ethnic Cleansing* (2005), stresses that his is essentially a *political theory* of ethnic cleansing. This is to say that groups become involved in what he calls ethnic cleansing, murderous ethnic cleansing and sometimes just murderous cleansing, when 'movements claiming to represent two fairly old ethnic groups both lay claim to their own state over all or part of the same territory' (p. 6). Note that Mann refers not to ethnic groups in conflict, but to movements claiming to represent ethnic groups: a significant difference. Second, we should note that he refers to 'fairly old groups', suggesting that the ability to call up historical memory of past conflicts will be crucial in the formation of an ethnic ideology. Groups must also, as we discussed above, have a plausible expectation of success, which can include a reasonable expectation of external support. This support can come from expatriate co-ethnics or co-nationals as was the case in the conflicts occurring in the wake of the collapse of Yugoslavia. When the less powerful side, believing it may have outside support, decides to fight on, the scene is set for 'murderous cleansing'.

Mann's comprehensive and much-debated theory (see Breuilly et al. 2006) starts by arguing that in modern states there is always the possibility of a confusion of the categories *demos* and *ethnos*; the first, *demos*, is a simple political definition of the people of a country, the second is the construction of those people, or crucially some of those people, as a nation (*ethnos*) with a common culture and heritage and 'distinct from others' (Mann 2005, p. 3). In the forming of democracies, there is a risk of ethnic cleansing. For a *demo*cracy – which contains the first term, *demos*, as rule by and for the people – must raise the question 'who are the people?' Conflicts over land, material resources and access to political power, typical of conflicts between social classes, can be reframed as being between 'peoples'. As we have argued in this book, these conflicts have a class context, and may take some of their energy from class resentments or from the defence of class privileges. But where, in Mann's words, 'ethnicity trumps class', serious conflict becomes a possibility.

The possibility comes closer when two further conditions are met: the emergence of fragments and factions within an existing or newly forming state and an unstable geopolitical environment as we shall see below in the case of Yugoslavia, destabilized by the collapse of the Soviet Union. In states which lack stability and cohesion, murderous conflict is more likely. Mann here discusses states which break into factions, struggling over control of the state; states consolidating themselves against internal opposition; and new states which are struggling to become cohesive (Rwanda, the Nazi state and Bosnia and Croatia being examples of these three situations respectively; 2005, p. 7). Mann makes a crucial adjustment to the arguments that (1) weak states fail to protect individuals and communities against violence and (2) the weak central authority leaves a vacuum or space which is filled by communal violence (cf. Wieviorka 1994). For Mann argues that ethnic cleansings are often *carried out by the state*. To do so the state must have some level of cohesion so as to be capable of organized action.

This distinction, between murderous actions of the state and the state's failure to control the murderous actions of others, can sometimes be difficult to sustain. This is because a state may instruct or permit militia and armed gangs to act on its behalf, or ignore and tacitly condone the actions of such gangs. Where militia groups, not being regular army or police units, act at some distance from the state itself, the state has 'deniability'. It can accept and welcome the actions whilst claiming that these actions were not endorsed by the state. In the former Yugoslavia Serbian militias committed atrocities in Bosnia: the concentration camps full of captured Muslims provided a grim reminder of the Nazi regime. The critical question was: how directly responsible for the actions of the militias was Mr Milosevic as the leader of the Serbs (see *The New York Times* 24 March 1999)? Similarly, Milosevic was believed to have assisted the arming of Serb militias in Croatia in order to detach Serb areas from Croatia and add them to Serbia. In countless instances of conflicts of this kind, state leaders seek to distance themselves from militias who act on their behalf. Indeed, Mann's formulation includes his typology of those who become involved in murderous cleansing: elite leaders, militias, with some elements of mass support, and finally ordinary people who are drawn into participation. The riots and pogroms against Chinese in Indonesia (a weakening authoritarian state) provide an example:

> [In the] anti-Christian and anti-Chinese pogroms in 1996 and 1998 . . . the police were mysteriously absent from the riot areas, while the initial rioters were organized black-garbed paramilitaries trucked in from outside (probably disguised policemen or soldiers). Then a large number of ordinary Indonesians joined in. (Mann 2005, p. 497)

Finally, Mann is at pains to emphasize that, under the right conditions, murderous ethnic cleansing can occur anywhere. Stunningly, his book opens (Preface, p. ix) with a quotation from US President Thomas Jefferson, that in the name of the advance of civilization, the extermination of native American Indians was 'justified', 'ultimately beneficial and inevitable'. In the US, as in Australia, people with a legitimate claim to the land, whose labour was not needed, stood in the way of another people who were determined to secure the land for themselves. These actions were part of what Mann describes as 'genocidal democracies in the New World' (pp. 70ff; see also Stannard 1992).

Ethnicity and geopolitics

Sekulic's theorization of the dissolution of Yugoslavia (Sekulic 1997) is a comparable analysis of state security and ethnic mobilization. Frequently, the starting point for analysis of Yugoslavia in the 1980s and 1990s has been the nature of the communal identities and the history of their antagonisms. The academic response (cf. Bennett 1995) has often been to deny the inescapable solidity of ethnic hatreds, and instead to emphasize the relative inter-ethnic harmony of the post-Second World War period. The focus then has been on the manipulative nationalist rhetoric of unscrupulous political leaders, including Milosevic and Tudjman (for a detailed historical account, see Magas 1993; also Bennett 1995). The addition to this framing of the argument is analysis of the dissolution of the state within its *geopolitical or geo-strategic context*.

Sekulic begins with an understanding of the state as deriving its legitimacy from its 'external success', grounding this in a Weberian theory of legitimacy. He sees Weber as positing the state as an instrument which can 'hold its own' in the international arena; the creation of and subsequently the legitimation of states commonly reflect a particular historical point of balance between opposing or competing political and military systems. So in the early part of the twentieth century, the creation of a Slav kingdom was an expression of liberation from the Austro-Hungarian empire; Serbian autonomy was already bolstered by the earlier weakening of the Ottoman empire. The stronger position of the Serbs, compared to the Slovenes and Croats, meant that the latter two 'nations' were willing to lose some of their autonomy within a Serb-dominated federation, especially if this helped to protect them against encroachments from the north and the west. But despite the fact that Slovenes and Croats gained some protection under the unified kingdom, in the longer run Serb domination meant some curtailment of local rights, of, for example, the Catholic Croats' freedoms of religion, laying the foundations for Croat and Slovene distrust of the Serb elites. Under the Yugoslav state, the competition and distrust was between different elites (e.g. Serb and Croat) and was not shared by or communicated to the peasantry of the differing communities (Bennett 1995; cf. Ramet 1996), that is communities who differed along lines of language, religious persuasion and perceived descent.

In the post-Second World War period, the legitimacy of the Yugoslav state was based on the 'memories of the liberation war against Nazi occupation' rather than on communism, 'an ideology accepted by only a small minority of the population' (Sekulic 1997, p. 174). However, throughout the 1980s and quite emphatically at the end of the 1980s, the *geo-strategic position* altered quite dramatically. Although the Serbs looked to the Soviet Union as their Slav allies, Yugoslavia rested upon its independence from the Soviet Union, giving it a kind of freedom not experienced in Soviet client states. The decline and eventual collapse of the Soviet Union, and of the communist states tied to it, fundamentally altered Yugoslavia's geo-strategic position. The Soviet Union was no longer a threat but equally the West no longer 'needed' Yugoslavia as a buffer state between East and West. In this situation, Serbia manoeuvred to transform Yugoslavism into pan-Serbianism, a shift for which the Serb intelligentsia provided some of the justification in the mid-1980s (Magas 1993; Pavkovic 1998). Not only did they glorify Serb history but also portrayed Serbia and Serbs past and present as a victim state always in need of watchfulness against its multitudinous enemies and always ready to 'fight for its very survival'. The achievement of Serb aims within a

federal Yugoslavia could only be by centralizing at the expense
of multinational autonomies; Yugoslavism was replaced by
Serbian imperialism, which, crucially, included defending
'imperilled' Serbs outside Serbia, that is in Croatia, Bosnia
and Kosovo but scarcely at all in Slovenia.

Although the West had lost interest in Yugoslavia as a
buffer state, western states (e.g. Italy) no longer posed a significant threat to Slovenia as the western-most Yugoslav
republic. As Sekulic argues 'their [Croatia and Slovenia] main
preoccupation became how to join Europe and not how to
escape it' and now Europe had become 'attractive for the
reform-minded, communist leaders of Slovenia and Croatia'
(1997, p. 178)

As Europe no longer posed a threat (to Slovenia and
Croatia), the real menace was now represented by Serb imperialism; the West was slow to recognize this (Janša 1994).
Whereas the Yugoslav state had stood at a point of balance
between East and West, this situation was transformed when
the Soviet Union began to disintegrate:

> The disappearance of the Soviet threat removed the sources
> of internal legitimacy of the regime and allowed the explosion
> of pro-Western sentiments. Consequently the shifts in external
> pressures, the attractiveness of the West and the disappear-
> ance of the threat from the East, totally destroyed the internal
> consensus and Yugoslavia exploded under cross-pressures and
> the attractions provided by the changes in the geopolitical
> environment. (Sekulic 1997, p. 178)

The account in the preceding paragraphs is largely based on
Sekulic's analysis, and his concepts of geo-strategic position
and the Weberian notion of legitimacy. Geo-strategy was
important in both the creation and collapse of Yugoslavia,
but at the beginning and the end the geo-strategic position
was quite different:

> The geostrategical explanation is important in understanding
> the dynamics of the creation and dissolution of Yugoslavia.
> Geostrategy operates on three different levels. First on
> the level of international actors and their perception of
> the importance of the creation or the dissolution of an entity
> like Yugoslavia; Second on the level of the interaction of

geostrategical considerations and internal elite strategies; Third on the production of legitimacy as the result of geostrategical success or failure. (Sekulic 1997, p. 177)

This case analysis is a good example of what Mann also describes as (unstable) geopolitical conditions. The concept of the state is taken seriously and indeed is the first point of reference – rather than 'the nation'. The Serbs had most to lose from the demise of Yugoslavia. Thus Sekulic looks outwards rather than inwards to establish an analysis of the conflict in Yugoslavia. This is following Weber's recommendation that state legitimacy must be understood in terms of the state's relationship with external powers. In a causal analysis this is a step prior to understanding the processes of nationalist mobilization and ethnic cleansing which followed.

Using Sekulic's model it is possible to construct a theorized explanation of ethnic conflict *with very little reference to ethnicity itself*. He is not mesmerized by the word 'ethnic' in the phrase 'ethnic conflict'. A complete analysis would explain how the ethnicities 'Serb', 'Croat' and 'Slovene' are constructed both in the public imagination and in the routine exchanges of everyday life. At this point we would have a theory of how people came to choose to act and were forced to act in terms of these categories, under the kinds of conditions which Sekulic describes (cf. Banton 2000).

Post-Soviet Russia

Similar arguments are evident in an investigation of 'ethnic tensions and separatism in (post Soviet) Russia' (Stepanov 2000). The author looks at a wide array of ethnic or nationalist conflicts in Russia and examines those *variable* conditions which might prompt ethnic conflict. Political, territorial and demographic factors are important: nationalist sentiments might be more easily mobilized when a region is a 'national' territory, and ethnic sentiments might be mobilized when distinctive groups live side by side in the same territory or when forced migration has disturbed a demographic and economic balance. In the case of the North Caucasus we see evidence of the influence of what Stepanov calls 'contingent situations'. Two are especially important: the availability of arms and long-term economic crisis. The impoverishment of soldiers in the Red Army led them to sell their weapons, thus releasing arms into the population at large. The economic crisis placed increasing pressure on the countryside – where people might scrape an existence – and resulted in widespread overpopulation of the rural areas. The economic failure also produced populations of 'unemployed young men in the rural areas [which] further reinforces the incipient militarisation of the regions' (p. 310). The conditions for ethnic conflict are present in most respects. That is, under these kinds of circumstances, two things are facilitated or made more likely. First, elite political leaders or organized military bandit leaders (or both in tacit collaboration) may gain advantage by drawing on ethnic symbols of collective identity; they may also gain from acting to exacerbate ethnic loyalties by inventing or perpetrating atrocities. Second, individuals face situations where loyalty to kin or, by extension, 'ethnicity' becomes the 'sensible' choice, or virtually the only possible one in difficult or desperate circumstances. Michael Banton has summarized this type of situation as follows:

> We may conclude that firstly the significance of shared ethnic origin varies infinitely; secondly that it has to be considered in parallel with other potential bases for collective action including neighbourliness, and shared national origin, race, religion, and political interest. In local communities there are many such bases, making the relations between members multidimensional and enabling the different relationships to balance each other. When individuals are mobilised by appeal to shared ethnic origin this may appear to result in a distinctive kind of conflict but the underlying processes are common to many kinds of mobilisation. (Banton 2000, p. 496)

A pronounced emphasis on these *contexts of action* is necessary to avoid a mistaken emphasis on the apparently 'ethnic' nature of the conflict, when the change in external circumstances results in communally oriented action. People are motivated by a wish for economic security, for protection and guarantees of their future, and they are constrained by economic and political barriers and by fear. In the situations we have described above, these motives are associated with ethnic identities.

This may be a particularly necessary emphasis when the conflict is not only a matter of 'suspicion' or 'antipathy' but becomes murderous and ruthlessly violent. Then we need to understand 'why are people killing each other at all?' as well as understanding 'who is killing whom?' There are, in other words, questions of at least two kinds: why do people become desperate and violent and who are the targets of violence and aggression? At least five conditions would have to be explored.

1   The way in which social and cultural differences are available as 'markers' between people.
2   The conditions under which these may be peaceful or non-relevant markers, as against critical moments where they are transformed into serious divisions.
3   The particular circumstance of a group being seen as not legitimately present ('they have no right to be here'), as having things (rights, resources) 'to which they are not entitled', or as posing a threat to an 'inferiorizing' ideology.
4   The lack of restraint or the removal or collapse of restraint.
5   A reasonable expectation of impunity from punishment.

The exploration of this set of conditions and potentialities would bring together the kinds of information and theorization of the evidence which permit a plausible theorization of what is often described as 'ethnic conflict'. The Barthian model (discussed in chapter 5) is principally directed at condition 1. The question of how ethnic identities originate, are articulated and sustained is only part of the story. We must also allow that although for some groups under some conditions, ethnic identities are brought into action, for many others such identities are scarcely formed, or are no more than loosely stated and frequently non-relevant markers. This requires us to consider when (if ever) ethnic identities are a source of action at all, let alone a totalizing and decisive point of reference for action and mobilization. Beyond this, we are interested in when ethnic identities are not just part of a 'neutral' or benign pattern of difference, but are brought to bear as the main source of conflict and unequal power. Conditions 3 and 4 above, and the kinds of economic and political conditions we described earlier in this chapter, are the basis for the answer to these latter questions. This type of theorization is, of course, with the exception of condition 3, considerably less 'culturalist' than is found in much current sociology.

Summary

In this chapter we have highlighted the socioeconomic system and social class relations, and the arenas of politics and the state, as two contexts of ethnicity. In Los Angeles, economic changes influenced the social position of ethnically named populations. This affects the likelihood of ethnic solidarity as ethnic groups are highly concentrated in residential areas and in class position. Precise areas of origin, differing by country and region within a country, remain socially significant, but immigrants' experience in the USA engenders a strong pan-ethnicity as Latinos, blacks and Asians. The emphasis on class and economic change is not to present a case for class analysis over ethnicity, or to 'reduce' ethnicity to class, as 'ethnicists' frequently claim. Rather it is to place ethnicity *within* a framework of class analysis.

Torres, Valle and Darder have made critical scholarly interventions to shift US sociological analysis away from an exclusive focus on race, racism and race relations. They critique (Valle and Torres 2000, p. 11) what they call 'the zero-sum picture of the great melodrama of "race relations" in Los Angeles: "racial" groups are considered to be deeply at odds with each other, each group "naturally" apart from others and antagonistic towards members of other groups'. Instead, they concentrate on class and opportunity in the previously white working-class suburbs: the 'Latino community's arrival at the gates of these white suburbs coincided with the emergence of southern California's distinctly post-Fordist pattern of industrial development' (p. 24). In a more theoretical work (Darder and Torres 2004), they argue for the reinstatement of class analysis (see p. 42). Trapped in the 'narrow framework imposed by the dominant views of "race" in the United States (p. 43)', academics continue to racialize the world. They cite Omi and Winant (1986) as a 'classic example' of this academic tendency in their insistence on the centrality of race. In this chapter, we have tried to establish conceptually, and illustrate through examples, the economic contexts in which ethnic or racial identities are deployed, rather than treating ethnic groups or 'races' as the primary reality.

In the second half of the chapter, we followed a parallel analytical track but with an emphasis on the state and political power. We acknowledge that virtually all societies are multi-ethnic but not all are dominated ideologically by ethnic categories; nor are they all subject to sharp and violent ethnic conflict. Where they are, we must look to differential features of those societies (Fenton 2004); we identified two in particular – weakness or instability in the state and central authority and unstable geopolitical conditions. Mann and others would add that ethnic conflict is likely where power is monopolized by a mono-ethnic elite, and where state authority is uncertain in newly developing democracies. As Lake and Rothchild summarize it:

> Ethnic conflict is not caused directly by inter-group differences, 'ancient hatreds' and centuries-old feuds, or the stresses of modern life within a global economy. We argue instead that intense ethnic conflict is most often caused by collective fears of the future. As groups begin to fear for their safety . . . dilemmas arise that contain within them the potential for tremendous violence. (1996, p. 41)

8
Ethnic Majorities and Nationalism in Europe: Globalization and Right-Wing Movements

In this chapter we focus on the 'nation' as a political project. We explore how class sentiments and social resentment have influenced national identity, a theme taken through an examination of xenophobic populist movements in Europe. Xenophobic political parties are found in most contemporary European states; we look at how threats to national identity and class entitlements have led to a resentful nationalism.

The nation

In modern European and North American states, political legitimacy has been formed historically from the coupling of nation and state. The idea of nationhood has come to be firmly embedded in modern political culture and popular consciousness. The nation has a mythical element, grounded in a historical collection of stories and images.

National symbols are reproduced and re-inscribed in public spaces and in everyday life:

> flags, anthems, parades, coinage, capital cities, war memorials, ceremonies of remembrance for the national dead, passports, frontiers ... national recreations, the countryside,

popular heroes and heroines, fairy tales, forms of etiquette, styles of architecture, arts and crafts, modes of town planning, legal procedures, educational practices and military codes . . . all those distinctive customs, mores, styles and ways of acting and feeling that are shared by the members of a community of historical culture. (Smith 1991, p. 77)

The full significance of the idea of nation in the modern world lies in the way it is constantly coupled with its partner 'the state'. 'Nations' have come to be seen as (1) people who ought to have a state or as (2) the people of a state, the legitimate population within the state as a 'container'. As Mann (2005) has argued (see chapter 7), in democracies which have fostered a strong idea of nationhood, there is a political expression of 'peoplehood' which also expresses who are *not* 'the' people. Strong states are able to sustain strong concepts of national membership. If states are weakened – by for example the non-state (i.e. global) basis of economic power, or the creation of supra-state institutions – then we might speculate what happens to the cultural persuasiveness of 'nation'.

There are three ways in which the emphasis on the idea of nation and national community can have the effect of excluding 'others'. The first is if the nation is thought of as a kind of *ethnic category*, a community of people who share ancestors, however distant and indistinct this shared ancestry may be. The second is the idea of *long occupation* of the land, expressed by the terms 'natives' or 'indigenous people'. And the third is a strong idea of *shared culture,* represented by language, religion and the conventions of everyday life. The implication of these ideas for non-nationals is clear. In the first mode (nation as ethnic group), 'others' do not really belong to the national family. In the second mode (nation as long-time occupation of the land), others have only recently come to this country and are seen as having weaker claims to membership and entitlements. In the third mode (the cultural), others are believed not to 'really understand our way of life' or are viewed as failing to conform to it.

These discursive 'gaps' between us and others are not inevitable. They can be opposed by a concept of citizenship which is 'universal', inclusive and non-ethnic. People are

encouraged to have a sense of belonging (to the nation) irrespective of 'ethnic origin'. In this way, national membership
is defined in a *civic* rather than an *ethnic* way, a long-standing
distinction in the field (Brown 2000; Brubaker 1996). Thus
the nation is not regarded as a fixed ancestral entity, but as
a dynamic category which captures a continuing and changing sense of 'membership'. Where the concept of citizenship
is open and universalistic, new populations are not condemned to permanent status as 'ethnic groups' and 'minorities'. We shall return to this question of 'nation' and 'ethnicity'
in the case of Britain later in this chapter.

Nation, class and resentment

Historically, it is class and religion which have, in the examples of many European nation-states, been the keys to 'full
membership'. The creation of a strong, and political, concept
of nation has usually been carried forward by a specific class
or coalition of classes. The idea of a 'nation' is at first sight
a unifying idea. It expresses an idea of peoplehood which cuts
across other divisions, especially of class and regional difference. But both in history and the present, particular sections
of a society have a special interest in promoting the national
idea. In nation formation there have been groups with a
particular stake in the 'national idea' or specific classes which
advocated nationalist ideas, and in the present day most
nationalisms are internally divisive.

Liah Greenfeld (1992) offers a comprehensive account of
the origins of the concept of nation. Central to Greenfeld's
account is the idea of envy and bitter competition between
social classes – a set of social attitudes described as *ressentiment*. Out of this in England in the sixteenth and seventeenth
centuries grew an idea of nation. There were in England, as
the feudal order crumbled and new classes emerged, classes
whose members felt insufficiently recognized, and classes
whose members feared the threat posed by *arrivistes*, newcomers to power and eminence. There were upwardly mobile
groupings within an elite, or seeking entry to an elite, who
lacked for respect and recognition, or for the measure of

political power which they craved. The mobile groups may be fragments of a new class such as representatives of newly rich men of trade and commerce, or fragments of an older class, the aristocracy. Among the aristocracy, newer entrants to the class go unrecognized by older aristocratic families. The 'new' aristocrats, or newly wealthy, regret their lack of lineage and resent their less than full acceptance; the older aristocrats, especially if they are poor but honoured families, bitterly reject the credentials of their new class partners.

This sociological model of class envy and status insecurity, to be found in sixteenth- and seventeenth-century England and eighteenth-century France, has two features of special interest to us. The first is that the (total or partial) exclusion of a new class creates the space for the idea of nation, since the upwardly mobile stand to benefit from replacing the conventions of aristocracy, with an ideology of an 'open-membership' nation. The second is that the ideas of 'freedom' and 'equality' also serve the new classes, who benefit from the articulation of a 'national' society. The key to the emergence of a nation and of nationalism is the broadening acceptance of the idea of a single political community to which all belong. In this sense, 'national membership' is an equalizing idea. In England, a string of related circumstances aided 'the spread of these ideas by growing numbers of people in different social strata'. The most important circumstances:

> were the transformation of the social hierarchy and the unprecedented increase in social mobility throughout the sixteenth century; the character and the needs of the successive Tudor reigns; and the Protestant reformation. (Greenfeld 1992, p. 44)

This period of unprecedented mobility was 'sustained for a hundred years or so'. Meanwhile, the monarchy had an interest in 'the extinction of the old nobility' to be replaced by a new one which was more educated and drawn from many strata of society:

> The redefinition of nobility as a status based on merit, and not on birth, was a simple acknowledgement of this transfer of authority from one elite to another, which was virtually happening before one's eyes. A fundamental transformation

of this kind required a rationalisation. . . . It is at this juncture,
I believe, that nationalism was born. (p. 47)

In France too, resentments arose from competition between
old and newer elements of the rich and powerful. The vulgar
rich were maligned by the old rich but the aristocratic poor
hated both (p. 150). Status anxieties among the French aristocracy were augmented by feelings of envy towards England.
Both sets of feelings contributed to French national self-
consciousness. In the second half of the eighteenth century,
'the aristocratic-intellectual elite in France was . . . personally
wounded by the superiority of England and felt *ressentiment*
generated by the relative position of the country' (p. 178).

In a later commentary, Brown (2000) describes these and
similar political sentiments as nationalisms 'articulated by an
insecure class or status group' and being '*ressentiment*-based'
and usually illiberal. Greenfeld even suggests that this bitter
feeling of loss or threat to status may be the clue to nationalism and thus to modernity: 'it would be no over-statement to
say that the world in which we live was brought into being
by vanity' (p. 488).

Greenfeld's comments are directed towards a group of
nationalisms, associated with the formation of modern
nation-states in Europe. There are many other nationalisms,
including those of end-of-empire new and restored states,
as were founded at the end of the Ottoman and Austro-
Hungarian empires. New nations followed the end of the
British, French and Dutch empires in the mid-twentieth
century and the collapse of the Soviet empire and the Yugoslav
federation at the end of the twentieth century. The Greenfeld
analysis is important because it shows nationalist sentiments
are often linked, directly and indirectly, to a view of the future
held by particular groups in a society; they are linked to
social mobility and class position. Some groups have a special
interest in the furthering of the nation and a particular idea
of the nation – however much 'all' may benefit. In 'new
nations', of which the USA is the classic example, nationhood
was not created out of the class divisions which were typical
in Europe; the USA had no feudal past. On the other hand,
US citizenship initially, and for a long time, excluded a very
substantial proportion of its people – African Americans.

Nation and majority

Understanding nations and nationalism becomes an essential step in understanding ethnicities in the contemporary world. Racism and nationalism are not the same thing, the first focusing on an ideology of inherent difference (Fenton 2006) and the other on the elevation of the idea of nation to the highest value. But they are frequently closely allied to each other (Balibar and Wallerstein 1991), as we can see in ideas of empire, Britishness and white England or Britain during and after the imperial period (Kumar 2003). Similarly, an early peak of American imperialism, at the turn of the nineteenth and twentieth centuries, was marked by a surge of ideas about the manifest destiny of the (white) American people (Gossett 1965). Nationalist ideas are expressed *militantly*, where a nation-state proclaims its world mission; or *mundanely*, in the reiteration of what Billig has called 'banal nationalism', the daily acknowledgement of the flag or the repetition of the name of the country and the name of the people (Billig 1995).

Where a national self-image is strengthened it has a simultaneous effect of tacitly or actively excluding people defined as 'other'. People defined as 'ethnic minorities' meet with expressions of hostility, suspicion and rejection. Thus majoritarian ideas of nation and conceptions of who properly belongs to the nation are essential to the self-awareness of ethnic groups. There are no ethnic minorities without an ethnic majority, whilst the 'claims' of minorities may heighten the self-consciousness of the majority. Anthony Smith is making this point when he writes:

> Even dominant ethnic groups must turn a latent, private sense of ethnicity into a public manifest one, if only to ensure the national loyalty of their members against the claims of other groups. (1981, p. 19)

In the contemporary world, 'nationalisms' and 'racisms' are frequently found side by side and are often perfectly fused in a single ideology. This is the case with the nationalism–racism of the National Front led by Jean-Marie Le Pen in France (Marcus 1995) or the Serbian nationalism–racism led by Slobodan Milosevic in the former Yugoslavia (Magas 1993). These racism–nationalism fusions usually contain four elements: social changes which are feared and despised, ethnic exclusiveness, a group or class experiencing a sense of threat and disenchantment and the targeting of others as undesirable.

Changes in political identity are matched by, and partly caused by, far-reaching changes in economy and class formations in western capitalist societies. De-industrialization in the West has diminished the traditional working class, reorganized commodity production on a global basis and led to what Wieviorka calls 'the era of destructuration'. Most notably, the 'grande mutation' (Wieviorka 1994, p. 178) involves 'the decay of the working class movement as a social movement'.

This is matched by a marked weakening of the state's ability, or willingness, to soften the impact of a quickly changing and global capitalist system. The gap left by the state's inaction and the decline of the traditional working classes is a space to be filled by populism and racism.

> A second element of destructuration deals with the state and public institutions, which encounter increasing difficulties in trying to respect egalitarian principles, or in acting as welfare states. (p. 180)

Political debate about 'welfare' and state benefits has throughout Europe and North America become ideologically linked to 'undeserving' beneficiaries of state spending, frequently framed in a racist discourse (Faist 1995; Solomos 1993). In a regime of neoliberal capitalism, North American and European governments set out to reverse the gains of the welfare state; Blair (as British prime minister, 1997–2007) and others simultaneously moved their parties away from their longstanding working-class bases and began to portray 'welfare' not as security but as 'dependency' (Holmes 2000, p. 166).

Class, welfare, the state and immigrants

The discontents and insecurities of western societies have been attributed to anxieties about *modernity* itself (Rattansi

1994, 2002). Bauman has argued that, under conditions of modernity, anxiety and uncertainty, 'occasions for the "no control" experience become more frequent' (1989, p. 64). However, material arguments about class, welfare and the state – in relation to national identity and what Bauman calls 'heterophobia' – relate to a *specific* phase in the relatively recent development of capitalist societies. This phase is marked by a trend towards de-industrialization of the developed capitalist societies, and with it the shrinking of the traditional (manual, manufacturing) working class, the shift of commodity production to newly developing economies (India, China, Brazil, South Korea, etc.) and the creation of a truly global economic space. Since the 1980s, this phase of global capitalism has been promoted by a doctrine of neoliberalism. Until the stock market and financial crises of 2008, this neoliberal doctrine was barely contested, aided of course by the collapse of communism in the Soviet sphere.

Under these specific conditions, Bauman argues, 'national identity' has become highly problematic, and when national identity is questioned, one response is to seek ever more urgently to rediscover it. The state, he suggests, can no longer be relied upon as a source of our common welfare:

> The reduced powers of the state do not promise much. A rational person would no longer trust the state to provide all that is needed in case of unemployment, illness or old age, to assure decent health care or proper education for children. (Bauman 2006, p. 44)

As the state becomes detached from welfare, so we see what Bauman calls a 'looming divorce between state and nation' (p. 61). Under these conditions 'it is no wonder that so-called "cultural visions" of identity are coming back into fashion among the groups that seek stable and secure havens' (p. 61). In a state which honoured the working class and provided for their welfare, identity as 'working class' was an identity capable of being a *national* identity. In the earlier postwar period in Britain, this sense of national membership was reinforced by the routine repetition of the words 'British' and 'national' in major industries and institutions (see Mandler 2006, p. 214). Mandler has argued that in the 1940s and 1950s a political 'middle way' made possible 'pride in social democracy as a "peculiarly British" formula for national success' (p. 214). This allowed British people to think of themselves as engaged in a 'common project'. It is this sense of 'common project' which is one of the important foundations of national sentiment. So Miller has argued that 'In acknowledging a national identity, I am also acknowledging that I owe a special obligation to fellow members of my nation which I do not owe to other human beings' (Miller 1995, p. 49). The postwar realization of the British welfare state solidified this sense of a compact with others and national membership. It is precisely this basis of incorporation into the nation that the neoliberal project of global capitalism has, as Bauman argues, undermined.

These social changes, with local variations, can be traced across most European societies. So in most contemporary countries in Western Europe there has been a realization of goals of social protection under the aegis of a welfare state. These systems of welfare have been projected as the political and national achievement of the 'working class' or 'the ordinary people' and now they are under threat. One response to this has been a series of movements which have combined elements of populism, neo-nationalism, xenophobia and racism.

Right-wing movements in Europe

Most European democracies now have political parties which are variously described as populist, neo-nationalist, racist and xenophobic, and these parties have typically attracted from 10 to 20 per cent of the popular vote. Depending on the structure of the political system, these levels of support may or may not result in significant parliamentary representation. The new right-wing or far right parties appear in rather different forms. As most observers argue (see Golder 2003), it is important to make a distinction between neo-fascist and populist parties: the former being committed to explicit fascist principles; the latter (populist) distance themselves from fascism and overt racism, but trade on and appeal to popular prejudice and anti-immigrant attitudes. They share a number of political positions, typically including opposition to immigration, hostility towards the European Union and their country's membership of it and generally a defence of the country's national identity. They also vary because of local conditions, like the Flemish Block's orientation to the Walloon–Flemish division within Belgium, or the fact that Switzerland is not formally a member of the European Union. And Germany and Britain are distinctive by the fact that neither has seen the emergence, to the same degree, of nationally successful populist parties.

The reason why these parties and movements are significant in understanding ethnic identities is because they are symptomatic of an important trend in the mobilization of majority ethnic belonging. Insofar as they are 'nationalist' they are symptoms of attempts, by alienated ethnic majority social groupings, to recapture the nation for themselves. In this sense, the populist or neo-nationalist movements are not only grounded in material dislocation, principally the de-structuring of the traditional working class through neoliberal economic changes, they are also grounded in a renewed search for meaning and belonging. Indigenous inhabitants, writes Holmes, are 'faced with what they believe to be a burgeoning immigrant population' and 'struggle with a rupture in their sense of belonging interleaved with fears that their way of life is doomed' (Holmes 2000, p. 105). These social and cultural shifts are the basis of what Holmes defines as 'integralist politics'. He is particularly interested in neofascist parties and their leaders but some of their ideologies, like anti-immigration, and their social roots in the declining old working class, are the same as can be found in the wider populist appeals.

The sentiments expressed by these parties, and by those who follow them, combine material/instrumental and symbolic/ideological themes (Golder 2003). The material/instrumental themes relate to jobs, housing and welfare and what are perceived to be 'loss of entitlements'. These would include the argument that indigenous populations have a special entitlement to welfare protection. The 'material' views are allied to symbolic/ideological themes about the loss of community and the 'threat to national identity'. In purely political and institutional terms, the populist parties occupy a space partially vacated by the (changed) labour parties and the weakened trade unions. The old working class has itself changed, undermined by de-industrialization, new forms of self-employment and the introduction of flexible working. As most commentators agree, there is no single causal chain that can explain voting support for populist or neo-nationalist parties (Eatwell 2000; Golder 2003; Lubbers et al. 2002), but most of these parties exhibit and express a contempt for mainstream party elites, seen as corrupt and detached from the true people, and contempt for cosmopolitan and 'multi-culturalist' attitudes.

At the turn of the century, Eatwell (2000) listed the levels of success of various European populist parties. Showing the percentage support and the date of a parliamentary election, these included the Austrian Freedom Party (27 per cent, 1999), the Swiss People's Party (23 per cent, 1999), the Norwegian Progress Party (15 per cent, 1997), the Danish Popular Party (7 per cent, 1998) and the Flemish Block (Belgium: 16 per cent, 1999). Comparing those figures with the most recent elections gives us some sense of the apparent relative stability of support for the new parties. Some six to nine years later, we see the following results: the Austrian Freedom Party (2008), 18 per cent; the Swiss People's Party (2007), 29 per cent; the Norwegian Progress Party (2005), 22 per cent; the Danish Popular Party (2007), 14 per cent; and Flemish Interest (Belgium 2007), 12 per cent – two decreases and three increases. Like the National Front in France, these parties often do well in old working-class areas where there was formerly strong support for parties of the left. Clearly, the New Labour Party in Britain, which has similarly weakened its links with the working class and the trade unions, now fears that it may have prepared the ground for defections to the British National Party. The Labour Party's then Communities and Local Government minister, Hazel Blears, wrote that:

> The British National Party has made advances because main-stream political parties, including Labour, have abandoned sections of the white working class, ignoring people's needs

while taking their votes for granted. (*The Guardian*, 22 November 2008)

Oesch (2008) agrees that 'the working class has become the core clientele of the right-wing populist parties in Western Europe' (p. 349) along with support from the petite bourgeoisie – shopkeepers and small business people. In the countries which he examines (Austria, Belgium, France, Norway and Switzerland) via the European Social Survey, the broadly defined working class 'is responsible for two-thirds of votes received by right-wing populist parties in Austria, Belgium and France' (p. 358). Looking at under- and over-representation of classes in populist voting, Oesch (2008) concludes that the 'thesis of proletarianisation of the right-wing populist parties' electorate' is confirmed in all five countries (p. 356). Three major orientations to politics and society are significant in explaining support for these parties: the fear of wage pressure and competition over welfare benefits; immigration and a sense of threat to national identity; and a sense of alienation from the present workings of democracy. Of these, Oesch shows, the concern with 'national identity' is the most important.

The populist parties typically seek a restoration of national pride and a defence of national identity; restriction, if not an end to immigration; and opposition to 'multiculturalism'. Competition (with immigrants) for welfare benefits and jobs is a recurring theme. Swank and Betz are able to show that comprehensive social protection 'lessens the economic insecurities attendant to internationalisation and, in turn, weakens support for far-right parties' (2003, p. 215). Globalization, economic insecurities, increased immigration, the weakening of labour unions, welfare retrenchment and the development of the European Union all set the scene for the populist and right-wing parties. Particular policies of the parties differ – becoming, for example, more or less overtly xenophobic, more or less neoliberal. But they all benefit from what Kriesi et al. (2006) call the 'transformation of the national political space'. New parties and new politics benefit from the weakening of the left–right cleavage, with a new 'structural opposition' between 'globalisation winners and losers' (p. 921). The winners are 'entrepreneurs and qualified employees in sectors open to international competition . . . and cosmopolitan citizens'; the losers are entrepreneurs and workers in 'traditionally protected sectors' as well as unqualified employees and 'citizens who strongly identify themselves with their national community' (p. 922). These observations reinforce the notion of an intersection of material and symbolic interests. As Kriesi et al. argue, 'individuals do not perceive cultural and material threats as clearly distinct phenomena' but as 'mutually reinforcing' each other (p. 922).

Multiculturalism and identity politics

If a significant section of the voters of those countries with successful right-wing populist parties are voting 'against multiculturalism', then we can be sure that this is based on a broad prejudice rather than an intellectual critique of multicultural ideas. Academics and columnists pursue their debates about multiculturalism in the public sphere but it is unlikely that these debates have much influence on popular views. Multiculturalism, however, has come to play a highly significant part in the political thinking and policy-making of many western (USA, Canada, Australia, Britain) and some non-western societies such as South Africa's 'rainbow nation' and multilingual, multi-religious India. Its historical home is Canada, where multiculturalism emerged from the tension between English-speaking and French-speaking Canada, and was developed by its best-known advocate, Kymlicka (1995). Since the 1970s, multiculturalist ideas have been adopted as explicit policies, as in Canada and Australia, or as guiding ideas in political pronouncements and policy discussion, as we find in the UK, the USA and the Netherlands. The subject of multiculturalism has a huge literature, which cannot possibly be covered here (for a pro-multiculturalist overview, see Modood 2007). But for a text on ethnicity, it is an important issue because 'multiculturalism' is a key word for significant governmental policies in a number of countries. And it is a policy which claims to address the public questions relating to 'ethnic and cultural difference'.

Here we identify three facets of multiculturalism: the demographic, the anti-discriminatory or anti-racist and the identitarian. The demographic emphasis is a seemingly simple statement that most societies have become 'more multicultural', meaning that diversity of religion, ethnic origin and language has increased in the population, largely through modern migration. In this respect it is unquestionably the case that the UK in the twenty-first century is a more multicultural society than it was in 1950. In truth, many societies which now describe themselves as 'multicultural' in the demographic sense have been multi-ethnic for much longer than the last three decades in which multiculturalism as an idea has grown. The crucial new fact is not so much simple demographic diversity, as a heightened deployment of symbols of cultural difference in the public political sphere. And the reasons for this 'heightened awareness of cultural difference' lie in the retreat from assimilationist ideas (see chapter 6), the global movement of people and ideas and the weakening of the nation-state (see Bauman 2006).

The second sense, the anti-discriminatory and anti-racist, is apparent in the public use of the term – in for example the speeches of politicians – to represent a call for a more tolerant and open society. Even in a speech which was widely interpreted as a 'retreat from multiculturalism', the British prime minister called for people to continue to 'celebrate multiculturalism' – a very non-specific rallying cry. The speech also stressed 'belief in democracy, the rule of law, tolerance, equal treatment for all, respect for this country and its shared heritage' (BBC News online, 8 December 2006). But 'tolerance' and 'equal treatment for all' are values which are very broadly accepted, even if not very well observed. Where multiculturalism means tolerance, respect and equal treatment, it does not depart from previous concerns for civil rights and equality of treatment. In this framing, multiculturalism carries with it the idea that a just, open and fair-minded society should respect ethnic and religious differences and should take all reasonable steps to ensure non-discrimination in employment, education and access to all kinds of goods and facilities. In the UK, these aims are given legal expression in the Race Relations Act of 1976 and its amendment in 2000.

It is the third sense, the identitarian, which has come to be the most contested. Here the emphasis is on ethnic groups and the cultural identities which they are said to represent. In its barest outline, the identitarian element of multiculturalism is the argument that individuals belong to (ethnic) groups; each of these groups has a distinctive culture; and that membership of the group bestows on the individual a crucial cultural identity. It follows that just treatment of an individual must respect this identity, and that a just and non-oppressive society will give some public recognition to cultural difference. So 'a denigration of a group identity, or its distortion, or its denial . . . the withholding of recognition or misrecognition is a form of oppression' (Modood 2007, p. 53: see also Taylor 1994). Modood is much influenced by Parekh, and both have become leading advocates and exponents of multicultural ideas in the UK and beyond. Some of these ideas were incorporated into the Commission on the Future of Multi-Ethnic Britain (the 'Parekh Report') (2000).

The intellectual and political critiques have, in the late twentieth and early twenty-first centuries, grown in number, force and persuasiveness. These include Barry's *Culture and Equality* (2001), a critique from the left and on behalf of a universalistic concept of justice and equality; and more recently, Benn Michaels' *The Trouble with Diversity* (2006), also a critique from the left and concentrating on the follies of multiculturalism in the USA. Three problems may be mentioned here. One is that, in effect, in countries like the USA and the UK, multicultural recognition is sought for groups which are argued to be 'culturally distinctive' *and* 'socially marginalized'. This 'groupist' idea makes it difficult to accommodate the fact that the 'groups' as defined are highly heterogeneous and, usually, not at all uniformly disadvantaged. The second is that multiculturalism tends to incorporate an inflexible and immobile notion of both 'groups' and 'cultures': indeed, it is not an idea which is informed by theoretical sociology, rather it is a wish or normative standpoint and an orientation in public policy. (This sociological weakness – the groupist fallacy – is discussed in chapter 5). Joppke has put it this way:

The world of multiculturalism is populated not by individuals with a multitude of overlapping, and often conflicting, group affiliations and interests, but by groups of 'communities' that are inert, homogeneous and mutually exclusive, such as gays, Latinos or Muslims. (1996, p. 449)

The third problem is not inherent in multiculturalism itself but does undermine its pretensions to lead public policy: this is the fact that multiculturalism finds only weak support in some sectors of society, and fierce opposition in others – what Joppke (2004, p. 237) calls the 'chronic lack of support for multiculturalism policies'. Political criticism comes from both the right and left, from the right because 'multiculturalism' is taken to be another symptom of the decline of 'national identity' (see above on right-wing parties) and from the left as infringing universalist principles. In the British case, Joppke comments that 'it is very much a liberal elite strategy . . . multi-culturalism is challenged by an openly racist right that seeks to remodel British nationhood along isolationist white "little England" lines, and a radical left that prefers anti-racist militance over multicultural accommodation' (1996, p. 455).

Summary: reflections on nation, resentment and identity

The emphasis in this chapter has been on the ethnic majority, class-based resentment and right-wing populist/xenophobic parties in Europe. We described Greenfeld's thesis on the origins of nationalism in England. This thesis has been subject to critical review. In particular Kumar (2003, pp. 122ff) has expounded his doubts about the Greenfeld thesis, suggesting that the equation of 'nation' with 'people' was not sustained, as 'nation' came to be associated more conservatively with 'the land' and government. It is certainly true that the close link of 'nation' with *all* the people, as a popular and 'equalizing' national identity, did not emerge at a point as early as Greenfeld claims. But this tends to reinforce the idea that interested me in Greenfeld: that even at its earliest origins the idea of 'nation' was allied to the material and symbolic interests of certain classes, especially those who were excluded from the inner circles of the aristocracies. English, and later British, nationalism gradually extended itself, in class terms, to a more popular and inclusive version. In other countries – the USA and Australia are prime examples – concepts of nationhood are much more overtly democratic and equalizing, in that they speak of a sense of national membership without distinction. Of course, we have to keep making qualifying comments for the USA given its long-term exclusion of African Americans; similarly Australia, for its treatment of Aboriginal peoples. Nonetheless, they achieve a more equalizing sense of national identity when compared with many European societies.

Later we saw how the articulation of nation with class continues to be one vital way of understanding nationalism, in this case new nationalistic populism in European countries. This is because the individual's sense of national membership is partly grounded in material experience. The second is that when 'nationhood' does become a popular idea, it has the potential to become 'exclusivist' – to articulate an idea not just of who does belong but also of who does not. In the context of some important social and economic changes that we described, this makes possible the development of a xenophobic nationalism and the tacit appearance of the un-marked 'we' – the 'ethnic majority'.

The socioeconomic changes to which we referred were implicated in the de-industrialization of many Western European economies and the growing importance of supranational economic movements – typically described as 'globalization'. As Bauman argues, the nation-state is materially and symbolically undermined. These changes, in both the material world and in the politics of culture and identity, underpin ethnic majoritarian consciousness. If we are interested in 'ethnicity' then this complex of changes are at the heart of the matter. We are not here making a case for a class theory of ethnicity and nationalism or for a reductionism or 'economism'. Rather, it is a case for understanding the material and the symbolic, together, and each in the context of the other.

Finally in this chapter, we turned to multiculturalism, the political policy orientation largely articulated by elites in western societies in a public attempt to address pressing questions of discrimination, the racist attitudes of some of the ethnic majority and recurring crises in the 'integration' of new citizens, immigrant populations and their families and descendants. We suggested possible flaws, especially in the identitarian mode of multiculturalism, flaws which are well rehearsed in the cited literature (e.g. Barry, Joppke, Michaels). But these difficulties in multicultural thinking should not detract from the importance of combating racism and discrimination, and creating a just and cohesive society. The fact that multiculturalism gains very little ground in much of the majority population is a primary difficulty, but not a surprising one. As a policy idea it has, on the face of it, little to offer to the ethnic majority and may appear to take away something to which they feel attached. The multicultural project will have to be reformed in ways that are not currently visible or advocated, before it can overcome the difficulties we have identified.

9
Ethnicity and the Modern World: General Conclusions

As a general rule it should be understood that there cannot be a theory of ethnicity, nor can 'ethnicity' be regarded as a theory. Rather, there can be a theory of the modern social world, as the material and cultural context for the expression of ethnic identities. This is to reject all separation of 'ethnicity' or 'racism' or 'national identity' from the social and theoretical mainstream. It is to re-position the interest in ethnicity within the central domain of the sociological imagination – the structuring of the modern world, class formations and class cultures, and the tensions between private lives, politics and the cohesion of communal and public life. The study of 'ethnicity' should, it follows, address the ethnic majority as much as the ethnic minorities.

A theory of ethnicity?

The argument that there cannot be a 'theory of ethnicity' has been sustained, explicitly or implicitly, throughout this book. There are two reasons for this. The *first* is that there is not a single unitary phenomenon 'ethnicity' but rather an array of private and public identities which coalesce around ideas of descent and culture. But the contexts in which these identities are found are multifold and multiform. This does not mean simply that there are 'ethnicities' rather than 'ethnicity', that is the 'same' phenomenon in different situations. Rather, it means that the contexts are sufficiently different so as to give an entirely different sense, force and function to ethnic identities according to the social, economic and political site of their emergence or their rise to importance.

The *second* is that in the 'contexts of ethnicity', it is the context that matters more than the ethnicity. This we have illustrated by showing how the significance or salience of ethnic identities is, in many if not most instances, influenced by external coordinates of the ethnic action rather than by internal characteristics of the ethnic identity itself. This is not to write ethnicity out of the picture, but it is a serious demotion. It suggests that our attention should be primarily turned to these 'coordinates' which form part of an explanation of why 'ethnicity' has become a focus of action. This is true at the aggregate level, where the question can be posed as 'how do we account for the fact that ethnicity has salience in the organization of private, communal and public affairs in the country, state or region?' It is also true at the individual level, where the question can be posed as 'why does the individual act – in these or those circumstances – in response to ethnic identities and interests? Why in these circumstances is the individual's action oriented to ethnicity?' This is the classic posing of the sociological question by rational choice theorists (Banton 1987; Hechter 1995). Something, they are saying, must influence why an actor acts in accordance with ethnicity in this circumstance but not in that one. Our interest then is not just in 'ethnicity' but in ethnicity as a component of the sociology of modernity.

Ethnicity as theory

If this is why we are not seeking out a 'theory of ethnicity', the reasons why 'ethnicity' is not a theory are considerably more straightforward. The idea of ethnicity could only be theoretically dominant if any of three conditions were met:

1 that ethnicity is seen to be a source of motivation, or
2 seen as the principal framework of social organization, or
3 ethnicity is seen as a quite autonomous and fundamental principle of action.

The first is rarely the case, although it is common to see problems of both human dignity and *recognition* and problems of social *allocation* significantly invested with ethnic meaning. It is true that Weber, in effect, tried to assimilate 'ethnically oriented action' to the category of 'affect': that is, it could be distinguished from rational action by the fact that ethnic ties were defined as 'emotional' rather than guided by reason or calculation. But much of the inclination of subsequent thinking about ethnicity has been *in precisely the opposite direction* – to assimilate 'ethnic action' to rational or instrumental action.

The closest approximation to the second condition can be found in societies such as the USA and South Africa, where almost all social principles of difference are – or were – reduced to a single line of division along a binary black/white coding. Even in these cases, where racial or ethnic difference is the dominant form of structuration, it remains difficult to explain social change in terms exclusively referring to ethnic oppositions. The third case is where ethnicity is seen as a primary source of action because ethnic difference is seen as being in some sense 'fundamental'. Very few commentators advocate this, although it is clear that in some social and historical settings, ethnic boundaries are very important indeed. Few people argue, in the manner of racial theory, that ethnic groups are basic population divisions. Van Den Berghe (1981) is an exception. He has argued that the inclination to act in accordance with ethnic group interests is a manifestation of a natural investment that the individual has in group preservation. This kind of social biologism has few supporters, partly because the status of the concept of 'group' is quite problematic. If we are to act in defence of a group that is 'ours' it must always be unmistakably clear which or what that group is. All the arguments, including the arguments in this book, about the situational and contextual nature of ethnicity, would run counter to a biologistic view of ethnicity.

Sociology of ethnicity: identity and action in context

The preceding section is suggesting that we should not be searching for a unitary theory of ethnicity and, equally, that 'ethnicity' is not a primary or autonomous source of action and structuration. The importance of ethnicity is conditional. We shall, therefore, attempt to set out in this final chapter a framework of argument addressing the problem of ethnicity and racism in the modern world. This requires above all that we essay a speculative sociology of modernity encompassing the place of ethnicity within it.

In the theorizing of ethnicity and modernity there are, broadly speaking, two sets of arguments. The first set deals with how ethnic identities are formed and how relationships with 'others' are articulated. The second set deals with how these ethnic identities come to take on primary importance *either* in particular circumstances, *or* in a 'totalizing' way. The key to answers to the first set of questions lies in the historical accounts of slavery and post-slavery identities, of colonial and postcolonial social orders, of labour and trader migration and settlement, of the conquest of indigenous peoples in New World societies settled by Europeans and in the – often arbitrary – making of the boundaries of modern states. The work of Barth and more recently Eriksen (Barth 1969; Eriksen 1993) shows how people can and do relate to others in ways which are designed to sustain the boundaries between communities, and how people cope when boundaries are threatened with a breach. In the present book, we have mostly concentrated on the formation of ethnic boundaries in relation to slavery and post-slavery identities, and labour and trader migration and settlement.

But the much wider questions are those addressed to the problem of the situational relevance of ethnic identities, that is towards understanding the conditions under which ethnicity becomes important or even decisive in everyday discourse and exchanges, or in major political events and conflicts. This requires an outline of a theory of modernity. It is, of course, only an 'outline', with selected features of the contemporary world singled out and highlighted, as they bear upon questions of ethnicity, nation and racism.

Late capitalism and the modern social world

In late capitalism, the twin doctrines of economic freedom and political democracy are intensified both in depth and in breadth. The 'deepening' of economic freedom, in its implications for people as individuals, is in the perpetual raising of the material stakes for consumers: what was once desirable becomes indispensable. The broadening of economic and political freedoms lies in the historical progression of extending the scope of those to whom they are seen to apply. The inner logic of a doctrine that 'all men (and women) are created equal' is that exclusions are not justifiable; those who are excluded but nonetheless 'hear' the doctrine, like African Americans or India's scheduled castes, are bound to find it to be an inexcusable and intolerable exclusion. The inner logic of a consumerist society is that no one can be exempted from the material and psychological ambitions which are proffered. Neither of these principles, one of *recognition* and the other of personal *accumulation* of material and psychological goods, can be fully realized. This is partly because they are in their nature unrealizable – we can never get enough recognition, we can never accumulate 'enough' – and partly because there are powerful contradictory tendencies in capitalist democracy. These two principles bear upon the politics of distribution and the politics of recognition (Taylor 1994). Ethnicity and racism in ethnic and nationalist politics are reinforced by the 'politics of recognition'. This would be true both of groups 'starved of recognition' and of groups (e.g. ethnic majorities) and classes who feel that their assumed pre-eminence is threatened. Ethnicity is tied into the 'politics of distribution' by the fact that access to resources follows ethnic lines, and by the way privileged minorities or a majority acquire a sense of entitlement to public and private benefits.

The problem of material distribution is relatively straightforward. Late modern capitalist societies (capitalist, post-industrial economies with an ever-increasing power and range of communications media) promise more rewards to more people than can possibly be satisfied. At the same time, there are dramatic shifts in the definition of who is useful and productive and whose skills are needed. Hence whole classes or fragments of classes are come to be seen as, and may see themselves as, 'dispensable' or outmoded. Even those who remain 'incorporated' either as the 'bankable' or as the employed but exploited classes described by Hoogvelt, may see their worth diminish or made precarious. This is a factor which we discussed in relation to ethnic groups in America: the de-industrialization of the USA has disproportionately affected groups who are least well situated to succeed in the post-industrial economy. (For the relation between ethnicity, class and economy, see Conley 1999; Fenton and Bradley 2002; Shapiro 2004; Steinberg 1981, 2000; Wilson 1980; Woo 2000; and chapter 7).

Thus universalism (as, for example, a meritocratic and equal regard for all) cannot be sustained in a continuous, progressive and undiluted fashion. In Balibar and Wallerstein's (1991) phrase, switching back and forth from universalism to particularism forms the contradictory zizzag motion of capitalist modernity. In this context, 'particular' means treating people by 'particular' criteria, including ethnic criteria. The wish to make best use of all talent and energy promises universalism; the wish to exploit some more than others leads to particularist super-exploitations of, for example, women and lowly regarded ethnic groups. Furthermore, *some* of those who are exploited and subsequently made redundant belong to a 'privileged' gender and ethnicity but a decidedly dis-privileged class. To some of them, the sight of temporary or enduring signs of success among minoritized ethnic groups and women is a classic source of *ressentiment*.

Furthermore, the speed of economic change – for example the disappearance of ship building (virtually) and coal mining (entirely) from Britain within a generation and the rapid growth of super- and hyper-markets – is also accompanied by stark changes in the social landscape. These include in Britain's case the transformation of work, of neighbourhoods and of the place of women. In work, craft skills and apprenticeships are lost, neighbourhoods become multi-ethnic, high streets lose their family grocers and hardware shops, and women appear where once only men were found. At the same time, the endless search for material satisfaction, coupled with the inability of many to realize their aims, produces cycles of rising utilitarian crime (Field 1990). The bankable classes and especially the less-favoured but employed wage-earners are some of the bitter victims of these crimes. These changes in the social landscape are experienced as a 'loss of community', the loss of a world in which people did not lock their doors, or fit alarms to their cars and houses, and knew their neighbours. These scenarios are often viewed through an ethnic lens, especially with respect to residential distributions and perceptions of neighbourhood and crime (Solomos 1993).

Global economic changes have sharpened and accelerated the changes in nation-states, whose ability to direct their own economic futures has diminished. This is true in the developing economies such as China, where vast numbers of rural village residents are drawn into the urban and manufacturing economy; and in the developed economies, where industries and indeed services that once employed many workers are shifted overseas. By 2009, these changes and the consequences of them are being exposed by the global recession.

The contradictions of late capitalist modernity

In approaching a sociology of the modern world, we need to address three problematics: the macro-sociology of economic and political formations, changes and events; the problem of social and communal cohesion; and the problem of private discontents. The sociology of right-wing populist parties in Europe (see chapter 8) illustrates this via an account of global economic change, and its repercussions for traditional working classes and for communal cohesion. These changes generate a resentment in private lives which is translated into a resentment-driven politics.

Wieviorka addresses both the 'class problematic' and the 'community problematic'. He attaches primary importance to classes within capitalism: class-based movements are essentially 'modern' in form and in principle. But he is also concerned with another and related dimension of the contemporary world and that is the persistent tension between 'individualism and community'. Wieviorka is taking his cue from Louis Dumont's distinction between 'holism and individualism', where Dumont (1986) first suggests that racism can be explained as a response to the transition from the former to the latter. Thus Dumont's account would be similar to other general accounts of the rise of a modern social order which view modernity as a 'loss of community'; this loss creates tensions which may be resolved by antagonistic or 'irrational' social movements. But Wieviorka is especially concerned not just with a transition to modernity but with *a persistent tension within modernity itself*. This concern, Wieviorka argues, is reflected in Dumont's later work:

> The problem is in fact no longer seen as one of transition, or of the mutation of one societal type into another, but rather as involving the necessary and impossible cohabitation of two modes of thinking: the old holistic one with life still in it, the new individualistic one not yet triumphant. (Wieviorka 1995, p. 29)

This Wieviorka–Dumont framework provides us with a way of thinking about 'the individual' and 'community' within the setting of late capitalism. Dumont's suggestion that racism can be partly understood as a consequence of a tension in modernity between 'individual' and 'community' could prove to be very fruitful. As Wieviorka suggests, the tension of holism–individualism becomes the basis of a theory of racism in terms of the dissociation it expresses between modernity and the particularism of the nation, or more broadly, the community (Wieviorka 1995).

In the modern world, we inhabit multiple identities in different life-situations and (partly as a consequence) internalize universalistic values. At the same time, countervailing social tendencies – many of which are described in this book – tend to reinforce communalist identities. In my view, it is at that meeting point of these contradictions that racism and ethnic conflicts are reproduced.

This way of thinking enables us to place an understanding of ethnicity, race and nation within a general understanding of the modern world and changes within it; in other words, within a general theory of modern social orders. This requires viewing 'modernity' as posing problems along two distinct if related axes: one an axis of exploitation and inequality, the second an axis of isolation and dissociation. The two are recombined through the general principle of 'individualism' since this is, in the great traditions of sociological thought, a principle of an unequal economic order (a market economy) and a principle of social organization and culture (the breaking of traditional ties and hallowing of the individual).

Individualism

Individualism was constituted *morally* and *culturally* by the cult of the individual. This was the growth of a culture in which regard for the individual and the sacredness and dignity of the individual became the ultimate human value. So the cult of the individual (Durkheim 1933; Fenton 1984), which could be equated to all those values which have been called 'universal' and the foundation of 'human rights', is a demonstration of a sociological 'law': the less collective life embraces and enfolds the individual, the more the individual breaks from the 'natal milieu', and the more society places a value on the individual. This value, or set of values, has the potential to be the foundation of a new civic morality and thus restore some of the moral binding power to a social order whose collectivities have been progressively weakened. It is a tendency which led Durkheim to believe that racial or ethnic groups would progressively lose their hold over individuals.

Two worlds – the liberal and the authoritarian

But individualism is also seen as the process of social detachment of individuals from communities, as fragmentation and isolation. Individualization is not simply a myth of modernity; *it has a foundation in the real experience of people*. At the same time, it takes on many of the characteristics of a myth in the multiple portrayals of modern life as disruptive and destructured: in most contemporary western societies and many non-western ones too, there is an abiding social imagery of a lost world of community, authority and trust. On this view, there is a time when 'people had regard for one another', 'children obeyed their parents' and no one lived in constant fear of crime. This spectre of social breakdown is a repeated and powerful theme of both politicized commentary and everyday discourse; the fact that it is part of everyday discourse is the reason why political actors always suspect or hope that they can trade on these very fears, whether they share them or not.

But in the world of moral politics there is a further contradiction: on the one hand, there is a broad group of values which comes close to Durkheim's civic morality rooted in regard for the individual, personal liberties and freedom of conscience; on the other hand, there is another diffuse set of values which places 'family values', authority, punishment and control at the head of its moral priorities and derives much of its momentum as a political force from its mocking rejection of the individualist principles. There is here a contradiction between universalistic-cosmopolitan identities and local-communal particularisms. In ethnic minority groups, especially urban migrants, the country of new settlement is perceived as devoid of moral control. In the ethnic majority population, multi-ethnicity is combined with a view of 'loss of control'. These are arguments which we discussed in chapters 6 and 8.

Four principal problematics

Capitalist modernity, then, presents a series of interlinked problematics, all of which are indicated directly or indirectly in the preceding passages. There is a *social class problematic*, where the idea of 'equality', and in particular equality of worth and of opportunity, continuously runs up against de facto inequalities both of outcome and opportunity. Sustaining ideas of equality under these circumstances is difficult.

Those who gain least learn a contrary message from real experience. Furthermore, the secure classes actively promote the idea that the 'failures' are unworthy and responsible for their own position.

There is too a *cohesion problematic*, described above as the contradiction between 'individual' and 'community'. There are real losses in community cohesion when the sociological processes of individuation press people more and more into 'individual lives' both materially and symbolically.

There is a *state and 'order' problematic*, which we have discussed in chapter 7. In many newer states, the state is barely established as the guarantor of material and legal security, let alone of advanced individual rights. In 'established' states, the state machinery is the repository of procedures for the protection of individual rights; thus the state may make extraordinary interventions to defend a humane principle. Such was the case in Britain when the courts insisted on the release of child-murderers on reaching maturity. Here the state acted to protect individual dignity against a background of moral outrage. In other instances, the state utterly fails the test of universality, as evidenced by the treatment of minorities in custody.

There is, fourthly, a *morality problematic*, which transcends each of the first three. This lies in the opposition between sanctity values and control values. Sanctity values are the ones which are often seen as being 'on the side of modernity' – progress, individual freedoms, moral 'liberations'. Control values are the ones which are on the side of common sense, common experience and authority. Sanctity values support an end to physical punishments because they demean the individual; control values support punishment because it is 'common sense' that miscreants will respond to 'toughness'.

Progressive responses are grounded in the wish to realize universalism. In the political space, we find those movements of minority ethnic groups which are directed towards the realization of civil rights and the removal of barriers to inclusion and mobility. The fact that 'minorities' in pursuit of their interests also express the interests of everybody indicates that they are giving voice to values – universalist human rights – which are in principle held by all. Hence Martin Luther King was able to speak of realizing the American Dream; he was setting out the terms of existence for an America which was not just a better place for black Americans but a better place for all Americans. Most (but definitely not all) social movements, of under-recognized populations and of people who are socially and economically excluded, are capable of assuming this universalist voice. But some responses, driven by *ressentiment*, typically press in quite the opposite direction (see chapter 8). It is here that we find the links between *ressentiment*, modernity, racism and the crises of national identity. For some, the 'opening up' of cultural and political space to previously disregarded communities is precisely the kind of apprehension of threat which generates feelings of *ressentiment*.

Modernity and ethnicity

In the immediately preceding passages I have tried to sketch out some of the sociological themes of the modern world – or late capitalist modernity – whilst 'trailing' themes of ethnicity through the argument. Although this is very much a 'contextualization' of ethnicity, nonetheless many familiar ethnic themes are apparent.

1 *Class and ethnicity:* Ethnic identities cannot be reduced to class experience but class experience and class culture give shape or form to ethnicity especially when class fortunes and ethnic fortunes are closely allied.

2 *Social mobility and individuation:* A key theme of much interest in ethnicity is social mobility and the effect of social mobility on ethnic solidarity. The same is true of residential mobility and community formation. By and large, the sociological argument has been that social mobility undermines ethnic solidarity. The politics of equal opportunities is also about social mobility – rather than social distribution. The evidence of class-ethnic concentrations is taken as an indictment of the opportunity structure.

3 *Individual and collective dignity:* In disadvantaged ethnic groups the routine unequal treatment of group members means that individuals are likely to experience the slight on the group as a slight on themselves. The options are to identify and 'fight' or to dis-identify in order to escape the prejudices towards the group.

4 *Racism and ethnicity:* The social changes of modernity are met with both exhilaration and apprehension. Ethnic majorities, or rather some among them, raise their voices against new sexuality mores, failures of punishment and social order, gender equalities – and multi-ethnicity. Rather dolefully, this makes racism appear not as an aberration from modernity but as a feature of it. More optimistically, the *ressentiment* and control values do not always succeed; rather they remain in tension with sanctity values.

This merely sketches out how an integration of sociological themes of ethnicity with sociological themes of modernity might take shape. In the final paragraphs of this chapter, we try to re-state some principal themes of the book.

Ethnicity in its place

In this book we have attempted two things: first, to provide a clear introduction to the field of ethnicity, and second, to essay an interpretation of the place of ethnicity in the contemporary world. In the 'introductory' phase, mostly the first four chapters, we examined the defining meanings of 'ethnicity' and 'ethnic group' and closely related terms.

In the first chapter, we considered the possible meanings of the term 'ethnic' and of the closely related words 'race' and 'nation'. An etymological view of the terms 'ethnic' ('group'), 'race' and 'nation' showed that there is a very considerable core of shared meaning and that this refers to the idea of 'our people', 'our origins' and the concepts of descent and ancestry. Since ethnicity is always relational, it can also mean '*those* people' with '*their* origins and ancestry'. The shared core of meaning is revealed by the fact that each of these words appears in the definitions of the other two. 'Ethnic group' and 'racial group' (or 'race') are particularly closely allied and there is considerable support for abandoning 'race' and replacing it with 'ethnic group'. The US Census, for example, has recognized these difficulties but continues to use the concept of race, whilst disavowing the idea of race as a biological classificatory system (Rodriguez 2000). And the US Census still uses a terminology (e.g. 'Asian', 'White or Caucasian') which is remarkably similar to the categories of nineteenth-century racial theory (Hollinger 1995).

In chapter 2, we explored how, in popular consciousness, in the political imagination and in academic debates, the history of a particular country or region influences the discourses and languages of ethnicity. For example, the American distinction between 'race' and 'ethnicity' would have no obvious meaning in Malaysia where in English 'races' and 'ethnic groups' are used interchangeably and in Bahasa Malaysia, Malaysia's official language, both are captured by the term *bangsa*. In the USA, 'ethnic groups' has acquired an association with whiteness, and with the countries of origin of successive European immigrations; in the UK, 'ethnic groups' has an association with non-whiteness. The idea of whites as an ethnic majority in the UK, which we discussed later, has scarcely taken hold. In chapter 3, we saw how the words 'ethnic' and 'ethnic group' had been used in some early scholarly work, including Robert Park and Lloyd Warner in the USA; and in the classic work of Max Weber.

Chapter 4 addressed the question of 'primordialism', whether ethnic groups can be regarded as naturally occurring social groups, or basic forms of social belonging. The primordialism debate had been informed, we argued, by a misunderstanding of Geertz's landmark essay, in particular of three analytically distinct issues. These could be summed up in three questions: Are ethnic groups real? Are ethnic groups corporate? Are ethnic 'motives' calculated? The first is a debate about 'social construction' wherein ethnicities are not seen as somehow 'fundamental' but as dependent on the way they are defined by 'us', by 'them' and by the state. The second is about the extent to which groups and communities defined as ethnic have any form of corporate organization. And the third is about the nature of ethnicity as a calculated affiliation as against an unreflective status and identity. Here we drove a broad path right up the middle of these arguments. Ethnicities are, in our phrase, 'grounded' as well as constructed. Ethnic identities take shape around real, shared material experience, shared social space, commonalities of socialization and communities of language and culture. Simultaneously, these identities have a public presence; they are socially defined in a series of presentations (public statements, assertions, images) by ethnic group members and non-members alike. These social definitions are part of the continuous construction and reconstruction of ethnic identities. The second and the third elements are in fact variable features of ethnic groups. They vary from highly organized groups to what Nagata called 'diffuse identities'. Similarly, ethnic groups vary in the degree of collective self-consciousness and thus in the extent to which individual and collective action is calculated or instrumental in the pursuit of ethnic ends.

In chapter 5, we turned to a relational model of ethnic groups. The question is not so much 'how do we define a group and group membership?' but 'how and when do individuals bring ethnic identities into "play" in their relationships with others?' We examined the work of the anthropologist Barth, whose work has made an enduring contribution via the concept of 'ethnic boundary'. This suggests that the crucial social action is the maintenance of boundaries in the relationship of ethnic groups. This represents a significant shift away from a conceptualization of ethnic groups as groups who differ by culture. This concept of ethnic boundary was deployed by competition theory, applied in cases of anti-progressive voting, violence against black Americans, the spread of the Ku Klux Klan and resistance to de-segregation in schooling. In the last part of the chapter, we discussed a critical argument against 'groupism' in theoretical approaches to ethnicity. In this chapter and later chapters, we addressed two key questions: In what contexts are ethnic identities formed? And in what circumstances do these identities assume importance for structure and action? This latter question contains within it the assumption that ethnic identities and cultural difference may be present in any society *but their relevance for action can change* quite dramatically for reasons which lie outside the ethnicities themselves.

In later chapters of the book, we move from the key terms of the subject and key items of the literature, and towards the *application* of explanatory and interpretative models. The emphasis here is on the exploration of the sociological conditions of ethnically informed action and structure. One of these conditions is the movement of peoples within countries, from country to country and across regions and continents. These movements have been both under compulsion and voluntary and all the historical evidence suggests that this difference is crucial to subsequent social outcomes (Ogbu 1987; Steinberg 2000). Some of these movements were established during the period of New World slavery (Degler 1971; Marx 1998), some during the colonial regimes of the nineteenth century and first half of the twentieth century (Fenton 1999) and yet others in the great nineteenth-century migrations from Europe to North America (Handlin 1973). Most of these migrations were of agricultural and industrial workers. Some were movements of traders, such as the establishment of Chinese trading communities in South East Asia. By the end of the twentieth and start of the new century, these labouring and trader migrants are joined by professional workers who migrate to the nodal points of demand for intellectual and professional services (Castles 2000; Khoser and Salt 1997). In the USA since the 1960s, there has been a change in the source countries of immigration, with increased in-migration from Asian countries and Central and South America. This has influenced the ethnic composition of several zones in the USA, but especially Los Angeles and the American southwest.

People who move in this way clearly 'carry with them' cultural and visible differences which become established as group difference in the new context. These movements also have a class character, so that migrant groups acquire a class *and* ethnic distinctiveness (e.g. Jamaican nurses in Britain). A great deal of the sociology of ethnic groups is concerned with the class position and social mobility of migrants. As John Rex has correctly argued (Rex and Tomlinson 1979), indigenous workers are likely to protect their own class gains against the claims of newcomers. This question takes on significance in social policy too, as governments give formal backing to 'equal opportunities' for minorities. Thus 'ethnic relations' take on a class character, and class processes take on an ethnic character.

In chapter 7, the main 'conditions' of ethnicity which we examined were the insecurity of the state and global inequalities. In insecure or precarious states individuals cannot rely upon the rule of law to protect them physically, materially or in terms of civic human rights. Where ethnic, regional, cultural and language differences exist, they provide an alternative support and system of trust. Under these circumstances, and especially if the state itself is closely identified with one ethnic (regional, language) group, ethnic group affiliation can become not just important but crucial and fateful. We also discussed economic inequalities in the developed world, notably the USA and the case of Los Angeles. In chapter 8, we traced out a sociology of late capitalist modernity in which majority and minority ethnicities are politicized within the contexts of modern discontents. This we have argued, in this final chapter, was an illustration of the need to integrate the sociology of ethnicity with the sociology of modernity and the modern world. In this argument, the fusion of ethnicity with nationalism and racism is made evident.

We have therefore, in this book, sought to clarify the meaning of the discourse of ethnicity, and its closely related discourses of race and racism and nationalism. We have done so by seeking to embed the sociology of ethnicity in a broader sociological discourse, a sociology which escapes the narrow confines of a cultural sociology of ethnic groups and re-inserts ethnicity into a sociology of class, community and power.

Bibliography

Alba R., 1999, Immigration and the American realities of assimilation and multiculturalism, *Sociological Forum*, 14(1): 3–25.

Alba R. and Nee V., 1997, Rethinking assimilation theory for a new era of immigration, *International Migration Review*, 31(4): 826–74.

American Community Survey Report – Blacks, 2004, February 2007, Washington DC: US Census Bureau.

Andaya B. W. and Andaya L. Y., 2001, *A History of Malaysia* (2nd edn), Basingstoke: Palgrave.

Anderson B., 1983, *Imagined Communities: Reflections on the Origin and Spread of Nationalism*, London: Verso.

Anderson B., 2000, *Doing the Dirty Work? The Global Politics of Domestic Labour*, London and New York: Zed Books.

Anderson E., 2000, *Beyond the Melting Pot* reconsidered, *International Migration Review*, 34(1): 262–70.

Anthias F. and Yuval-Davis N. in association with Cain H., 1992, *Racialised Boundaries: Race, Nation, Gender, Colour and Class and the Anti-racist Struggle*, London: Routledge.

Balibar E. and Wallerstein I., 1991, *Race, Nation, and Class: Ambiguous Identities*, London: Verso.

Ballard R. (ed.), 1994, *Desh Pardesh: The South Asian Presence in Britain*, London: Hurst.

Ballard R. and Ballard C., 1977, The Sikhs: the development of South Asian settlements in Britain, in Watson J. L. (ed.), *Between Two Cultures: Migrants and Minorities in Britain*, Oxford: Blackwell, pp. 21–56.

Banks M., 1996, *Ethnicity: Anthropological Constructions*, London: Routledge.

Banton M., 1977, *The Idea of Race*, London: Tavistock.

Banton M., 1983, *Racial and Ethnic Competition*, Cambridge: Cambridge University Press.

Banton M., 1987, *Racial Theories*, Cambridge: Cambridge University Press.

Banton M., 1995, Rational choice theories, *American Behavioral Scientist*, 38(3): 478–97.

Banton M., 2000, Ethnic conflict, *Sociology*, 34(3): 481–98.

Banton M., 2007, Max Weber on 'ethnic communities': a critique, *Nations and Nationalism*, 13(1): 19–35.

Barret J. and Roediger D., 1997, In between people: race, nationality and the 'New Immigrant' working class, *Journal of American Ethnic History*, 16(3): 3–44.

Barry B., 2001, *Culture and Equality: An Egalitarian Critique of Multiculturalism*, Cambridge: Polity.

Barth F. (ed.), 1969, *Ethnic Groups and Boundaries: The Social Organization of Culture Difference*, London: Allen and Unwin.

Barzun J., 1965, *Race: A Study in Superstition*, New York: Harper and Row.

Bauman Z., 1989, *Modernity and the Holocaust*, Cambridge: Polity.

Bauman Z., 2006, *Identity*, Cambridge: Polity.

Baumann G., 1996, *Contesting Cultures: Discourses of Identity in Multi–ethnic London*, Cambridge: Cambridge University Press.

BBC News online, 8 December 2006, 'Conform to our society says PM': http://news.bbc.co.uk/1/hi/uk_politics/6219626.stm: consulted 25 February 2008.

Bélanger S. and Pinard M., 1991, Ethnic movements and the competition model: some missing links, *American Sociological Review*, 56(4): 446–57.

Benn Michaels W., 2006, *The Trouble with Diversity*, New York: Holt.

Bennett C., 1995, *Yugoslavia's Bloody Collapse: Causes, Course and Consequences*, London: Hurst.

Bennett C., 2000, Racial categories used in the decennial censuses, 1790 to the present, *Government Information Quarterly*, 17(2): 161–80.

Billig M., 1995, *Banal Nationalism*, London: Sage.

Blalock H. M., 1967, *Towards a Theory of Minority-Group Relations*, New York: Wiley.

Bloemraad I., 2006, Becoming a citizen in the United States and Canada: structured mobilization and immigrant political incorporation, *Social Forces*, 85(2): 667–95.

Blumer H., 1958, Race prejudice as a sense of group position, *Pacific Sociological Review*, 1(1): 3–7.

Boas F., 1982, *Race, Language and Culture*, Chicago: University of Chicago Press.

Bobo L., 1983, Whites' opposition to busing: symbolic racism or realistic group conflict?, *Journal of Personality and Social Psychology*, 45(6): 1196–210.

Bonacich, E., 1972, A theory of ethnic antagonism: the split labor market, *American Sociological Review*, 37(5): 547–59.

Bonacich E., 1973, A theory of middleman minorities, *American Sociological Review*, 38(5): 583–94.

Bonacich E., 1975, Abolition, the extension of slavery, and the position of free blacks: a study of split labor markets in the United States, 1830–1863, *American Journal of Sociology*, 81(3): 601–28.

Bourdieu P., 1990, *In Other Words: Essays towards a Reflexive Sociology*, Cambridge: Polity.

Bradley H., 1996, *Fractured Identities: Changing Patterns of Inequality*, Cambridge: Polity.

Brass P. R. (ed.), 1985, *Ethnic Groups and the State*, Beckenham: Croom Helm.

Brass P. R., 1991, *Ethnicity and Nationalism: Theory and Comparison*, New Delhi: Sage.

Breuilly J., Cesarani D., Maleŝević S., Neuberger B. and Mann M., 2006, Debate on Michael Mann's *The Dark Side of Democracy: Explaining Ethnic Cleansing*, Nations and Nationalism, 12(3): 389–411.

Brown C., 1984, *Black and White Britain: The Third PSI Survey*, London: Heinemann.

Brown D., 2000, *Contemporary Nationalism: Civic, Ethnic and Multicultural Politics*, London: Routledge.

Brown M. E., 2001, *Nationalism and Ethnic Conflict* (revised edn), Cambridge, MA: MIT Press.

Brubaker R., 1996, *Nationalism Reframed: Nationhood and the National Question in the New Europe*, Cambridge: Cambridge University Press.

Brubaker R., 2002, Ethnicity without groups, *Archives Européennes de sociologie*, 43(2): 163–89.

Brubaker R., 2003, Neither individualism nor 'groupism': a reply to Craig Calhoun, *Ethnicities*, 3(4): 553–7.

Brubaker R., 2004, *Ethnicity without Groups*, Cambridge, MA: Harvard University Press.

Brubaker R. and Laitin D. D., 1998, Ethnic and nationalist violence, *Annual Review of Sociology*, 24: 423–52.

Bulmer M. and Solomos J. (eds), 2000, *Racism*, Oxford: Oxford University Press.

Calandruccio G., 2005, A review of recent research on human trafficking in the Middle East, *International Migration*, 43(1/2): 267–99.

Califa A. J., 1989, Declaring English the official language: prejudice spoken here, *Harvard Civil Rights-Civil Liberties Law Review*, 24(2): 293.

Camejo P., 1976, *Racism Revolution Reaction, 1861–1877*, New York: Monda Press.

Carvalho J. A. M., 2004, Estimating the stability of census-based racial/ethnic classifications: the case of Brazil, *Population Studies*, 58(3): 331–43.

Cashmore E. E., 1987, *The Logic of Racism*, London: Allen and Unwin.

Castles S., 2000, *Ethnicity and Globalization*, London: Sage.

Castles S., 2003, Why migration policies fail, *Ethnic and Racial Studies*, 27(2): 205–27.

Castles S. and Miller M. J., 1993, *The Age of Migration: International Population Movements in the Modern World*, Basingstoke: Macmillan.

Cohen A. (ed.), 1974, *Urban Ethnicity*, London: Tavistock.

Colley L., 1992, *Britons: Forging the Nation 1707–1837*, New Haven, CT and London: Yale University Press.

Commission on the Future of Multi-Ethnic Britain (The Parekh Report), 2000, *The Future of Multi-Ethnic Britain*, London: Profile Books.

Condor S., 2000, Pride and prejudice: identity management in English people's talk about 'this country', *Discourse and Society*, 11(2): 175–205.

Conley D., 1999, *Being Black, Living in the Red*, Berkeley: University of California Press.

Conversi D., 2000, Autonomous communities and the ethnic settlement in Spain, in Ghai Y. (ed.), *Autonomy and Ethnicity: Negotiating Competing Claims in Multi-ethnic States*, Cambridge: Cambridge University Press, pp. 122–46.

Coope A. E. (ed.), 1993, *Hippocrene Standard Dictionary: Malay–English, English–Malay Dictionary*, New York: Hippocrene Books.

Cornelius W., 2005, Controlling 'unwanted' immigration: lessons from the United States, 1993–2004, *Journal of Ethnic and Migration Studies*, 31(4): 775–94.

Cornell S., 1996, The variable ties that bind: content and circumstance in ethnic processes, *Ethnic and Racial Studies*, 19(2): 265–89.

Creech J. C., Corzine J. and Huff-Corzine L., 1989, Theory testing and lynching: another look at the power threat hypothesis, *Social Forces*, 67(3): 626–30.

Cunningham D. and Phillips B. T., 2007, Context for mobilization: spatial settings and Klan presence in North Carolina, 1964–1966, *American Journal of Sociology*, 113(3): 781–814.

Darder A. and Torres R. D., 2004, *After Race: Racism after Multiculturalism*, New York and London: New York University Press.

Davis A., Gardner B. and Gardner M., 1941, *Deep South: A Social Anthropological Study of Caste and Class*, Chicago: University of Chicago Press.

Davis F. J., 2001, *Who is Black?: One Nation's Definition*, University Park: Pennsylvania State University Press.

Davis M., 2001, *Magical Urbanism: Latinos Reinvent the City*, London: Verso.

Degler C. N., 1971, *Neither Black nor White: Slavery and Race Relations in Brazil and the United States*, New York: Macmillan.

DeWind J. and Kasinitz P., 1997, Everything old is new again? Processes and theories of immigrant incorporation, *International Migration Review*, 31(4): 1096–111.

Diamond L. and Plattner M. F. (eds), 1994, *Nationalism, Ethnic Conflict and Democracy*, Baltimore: Johns Hopkins University Press.

Dikotter F., 1992, *The Discourse of Race in Modern China*, Stanford: Stanford University Press.

Dollard J., 1937, *Caste and Class in a Southern Town: White Caste Aggression against Negroes*, New York: Doubleday.

Dumont L., 1986, *Essays on Individualism: Modern Ideology in Anthropological Perspective*, Chicago: University of Chicago Press.

Durkheim E., 1893, *De la division du travail social*, Paris: Alcan.

Durkheim E., 1933, *The Division of Labour in Society*, New York: Macmillan.

Eatwell R., 2000, The rebirth of the 'extreme right' in Western Europe?, *Parliamentary Affairs*, 53 (July): 407–25.

Ejiogu E. C., 2001, The roots of political instability in an artificial 'nation-state': the case of Nigeria, *International Journal of Comparative Sociology*, 42(3): 323–43.

Eller J. D. and Coughlan R. M., 1993, The poverty of primordialism: the demystification of ethnic attachments, *Ethnic and Racial Studies*, 16(2): 185–202.

Epstein A. L., 1978, *Ethos and Identity*, London: Tavistock.

Eriksen T. H., 1993, *Ethnicity and Nationalism: Anthropological Perspectives*, London: Pluto Press.

Esman M. J., 2004, *An Introduction to Ethnic Conflict*, Cambridge: Polity.

Evans-Pritchard E. E., 1962, *Essays in Social Anthropology*, London: Faber.

Faist T., 1995, Ethnicization and racialization of welfare-state politics in Germany and the USA, *Ethnic and Racial Studies*, 18(2): 219–50.

Feagin J. R., 1991, The continuing significance of race: anti-black discrimination in public places, *American Sociological Review*, 56(1): 101–16.

Fearon J. D. and Laitin D., 1996, Explaining interethnic cooperation, *American Political Science Review*, 90(4): 715–35.

Feng W., Zuo X. and Ruan D., 2002, Rural migrants in Shanghai: living under the shadow of socialism, *International Migration Review*, 36(2): 520–45.

Fenton S., 1980, Race, class and politics in the work of Emile Durkheim, in *Sociological Theories: Race and Colonialism*, Paris: UNESCO, pp. 43–82.

Fenton S., 1981, Robert Park: his life and sociological imagination, *New Community*, 9(2): 294–301.

Fenton S., 1984, *Durkheim and Modern Sociology*, Cambridge: Cambridge University Press.

Fenton S., 1996, Counting ethnicity: social groups and official categories, in Levitas R. and Guy W. (eds), *Interpreting Official Statistics*, London: Routledge, pp. 143–65.

Fenton S., 1999, *Ethnicity: Racism, Class and Culture*, London: Macmillan.

Fenton S., 2004, Beyond ethnicity: the global comparative analysis of ethnic conflict, *International Journal of Comparative Sociology*, 45(3–4): 179–94.

Fenton S., 2006, Race and nation, in Kumar K. and Delanty G. (eds), *Handbook of Nations and Nationalism*, London: Sage.

Fenton S., 2007, Indifference towards national identity: what young adults think about being English and British, *Nations and Nationalism*, 13(2): 321–39.

Fenton S. and Bradley H. (eds), 2002, *Ethnicity and Economy: 'Race and Class' Revisited*, London: Palgrave.

Fenton S. and May S. (eds), 2003, *Ethnonational Identities*, London: Palgrave.

Field S., 1990, *Trends in Crime and Their Interpretation*, London: HMSO.

Frankenberg R., 1993, *White Women Race Matters: The Social Construction of Whiteness*, Minneapolis: University of Minnesota Press.

Fredrickson G. M., 1972, *The Black Image in the White Mind: The Debate on Afro American Character and Destiny, 1817–1914*, New York: Torchbook, Harper and Row.

Fredrickson G. M., 1988, *The Arrogance of Race: Historical Perspectives on Slavery, Racism and Social Inequality*, Hanover, NH: Wesleyan University Press.

Freyre G., 1959, *New World in the Tropics: The Culture of Modern Brazil*, New York: Knopf and Random House.

Gans H., 1979, Symbolic ethnicity: the future of ethnic groups and culture in America, *Ethnic and Racial Studies*, 2(1): 1–20.

Gans H., 1994, Symbolic ethnicity and symbolic religiosity: towards a comparison of ethnic and religious acculturation, *Ethnic and Racial Studies*, 17(4): 577–92.

Gans H., 1997, Toward a reconciliation of 'assimilation' and 'pluralism': the interplay of acculturation and ethnic retention, *International Migration Review*, 31(4): 875–92.

Geertz C., 1973, *The Interpretation of Cultures*, New York: Basic Books.

Ghai Y. (ed.), 2000, *Autonomy and Ethnicity: Negotiating Competing Claims in Multi-ethnic States*, Cambridge: Cambridge University Press.

Gilens M., 1996, 'Race coding' and white opposition to welfare, *American Political Science Review*, 90(3): 593–604.

Gil-White F. J., 1999, How thick is blood? The plot thickens . . . if ethnic actors are primordialists, what remains of the circumstantialist-primordialist controversy?, *Ethnic and Racial Studies*, 22(5): 789–820.

Glazer N. and Moynihan D. P., 1963, *Beyond the Melting Pot*, Cambridge, MA: Harvard University Press (reprinted MIT Press, 1970).

Glazer N. and Moynihan D. P. (eds), 1975, *Ethnicity: Theory and Experience*, Cambridge, MA: Harvard University Press.

Golder M., 2003, Explaining variation in the success of extreme right parties in Western Europe, *Comparative Political Studies*, 36(4): 432–66.

Goldman Sachs Global Economic Research, 2007, *BRICs and Beyond*, London: Goldman Sachs Group.

Gordon M., 1964, *Assimilation in American Life: The Role of Race, Religion, and National Origins*, New York: Oxford University Press.

Gossett T. F., 1965, *Race, the History of an Idea in America*, New York: Schocken Books.

Gottlieb R., Vallianatos M., Freer R. M. and Dreier P., 2005, *The Next Los Angeles: The Struggle for a Liveable City*, Berkeley: University of California Press.

Grebler L., Moore J. and Guzman R. C., 1970, *The Mexican American People*, New York: Free Press.

Greenfeld L., 1992, *Nationalism: Five Roads to Modernity*, Cambridge, MA: Harvard University Press.

Guibernau M. and Rex J. (eds), 1997, *The Ethnicity Reader: Nationalism, Multiculturalism and Migration*, Cambridge: Polity.

Hall J. A., 1998, *The State of the Nation: Ernest Gellner and the Theory of Nationalism*, Cambridge: Cambridge University Press.

Handlin O., 1973, *The Uprooted*, Boston: Little, Brown.

Hartman A., 2004, The rise and fall of whiteness studies, *Race Class*, 46(2): 22–38.

Hechter M., 1995, Explaining nationalist violence, *Nations and Nationalism*, 1(1): 53–68.

Held D. and McGrew A. (eds), 2000, *The Global Transformations Reader*, Cambridge: Polity.

Hirschman C., 1986, The meaning and measurement of ethnicity in Malaysia, *Journal of Asian Studies*, 46(3): 552–82.

Hirschman C., 1987, The making of race in colonial Malaya: political economy and racial ideology, *Sociological Forum*, 1(2): 330–61.

Hirschman C., Alba R. and Farley R., 2000, The meaning and measurement of race in the US Census: glimpses into the future, *Demography*, 37(3): 381–93.

Hirst P. and Thompson G., 1999, *Globalization in Question*, Cambridge: Polity.

Hobsbawm E. and Ranger T. (eds), 1983, *The Invention of Tradition*, Cambridge: Cambridge University Press.

Hollinger D. A., 1995, *Postethnic America: Beyond Multiculturalism*, New York: Basic Books.

Holmes D. R., 2000, *Integral Europe: Fast Capitalism, Multiculturalism, Neofascism*, Princeton: Princeton University Press.

Hoogvelt A., 2000, Globalization and the postcolonial world, in Held D. and McGrew A. (eds), *The Global Transformations Reader*, Cambridge: Polity, pp. 355–60.

Horowitz D. L., 1989, Incentives and behavior in the ethnic politics of Sri Lanka and Malaysia, *Third World Quarterly*, 14(4): 18–35.

Hughey M. W. (ed.), 1998, *New Tribalisms: The Resurgence of Race and Ethnicity*, London: Macmillan.

Hutchinson J. and Smith A. D. (eds), 1996, *Ethnicity*, Oxford: Oxford University Press.

Huxley J. and Haddon A. C., 1935, *We Europeans*, London: Cape.

Ignatiev N., 1995, *How the Irish Became White*, New York: Routledge.

International Herald Tribune, 21 October 2008, Indian politician arrested for migrant violence.

Jacobs D. and Tope D., 2007, The politics of resentment in the post-civil rights era: minority threat, homicide, and ideological voting in Congress, *American Journal of Sociology*, 112(5): 1458–94.

Jacobson J., 1997a, Perceptions of Britishness, *Nations and Nationalism*, 3(2): 181–200.

Jacobson J., 1997b, Religion and ethnicity: dual and alternative sources of identity among young British Pakistanis, *Ethnic and Racial Studies*, 20(2): 238–56.

Jacobson, M. F., 1998, *Whiteness of a Different Color: European Immigrants and the Alchemy of Race*, Cambridge, MA: Harvard University Press.

Janša J., 1994, *The Making of the Slovenian State, 1988–1992: The Collapse of Yugoslavia*, Ljubljana: Mladinska Knijga Publishing House.

Johnson J. H., Farrell W. C. and Guinn C., 1997, Immigration reform and the browning of America: tensions, conflicts and community instability in Metropolitan Los Angeles, *International Migration Review*, 31(4): 1055–95.

Joppke C., 1996, Multiculturalism and immigration: a comparison of the United States, Germany, and Great Britain, *Theory and Society*, 25(4): 449–500.

Joppke C., 2001, Multicultural citizenship: a critique, *Archives Européennes de sociologie*, 42(2): 431–47.

Joppke C., 2004, The retreat of multiculturalism in the liberal state: theory and policy, *British Journal of Sociology*, 55(2): 237–57.

Jordan W., 1968, *White Over Black*, Baltimore: Penguin.

Kasinitz P., Mollenkopf J. and Waters M., 2002, Becoming American/becoming New Yorkers: immigrant incorporation in a majority minority city, *International Migration Review*, 36(4): 1020–36.

Kasinitz P., Mollenkopf J., Waters M. and Holdaway J., 2008, *Inheriting the City: The Children of Immigrants Come of Age*, Cambridge, MA: Harvard University Press.

Khoser K. and Salt J., 1997, The geography of highly skilled migration, *International Journal of Population Geography*, 3: 285–303.

Kinloch G. C., 1981, Comparative race and ethnic relations, *International Journal of Comparative Sociology*, 22(3–4): 257–71.

Koopmans R., Statham P., Giugni P. and Passy F., 2005, *Contested Citizenship: Immigration and Ethnic Relations Politics in Europe*, Minneapolis: Minnesota University Press.

Kriesi H., Grande E., Lachat R., Dolezal M., Bornschier S. and Frey T., 2006, Globalization and the transformation of the national political space: six European countries compared, *European Journal of Political Research*, 45(6): 921–56.

Kumar, K., 2003, *The Making of English National Identity*, Cambridge: Cambridge University Press.

Kymlicka W., 1995, *Multicultural Citizenship: A Liberal Theory of Minority Rights*, Oxford: Oxford University Press.

Lake D. A. and Rothchild D., 1996, Containing fear: the origin and management of ethnic conflict, *International Security*, 21(2): 41–75.

Lawson S., 1992, Constitutional change in Fiji, the apparatus of justification, *Ethnic and Racial Studies*, 15(1): 61–84.

Lawson S., 1997, *The Failure of Democratic Politics in Fiji*, Oxford: Oxford University Press.

Lawson S., 2004, Nationalism versus constitutionalism in Fiji, *Nations and Nationalism*, 10(4): 519–38.

Leach E. R., 1982, *Social Anthropology*, Glasgow: Fontana.

Lee M. A. and Mather M., 2008, US labor force trends, *Population Bulletin*, 63(2).

Lee S. M., 1993, Racial classification in the US Census 1890–1990, *Ethnic and Racial Studies*, 16(1): 75–94.

Leigh M., 1975, The population of Sarawak: baseline rural mapping of rural ethnic distribution prior to the new economic policy, *Sarawak Gazette* 1975–6 (reprinted in *Monographs of Institute of East Asian Studies*, University of Malaysia, Sarawak, 2000).

Liddell, H. G. and Scott R., 1897, *A Greek–English Lexicon*, Oxford: Clarendon Press.

Lind A., 1968, *An Island Community: Ecological Succession in Hawaii*, Westport, CT: Greenwood Press.

Little D., 1994, *Sri Lanka: The Invention of Enmity*, Washington DC: United States Institute of Peace Press.

López D. E. and Stanton-Salazar R. D., 2001, Mexican Americans: a second generation at risk, in Rumbaut R. and Portes A. (eds), *Ethnicities: Children of Immigrants in America*, Berkeley: University of California Press.

Lott J., 1998, *Asian Americans: From Racial Category to Multiple Identities*, London: Altamira Press.

Lu C., Menju T. and Williams M., 2005, Japan and the 'Other': reconceiving Japanese citizenship in the era of globalization, *Asian Perspective*, 29(1): 19–34.

Lubbers M. L., Gijsberts M. and Scheepers P., 2002, Extreme right-wing voting in Western Europe, *European Journal of Political Research*, 41(3): 345–78.

Magas B., 1993, *The Destruction of Yugoslavia: Tracing the Break Up 1980–1992*, London: New Left Books.

Malik K., 1996, *The Meaning of Race: Race, History and Culture in Western Society*, London: Macmillan.

Mandler P., 2006, *The English National Character: The History of an Idea from Edmund Burke to Tony Blair*, New Haven, CT and London: Yale University Press.

Mann M., 2005, *The Dark Side of Democracy: Explaining Ethnic Cleansing*, Cambridge: Cambridge University Press.

Marcus J., 1995, *The National Front and French Politics: The Resistible Rise of Jean-Marie Le Pen*, New York: New York University Press.

Martin P. and Martin S., 2006, GCIM: a new global migration facility, *International Migration*, 44(1): 5–12.

Marx A. W., 1998, *Making Race and Nation: A Comparison of South Africa, the United States and Brazil*, Cambridge: Cambridge University Press.

Massey D. and Denton N., 1993, *American Apartheid and the Making of the American Underclass*, Cambridge, MA: Harvard University Press.

Matsumoto M., 2008, *Making Koreans Japanese? Teachers' Mis-recognition and Non-recognition of Cultural Difference*, unpublished doctoral dissertation, University of Bristol.

Mauzy D. K. and Milne R. S., 1999, *Malaysian Politics under Mahathir*, London: Routledge.

Meyer J. B., Kaplan D. and Charum J., 2001, *Scientific Knowledge and the New Geo-politics of Knowledge*, Oxford: UNESCO.

Michaels W. B., 2006, *The Trouble with Diversity: How We Learned to Love Identity and Ignore Inequality*, New York: Holt.

Miller D., 1995, 'Reflections on British national identity', *Journal of Ethnic and Migration Studies* (incorporating *New Community*), 21(2): 49.

Mirza H. S. (ed.), 1997, *Black British Feminism, a Reader*, London: Routledge.

Modood T., 2007, *Multiculturalism: A Civic Idea*, Cambridge: Polity.

Modood T., Berthoud R., Lakey J., Nazroo J. and Smith P., 1997, *Ethnic Minorities in Britain, Diversity and Disadvantage*, London: Policy Studies Institute.

Morning A., 2008, Ethnic classification in global perspective: a cross-national survey of the 2000 Census round, *Population Research Policy Review*, 27(2): 239–72.

Morris H. S., 1968, Ethnic groups, in Sills D. L. (ed.), *International Encyclopedia of the Social Sciences*, New York: Macmillan Free Press.

Nagata J. A., 1974, What is a Malay? Situational selection of ethnic identity in a plural society, *American Ethnologist*, 1(2): 331–50.

Nagata J. A., 1981, In defence of ethnic boundaries: the changing myths and charters of Malay identity, in Keyes C. (ed.), *Ethnic Change*, Seattle: University of Washington Press, pp. 87–116.

Nagel J., 1995, Resource competition theories, *American Behavioural Scientist*, 38(3): 442–58.

National Intelligence Council, Council on Foreign Relations, 2008, *Global Trends 2025: A Transformed World – the National Intelligence Council's 2025 Project*, Washington DC: US Government Printing Office.

Neckerman K. M., Carter P. and Lee J., 1999, Segmented assimilation and minority cultures of mobility, *Ethnic and Racial Studies*, 22(6): 945–65.

New Straits Times, 1 December 2000, BN committed to ethnic cooperation despite loss.

New Straits Times, 17 April 2001, Bumiputera traders must be bold and emulate other races to succeed.

New Straits Times, 19 April 2001, Chinese seek knowledge earnestly, Malays don't.

Nisbet R. A., 1967, *The Sociological Tradition*, London: Heinemann Educational.

OECD (Organization for Economic Cooperation and Development), 2002, *International Mobility of the Highly Skilled*, Paris: OECD.

Oesch D., 2008, Explaining workers' support for right-wing populist parties in Western Europe: evidence from Austria, Belgium, France, Norway and Switzerland, *International Political Science Review*, 29(3): 349–73.

Ogbu J., 1987, Variability in minority school performance: a problem in search of an explanation, *Anthropology and Education Quarterly*, 18(4): 312–14.

Oliver M. and Shapiro, T., 1995, *Black Wealth/White Wealth: A New Perspective on Racial Inequality*, New York: Routledge.

Olzak S., 1989, Labor unrest, immigration and ethnic conflict in urban America, 1880–1914, *American Journal of Sociology*, 94(6): 1303–33.

Olzak S., 1990, The political context of competition: lynching and urban racial violence, 1882–1914, *Social Forces*, 69(2): 395–421.

Olzak S., Shanahan S. and West E., 1994, School de-segregation, interracial exposure, and antibusing activity in contemporary urban America, *American Journal of Sociology*, 100(1): 196–241.

Omi M. and Winant H., 1986, *Racial Formation in the United States*, London: Routledge and Kegan Paul.

Oxford English Dictionary: Compact Edition, 1993, London: BCA/ Oxford University Press.

Oxford Reference Dictionary, 1986, Oxford: Clarendon Press.

Park R. E., 1950, *Race and Culture*, New York: Free Press.

Park R. E. and Burgess E. W., 1921, *Introduction to the Science of Sociology*, Chicago: University of Chicago Press.

Parsons T., 1968, *The Structure of Social Action*, New York: Free Press.

Pavkovic A., 1998, From Yugoslavism to Serbism: the Serb national idea 1986–96, *Nations and Nationalism*, 4(4): 511–28.

Peixoto J., 2002, Strong market, weak state: the case of recent foreign immigration in Portugal, *Journal of Ethnic and Migration Studies*, 28(3): 483–97.

Portes A., Fernández-Kelly P. and Haller W., 2005, Segmented assimilation on the ground: the second generation in early adulthood, *Ethnic and Racial Studies*, 28(6): 1000–40.

Portes A. and Rumbaut R. G., 2006, *Immigrant America* (3rd edn), Berkeley: University of California Press.

Portes A. and Zhou M., 1993, The new second generation: segmented assimilation and its variants, *Annals of the American Academy of Political and Social Science*, 530 (November): 74–96.

Posner, A. J. P. S., 2004, Measuring ethnic fractionalisation in Africa, *American Journal of Political Science*, 48(4): 849–63.

Quillian L., 1995, Prejudice as a response to perceived group threat: population and anti-immigrant and racial prejudice in Europe, *American Sociological Review*, 60(4): 586–611.

Rallu J.-L., Piché V. and Simon P., 2004, Démographie et ethnicité: une relation ambiguë, in Caselli G., Vallin J. and Wunsch, G. (eds), *Démographie: analyse et synthèse*, Paris: Institut National d'Etudes Démographiques, pp. 481–515.

Ramet S. P., 1996, Nationalism and the 'idiocy' of the countryside: the case of Serbia, *Ethnic and Racial Studies*, 19(1): 70–87.

Rattansi A., 1994, 'Western' racisms, ethnicities and identities in a 'postmodern' frame, in Rattansi A. and Westwood S. (eds), *Racism, Modernity and Identity on the Western Front*, Cambridge: Polity.

Rattansi A., 2002, Racism, sexuality and political economy: Marxism/Foucault/'postmodernism', in Fenton S. and Bradley H.

(eds), *Ethnicity and Economy: 'Race and Class' Revisited*, London: Palgrave, pp. 42–63.

Rex J., 1973, *Race, Colonialism and the City*, London: Routledge and Kegan Paul.

Rex J., 1996, *Ethnic Minorities in the Modern Nation State*, London: Macmillan.

Rex J. and Tomlinson S., 1979, *Colonial Immigrants in a British City: A Class Analysis*, London: Routledge and Kegan Paul.

Robertson R., 1992, *Globalization: Social Theory and Global Culture*, London: Sage.

Rodriguez C., 2000, *Changing Race: Latinos, the Census, and the History of Ethnicity in the United States*, New York: New York University Press.

Rodriguez C. and Cordero-Guzman H., 1992, Placing race in context, *Ethnic and Racial Studies*, 15(4): 523–42.

Rothschild J., 1981, *Ethnopolitics: A Conceptual Framework*, New York: Columbia University Press.

Ruane J. and Todd J., 2004, The roots of intense ethnic conflict may not in fact be ethnic: categories, communities and path dependence, *European Journal of Sociology*, 45(2): 209–32.

Rumbaut R. and Portes A. (eds), 2001, *Ethnicities: Children of Immigrants in America*, Berkeley: University of California Press.

Santoro W. A., 1999, Conventional politics takes center stage: the Latino struggle against English-only laws, *Social Forces*, 77(3): 887–909.

Scott G. M., 1990, A resynthesis of the primordial and circumstantial approaches to ethnic group solidarity: towards an explanatory model, *Ethnic and Racial Studies*, 13(2): 147–71.

Sekulic D., 1997, The creation and dissolution of the multinational state: the case of Yugoslavia, *Nations and Nationalism*, 3(2): 165–80.

Shapiro T. M., 2004, *The Hidden Cost of Being African American: How Wealth Perpetuates Inequality*, Oxford: Oxford University Press.

Shaw A., 1988, *A Pakistani Community in Britain*, Oxford: Blackwell.

Shils E., 1957, Primordial, personal, sacred and civil ties, *British Journal of Sociology*, 8(2): 130–45.

Siddle R., 2003, The limits to citizenship in Japan: multiculturalism, indigenous rights and the Ainu, *Citizenship Studies*, 7(4): 447–62.

Simons A., 1997, Democratization and ethnic conflict: the kin connection, *Nations and Nationalism*, 3(2): 273–90.

Smith A. D., 1981, *The Ethnic Revival in the Modern World*, Cambridge: Cambridge University Press.

Smith A. D., 1986, *The Ethnic Origin of Nations*, Oxford: Blackwell.

Smith A. D., 1991, *National Identity*, London: Penguin.

Smith M. G., 1965, *The Plural Society in the British West Indies*, Berkeley: University of California Press.

Snipp C. M., 2003, Racial measurement in the American Census: past practices and implications for the future, *Annual Review of Sociology*, 29: 56–88.

Solomos J., 1993, *Race and Racism in Britain*, London: Macmillan.

Stannard D. E., 1992, *American Holocaust: The Conquest of the New World*, New York: Oxford University Press.

Steinberg S., 1981, *The Ethnic Myth: Race, Ethnicity and Class in America*, Boston: Beacon Press.

Steinberg S. (ed.), 2000, *Race and Ethnicity in the United States: Issues and Debates*, Oxford: Blackwell.

Stepanov V., 2000, Ethnic tensions and separatism in Russia, *Journal of Ethnic and Migration Studies*, 26(2): 333–55.

Swank D. and Betz H.-G., 2003, Globalization, the welfare-state and right-wing populism in Western Europe, *Socio-Economic Review*, 1(2): 212–45.

Taguieff P.-A., 1990, The new cultural racism in France, *Telos*, 83 (Spring): 109–22.

Tan E. G., 2005, Multiracialism engineered: the limits of electoral and spatial integration in Singapore, *Ethnopolitics*, 4(4): 413–28.

Taylor C. M., 1994, *Multiculturalism: Examining the Politics of Recognition*, Princeton: Princeton University Press.

The Guardian, 14 August 2001, Lifting the veil (Angelique Chrisafis).

The Guardian, 22 November 2008, How to beat the BNP (Hazel Blears MP).

The New York Times, 24 March 1999, Conflict in the Balkans: the negotiators (Roger Cohen).

Tishkov V., 1997, *Ethnicity, Nationalism and Conflict in and after the Soviet Union: The Mind Aflame*, London: Sage.

Tishkov V., 2000, Forget the nation: post-nationalist understanding of nationalism, *Ethnic and Racial Studies*, 23(4): 625–50.

Tolnay S. E., Beck E. M. and Massey J. L., 1989, Black lynchings: the power threat hypothesis revisited, *Social Forces*, 67(3): 605–23.

Tönnies F., 1963, *Community and Society*, New York: Harper and Row.

Triandafyllidou A., Calloni M. and Mikrakis A., 1997, New Greek nationalism, *Sociological Research Online*, 2(1): http://www.socresonline.org.uk/socresonline/ 2/1/7.html

US Census Bureau, 2000, Racial and ethnic classifications used in Census 2000 and beyond: http://www.census.gov/population/www/socdemo/race/racefactcb.html

US Census Bureau, 2001, *Census 2000 Brief: Overview of Race and Hispanic Origin*, Washington DC: US Department of Commerce.

US Census Bureau, 2003, *Language Use and English-Speaking Ability: 2000*, Washington DC: US Department of Commerce.

US Census Bureau, 2004, *The Foreign-Born Population of the United States: 2003*, August, Washington DC: US Department of Commerce.

US Commission on Civil Rights, 1973, *To Know or not to Know: Collection and Use of Racial and Ethnic Data in Federal Assistance Programs*, Washington DC: US Commission on Civil Rights.

Valle V. M. and Torres R. D., 2000, *Latino Metropolis*, Minneapolis: University of Minnesota Press.

Van Den Berghe P. L., 1978, *Race and Racism: A Comparative Perspective* (2nd edn), New York: Wiley.

Van Den Berghe P., 1981, *The Ethnic Phenomenon*, New York: Elsevier Press.

Vann Woodward C., 1963, *Tom Watson: Agrarian Rebel*, Oxford: Oxford University Press

Vann Woodward C., 1964, *American Counterpoint*, Boston: Little, Brown.

Vann Woodward C., 1974, *The Strange Career of Jim Crow* (3rd revised edn), New York: Oxford University Press.

Vasil R., 1995, *Asianising Singapore: The PAP's Management of Ethnicity*, Singapore: Institute of Southeast Asian Studies/Heinemann Asia.

Vertovec S., 1999, Conceiving and researching transnationalism, *Ethnic and Racial Studies*, 22(2): 447–62.

Wade P., 1997, *Race and Ethnicity in Latin America*, London: Macmillan.

Waldinger R., 2007, Did manufacturing matter? The experience of yesterday's second generation: a reassessment, *Ethnic and Racial Studies*, 41(1): 3–39.

Waldinger R. and Feliciano C., 2004, Will the second generation experience 'downward assimilation'? Segmented assimilation re-assessed, *Ethnic and Racial Studies*, 27(3): 376–402.

Walvin J., 2007, *A Short History of Slavery*, London: Penguin.

Warner W. L. and Srole L., 1945, *The Social Systems of American Ethnic Groups*, New Haven, CT: Yale University Press.

Waters M. C., 1990, *Ethnic Options: Choosing Identities in America*, Berkeley: University of California Press.

Waters M. C., 1999, *Black Identities: West Indian Immigrant Dreams and American Realities*, Cambridge, MA: Harvard University Press.

Waters M. C. and Eschbach K., 1995, Immigration and ethnic and racial inequality in the United States, *Annual Review of Sociology*, 21: 419–46.

Weber M., 1978, *Economy and Society*, Berkeley: University of California Press.

Wetherell M. and Potter J., 1992, *Mapping the Language of Racism: Discourse and the Legitimation of Exploitation*, London: Harvester Wheatsheaf.

Wieviorka M., 1994, Racism in Europe: unity and diversity, in Rattansi A. and Westwood S. (eds), *Racism, Modernity and Identity on the Western Front*, Cambridge: Polity, pp. 173–88.

Wieviorka M., 1995, *The Arena of Racism*, London: Sage.

Wilson W. J., 1980, *The Declining Significance of Race*, Chicago: University of Chicago Press.

Wilson W. J., 1991, Studying inner-city dislocations: the challenge of public agenda research: 1990 presidential address, *American Sociological Review*, 56(1): 1–14.

Wilson W. J., 1999, When work disappears: new implications for race and urban poverty in the global economy, *Ethnic and Racial Studies*, 22(3): 479–99.

Wimmer A., 1997, Who owns the state? Understanding ethnic conflict in post-colonial societies, *Nations and Nationalism*, 3(4): 631–66.

Winant H., 2000, Race and race theory, *Annual Review of Sociology*, 26: 169–85.

Woo D., 2000, *Glass Ceilings and Asian Americans*, New York: Altamira Press.

Worthman P. B., 1969, Black workers and labor unions in Birmingham Alabama, 1897–1904, *Labor History*, 10(3): 375–407.

Yamanaka K., 2000, Nepalese labour migration to Japan: from global warriors to global workers, *Ethnic and Racial Studies*, 23(1): 62–93.

Yinger M. J., 1994, *Ethnicity*, New York: State University of New York Press.

Zarrugh L., 2008, The Latinisation of the Shenandoah Valley, *International Migration*, 46(1): 19–58.

Index

rational choice theory 62,
72–3, 103, 114, 188–9
Rattansi, A. 175
refugees 37, 76
religion
and British identity 49
and culture, identity 20,
55, 58, 62, 90, 116, 165,
170, 182
and ethnic conflict 162
and migration 116
and nation 171
primordial debate 78
race discourse in
Malaysia 40
US 58
resentment, politics of 95–6,
144, 150, 159, 167, 171,
173, 184
ressentiment 198–9, 171,
173, 192
Rex, J. 53, 60, 85, 116, 202
right-wing movements,
Europe 169–86
support for, 180, 184
Rodriguez, C. 25, 30–3, 200
Rumbaut, R. 128, 138
Russia, ethnic conflict 165–68
Rwanda 157–9

sacred ties 75–8
sanctity values 197, 199
Sarawak 4–5, 43
Sekulic, D. 161–4
Serbs 158, 160–4, 174
Shapiro 132, 141, 192
Shils, E. 75–81, 84
Simons, A. 154
Singapore 8, 24, 45–6, 50
situational ethnicity 82, 87,
155, 189–90
slavery 10, 25–7, 46–50, 107,
115–17, 126, 190, 202
Slovenes 162–4
Smith, A. D. 21–2, 60, 170,
174

social action 6, 62, 73,
75, 104, 112, 139,
201
social breakdown 196
social categories 65–9
social class
and idea of nation 171–3
and migration 128–9
and right-wing
movements 169, 171,
175–80, 184–6
US 128–9, 131–6, 145,
149–52, 167–8
social cohesion 74–8
social constructionism 2–4, 5,
8–9, 34–6, 65, 71–4, 85,
93, 200–1
social context
contexts of ethnic action
82–4, 139–40, 190–1
social groups 7, 56, 66–7,
178, 200
social inclusion/exclusion 10,
29, 35–6, 58, 108, 142–4,
170, 172, 175, 185, 191,
197
social inequality *see* inequality/
equality
socialism 64, 142
socialization 85–7, 201
social mobility 10, 133, 135,
202
and ethnic loyalty 59, 111,
198
and nationalism 172–3
social organization 76, 91,
189, 195
social status 26
see also social class
social ties 74–82, 85, 109
sociology
centrality of ethnicity
187–90
key points in ethnicity
literature 51–70,
110–12